CONTENTS

ACKNOWLEDGEMENTS

The author wishes to thank the following for their help with the editing and production of the book: Jean Cox, Michael Fardon, Michael Gilbert, Jon Moore and Anita Sherwood. Particular thanks go to Roger Petheram of Worcester College of Technology for reading the text, commenting upon it, checking answers, and always being prepared to discuss any aspect of the book. The editorial staff at Osborne Books would like to thank the AAT tutors they have consulted about the interpretation of the revised Standards of Competence and are particularly grateful to Derek Street and Marjory Pierce for their practical guidance. Thanks are also due to the Association of Accounting Technicians for their generous help and advice and to the Lead Body for Accounting for permission to reproduce extracts from the Standards of Competence for Accounting.

AUTHOR

David Cox has had more than twenty years' experience teaching accountancy students over a wide range of levels. Formerly with the Management and Professional Studies Department at Worcester College of Technology, he now lectures on a freelance basis and carries out educational consultancy work in accountancy studies. He is author and joint author of a number of textbooks in the areas of accounting, finance and banking.

INTRODUCTION

Osborne tutorials

Financial Accounting Tutorial has been written to provide a study resource for students taking courses based on the NVQ Level 3 Accounting Unit 5 'Maintaining financial records and preparing accounts'. The companion Osborne text *Costing, Reports & Returns Tutorial* covers Units 6 and 7 in a single volume.

Financial Accounting Tutorial commences with the recording of business transactions in double-entry accounts, develops through the extended trial balance, and leads to an understanding of the structure of the final accounts of sole traders, partnerships, manufacturers and clubs. The emphasis at NVQ Level 3 – and in this text – is on the extended trial balance. The presentation of final accounts (developed fully at NVQ Level 4) is, however, covered in the text and the Appendix as preparation for later studies; many of the Student Activities which require figures to be set out in the form of an extended trial balance can, *if required*, be expanded to present lists of assets and liabilities, or conventional final accounts.

Financial Accounting Tutorial provides the student with the theoretical background to the subject while at the same time including plenty of opportunity to put theory into practice. The aim has been to introduce the right amount of material at the right level.

The chapters of *Financial Accounting Tutorial* contain:

- a clear text with worked examples and case studies
- a chapter summary and key terms to help with revision
- student activities – with answers at the end of the book

The tutorial text – with questions and answers – is therefore useful for classroom use and also for distance learning students. More extended student exercises, without answers in the text, are available in the *Financial Accounting Workbook* (see below).

Osborne workbooks

Financial Accounting Tutorial has been written to be used alongside the *Financial Accounting Workbook* which contains extended student activities and sample Central and Devolved Assessments.

The answers to these tasks are included in a separate Tutor Pack.

If you would like a workbook, please telephone Osborne Books Sales Office on 01905 748071 for details of how to order.

COVERAGE OF NVQ COMPETENCES

NOTE ON UNIT NUMBERING

In 2000 the reference number of the NVQ Unit covered in this book was changed from Unit 4 to Unit 5. This change is reflected in the introductory pages of this book. References in subsequent pages should be adjusted accordingly.

Unit 5: MAINTAINING FINANCIAL RECORDS AND PREPARING ACCOUNTS

element 1

maintain records relating to capital acquisition and disposal — *chapter*

	chapter
❑ *relevant details relating to capital expenditure are correctly entered in the appropriate records*	*16*
❑ *the organisation's records agree with the physical presence of capital items*	*16*
❑ *all acquisition and disposal costs and revenues are correctly identified and recorded in the appropriate records*	*16*
❑ *depreciation charges and other necessary entries and adjustments are correctly calculated and recorded in the appropriate records*	*16*
❑ *the records clearly show the prior authority for capital expenditure and disposal and indicate the approved method of funding and disposal*	*16*
❑ *profit and loss on disposal is correctly calculated and recorded in the appropriate records*	*16*
❑ *the organisation's policies and procedures relating to the maintenance of capital records are adhered to*	*16*
❑ *lack of agreement between physical items and records are identified and either resolved or referred to the appropriate person*	*16*
❑ *when possible, suggestions for improvements in the way the organisation maintains its capital records are made to the appropriate person*	*16*

element 2

record income and expenditure

	chapter
❑ *all income and expenditure is correctly identified and recorded in the appropriate records*	*2*
❑ *relevant accrued and prepaid income and expenditure is correctly identified and adjustments are made*	*5*
❑ *the organisation's policies, regulations, procedures and timescales in relation to recording income and expenditure are observed*	*2,5,6,7,12*
❑ *incomplete data is identified and either resolved or referred to the appropriate person*	*12*

element 3

collect and collate information for the preparation of final accounts

		chapter
❑	*relevant accounts and reconciliations are correctly prepared to allow the preparation of final accounts*	*9,11*
❑	*all relevant information is correctly identified and recorded*	*10,13,14,15*
❑	*investigations into business transactions are conducted with tact and courtesy*	*9,11,12,13*
❑	*the organisation's policies, regulations, procedures and timescales relating to preparing final accounts are observed*	*4,8,13,14,15*
❑	*discrepancies and unusual features are identified and either resolved or referred to the appropriate person*	*9*
❑	*the trial balance is accurately prepared and, where necessary, a suspense account is opened and reconciled*	*3,10*

element 4

prepare the extended trial balance

❑	*totals from the general ledger or other records are correctly entered on the extended trial balance*	*4*
❑	*material errors disclosed by the trial balance are identified, traced and referred to the appropriate authority*	*10*
❑	*adjustments not dealt with in the ledger accounts are correctly entered on the extended trial balance*	*5*
❑	*an agreed valuation of closing stock is correctly entered on the extended trial balance*	*8,15*
❑	*the organisation's policies, regulations, procedures and timescales in relation to preparing extended trial balances are observed*	*6,7*
❑	*discrepancies, unusual features or queries are identified and either resolved or referred to the appropriate person*	*10*
❑	*the extended trial balance is accurately extended and totalled*	*4,6,7,13,14,15*

Note

For the 'Knowledge and Understanding' requirements of the course, please refer to the index for individual subjects.

1 THE ACCOUNTING SYSTEM

this chapter covers . . .

Before studying financial accounting in detail, it is important to take an overview of the accounting system. Every organisation is unique and therefore no one accounting system will be exactly the same as another. This chapter provides:

- *an introduction to business transactions*
- *an explanation of how the transactions are recorded in an accounting system*
- *an introduction to some of the terms used in accounting*

NVQ PERFORMANCE CRITERIA COVERED

unit 4: MAINTAINING FINANCIAL RECORDS AND PREPARING ACCOUNTS

KNOWLEDGE AND UNDERSTANDING – THE BUSINESS ENVIRONMENT

- ❑ *methods of recording information for the organisational accounts of: sole traders; partnerships; manufacturing accounts; club accounts*
- ❑ *the need to present accounts in the correct form*
- ❑ *the importance of maintaining the confidentiality of business transactions*

KNOWLEDGE AND UNDERSTANDING – THE ORGANISATION

- ❑ *understanding of the ways the accounting systems of an organisation are affected by its organisational structure, its administrative systems and procedures and the nature of its business transactions*

ACCOUNTING AND THE ACCOUNTING SYSTEM

what is accounting?

Accounting is essential to the recording and presentation of business activities in the form of *financial accounts*. Accounting involves:

- recording business transactions in financial terms
- reporting financial information to the owner and managers of the business and other interested parties
- advising the owner how to use the financial reports to assess the past performance of the business, and to make decisions for the future

the role of the accountant

The accountant's job is to check, summarise, present, analyse and interpret the accounts for the benefit of the owner/owners and other interested parties. There are two types of specialist accountant:

- *financial accountant*, mainly concerned with external reporting
- *management accountant*, mainly concerned with internal reporting

The function of the *financial accountant* is concerned with financial transactions, and with taking further the information produced by whoever 'keeps the books'. The financial accountant extracts information from the accounting records in order to provide a method of control, for instance over debtors, creditors, cash and bank balances. The role also requires the preparation of year-end financial statements.

The *management accountant* obtains information about costs – eg the cost of materials, labour, expenses and overheads – and interprets it and prepares reports for the owners or managers of the business. In particular, the management accountant will be concerned with financial decision-making, planning and control of the business.

manual and computer accounts

This book looks at part of the accounting process and is concerned with the preparation of the accounting records so that the end-of-period financial statements can be drawn up.

Financial accounting records are kept in handwritten form and in many cases on computer. Computer accounting systems are sensibly backed up by handwritten records, in case of computer disasters such as total loss of data. The main record in a handwritten system is *the ledger* which, at one time, would be a weighty leather-bound volume, neatly ruled, into which the book-keeper would handwrite each business transaction into individual accounts.

Computers are now relatively cheap and generally affordable. The major advantage of computer accounting is that it is a very accurate method of recording business transactions. The word 'ledger' has survived into the computer age but, instead of being a bound volume, it is used to describe data files held on a computer disk.

Whether business transactions are recorded by hand, or by using a computer, the basic principles remain the same. In the first few chapters of this book we will concentrate on these basic principles.

keeping accounts – practical points

When maintaining financial accounts you should bear in mind that they should be kept:

- accurately
- up-to-date
- confidentially:
  - not revealed to people outside the business (unless authorisation is given)
  - revealed only to those within the business who are entitled to the information

Maintaining financial accounts is a discipline, and you should develop disciplined accounting skills as you study with this book. In particular, when attempting Student Activities and Assessments you should:

- be neat in the layout of your work
- use ink (in accounting, the use of pencil shows indecision)
- not use correcting fluid (errors should be crossed through neatly with a single line and the correct version written on the line below)

The reason for not using correcting fluid in handwritten accounts is because the accounts should always be available for auditing (checking by accountants): correcting fluid may hide errors, but it can also conceal fraudulent transactions.

the stages of the accounting system

The diagram on the next page should now be studied carefully.

The early stages of the accounting system are covered at level 2 of NVQ Accounting. Topics such as prime documents, primary accounting records, and some aspects of double-entry book-keeping are explained in Osborne Books' *Cash & Credit Accounting Tutorial.* In this book we will focus on the double-entry accounts system, the trial balance in its 'extended' form, and the final accounts. If you should at any time lose sight of where your studies are taking you, refer back to this chapter, and the diagram, and it should help to place your work in context.

the accounting system

PRIME DOCUMENTS

invoices – issued and received
credit notes – issued and received
bank paying-in slips
cheques issued
BACS documents

sources of accounting information

PRIMARY ACCOUNTING RECORDS

day books
journal
cash books (also used in double-entry)

gathering and summarising accounting information

DOUBLE-ENTRY BOOK-KEEPING

sales ledger – accounts of debtors
purchases ledger – accounts of creditors
general (nominal) ledger
– 'nominal' accounts for sales, purchases, expenses, capital, loans etc
– 'real' accounts for items, eg fixed assets
cash books
– cash book for bank and cash transactions
– petty cash book

recording the dual aspect of business transactions in the accounting system

TRIAL BALANCE

a summary of the balances of all the accounts
– 'extended' to produce data for final accounts

arithmetical checking of double-entry book-keeping

FINAL ACCOUNTS

- profit and loss account

and

- balance sheet

statement measuring profit (or loss) for an accounting period

statement of assets, liabilities and capital at the end of an accounting period

We will now look at each of these stages of the accounting system in turn.

PRIME DOCUMENTS

Business transactions generate documents. In this section we link the main documents to the type of transaction involved. Business documents are covered at level 2 of NVQ Accounting, and a full discussion of documents is contained in chapters 2 and 3 of Osborne Books' *Cash & Credit Accounting Tutorial.*

sales and purchases – the invoice

When a business buys or sells goods or services the seller prepares an invoice stating:

- the amount owing
- when it should be paid
- details of the goods sold or service provided

cash sales and credit sales – debtors and creditors

An invoice is prepared by the seller for:

- *cash sales* – where payment is immediate, whether by cash or by cheque. (note that not all cash sales will require an invoice to be prepared by the seller – shops, for instance, normally issue a receipt for the amount paid)
- *credit sales* – where payment is to be made at a later date (often 30 days later)

A *debtor* is a person who owes you money when you sell on credit.

A *creditor* is a person to whom you owe money when you buy on credit.

return of goods – the credit note

If the buyer returns goods which are bought on credit (they may be faulty or incorrect) the seller will prepare a credit note which is sent to the buyer, reducing the amount of money owed. The credit note, like the invoice, states the money amount and the goods and services to which it relates.

bank transactions – cheques, giro credits, BACS

Businesses need to pay in money, draw out cash and make payments. Paying-in slips and cheques are used as prime documents for bank account transactions as are documents generated by the BACS inter-bank computer payments system (eg debtors paying direct into the bank).

PRIMARY ACCOUNTING RECORDS

Many businesses issue and receive large quantities of invoices, credit notes and banking documents, and it is useful for them to list these in summary form, during the course of the working day. These summaries are known as *primary accounting records* (also called *books of original entry*). These primary accounting records include:

- *sales day book* – a list of sales made, compiled from invoices issued
- *purchases day book* – a list of purchases made, compiled from invoices received
- *sales returns day book* – a list of 'returns in', ie goods returned by customers, compiled from credit notes issued
- *purchases returns day book* – a list of 'returns out', ie goods returned by the business to suppliers, compiled from credit notes received
- *cash book* – the business' record of the bank account and the amount of cash held, compiled from receipts, paying-in slips and cheques
- *petty cash book* – a record of low-value cash purchases made by the business, compiled from petty cash vouchers
- *journal* – a record of non-regular transactions, which are not recorded in any other primary accounting record (this is covered in Chapter 10)

The primary accounting records are covered at level 2 of NVQ Accounting. They are fully explained in Osborne Books' *Cash & Credit Accounting Tutorial*, chapters 5 and 6 (day books), chapter 11 (journal), chapter 15 (cash book) and chapter 16 (petty cash book).

DOUBLE-ENTRY ACCOUNTS: THE LEDGER

The basis of many accounting systems is the *double-entry book-keeping system* which is embodied in a series of records known as the *ledger*. This is divided into a number of separate *accounts*.

double-entry book-keeping

Double-entry book-keeping involves making two entries in the accounts for each transaction: for instance, if you are paying wages by cheque you will make an entry in bank account and an entry in wages account. If you are operating a manual accounting system you will make the two entries by hand, if you are operating a computer accounting system you will make *one* entry on the keyboard, but indicate to the machine where the other entry is to be made by means of a numerical code.

accounts

The primary accounting records are the sources for the entries you make in the accounts. The ledger into which you make the entries is divided into separate accounts, eg a separate account for sales, purchases, each type of business expense, each debtor, each creditor, and so on. Each account is given a specific name, and a number for reference purposes.

computer accounts

As noted earlier, many small businesses and almost all large businesses use computers to handle their business transactions. Using an accounting program, transactions are input into the computer and stored on disk. The separate accounts are represented by data files held on disk. The principles of double-entry book-keeping remain the same; an input code is used to identify the two accounts involved in each transaction.

division of the ledger

Because of the large number of accounts involved, the ledger has traditionally been divided into a number of sections. These same sections are used in computer accounting systems.

- *sales ledger* – personal accounts of debtors, ie customers to whom the business has sold on credit
- *purchases ledger* – personal accounts of creditors, ie suppliers to whom the business owes money
- *cash books* – a cash book comprising cash account and bank account, and a petty cash book for petty cash account (low-value purchases); note that the cash books are also primary accounting records for cash transactions
- *general (or nominal) ledger* – the remainder of the accounts: *nominal accounts*, eg sales, purchases, expenses, and *real accounts* for items owned by the business

TRIAL BALANCE

Double-entry book-keeping, because it involves making two entries for each transaction, is open to error. What if the person keeping the books writes £45 in one account and £54 in another? The trial balance – explained fully in Chapter 3 – effectively checks the entries made over a given period and will pick up most errors. It sets out the *balances* of all the double-entry accounts, ie the totals of the accounts to date. As well as being an arithmetical check, it is the source of valuable information which is used – in the *extended trial balance* – to help in the preparation of the *final accounts* of the business.

FINAL ACCOUNTS

The final accounts of a business comprise the profit and loss account and the balance sheet.

profit and loss account

income minus **expenses** equals **profit**

The profit and loss account of a business calculates the profit due to the owner(s) of the business after the cost of purchases and other expenses have been deducted from the sales income.

The figures for these calculations – sales, purchases, expenses of various kinds – are taken from the double-entry system. Profit and loss accounts, which are discussed in more detail in Chapter 4, are invariably presented in a vertical format:

	income	**(£)**
minus	**expenses**	**(£)**
equals	**profit**	**(£)**

balance sheet

The balance sheet is so called because it balances in numerical (money) terms:

assets	minus	**liabilities**	equals	**capital**
what a business owns		*what a business owes*		*how the business has been financed*

The double-entry system contains figures for:

assets items the business owns, which can be:

- fixed assets – items bought for use in the business, eg premises, vehicles, computers
- current assets – items used in the everyday running of the business, eg stock, debtors (money owed by customers), and money in the bank

liabilities items that the business owes, eg bank loans and overdrafts, and creditors (money owed to suppliers)

capital money or assets introduced by the owner(s) of the business; capital is in effect owed by the business to the owner

Balance sheets, which are explained in Chapter 4 and the Appendix, are – like profit and loss accounts – usually presented in a vertical format:

	assets	**(£)**
minus	**liabilities**	**(£)**
equals	**capital**	**(£)**

the accounting equation

The balance sheet illustrates a concept important to accounting theory, known as the *accounting equation*. This equation has been explained above, namely:

assets minus **liabilities** equals **capital**

Every business transaction will change the balance sheet and the equation, as each transaction has a *dual effect* on the accounts. However, the equation will always balance. Consider the following transactions:

	Transaction	*Effect on accounting equation*
1.	Business pays creditor	decrease in asset (bank) decrease in liability (money owed to creditor)
2.	Business buys a computer	increase in asset (computer) decrease in asset (bank)
3.	The owner introduces new capital by paying a cheque into the bank	increase in asset (bank) increase in capital (money owed by business to owner)

How is the equation affected by these particular transactions?

Transaction 1 Assets and liabilities both decrease by the amount of the payment; capital remains unchanged.

Transaction 2 Assets remain the same because the two transactions cancel each other out in the assets section: value is transferred from the asset of bank to the asset of computer.

Transaction 3 Both sides of the equation increase by the amount of the capital introduced.

The equation always balances, as will the balance sheet of a business.

In conclusion, every business transaction has a *dual aspect*, as two entries are involved: this is the basis of the theory of double-entry book-keeping.

CHAPTER SUMMARY

- Accounting is used to record business transactions in financial terms
- Financial accounts are used by the owner(s) and managers of the business and also by other interested parties.
- The accounting system comprises a number of specific stages of recording and presenting business transactions
  - prime documents
  - primary accounting records
  - the double-entry system of ledgers
  - the trial balance and extended trial balance
  - final accounts
- The balance sheet uses the accounting equation:

  assets – liabilities = capital

KEY TERMS

In the course of this chapter a number of specific accounting terms have been introduced. You should now study this section closely to ensure that you are clear about these terms:

accounts	financial records, where business transactions are entered
ledger	the set of accounts of a business
assets	items owned by a business
liabilities	items owed by a business
capital	the amount of the owner's (or owners') stake in the business
debtors	individuals or businesses who owe money in respect of goods or services supplied by the business
creditors	individuals or businesses to whom money is owed by the business
purchases	goods bought, either on credit or for cash, which are intended to be resold later
credit purchases	goods bought, with payment to be made at a later date
cash purchases	goods bought and paid for immediately
petty cash	low-value cash purchases, often for expenses
sales	the sale of goods, whether on credit or for cash, in which the business trades

credit sales	goods sold, with payment to be received at an agreed date in the future
cash sales	goods sold, with immediate payment received in cash, by cheque, by credit card, or by debit card
turnover	the total of sales, both cash and credit, for a particular time period
profit	the gain made by a business from selling goods or services during a particular time period
expenses	the costs of running the business, eg wages, rent, rates, telephone, etc
trial balance	list of the balances of all the double-entry accounts

STUDENT ACTIVITIES

The answers to these Student Activities are printed in the back of this book. Further questions and more fully extended Student Activities and Assessments are to be found in the accompanying Osborne Books' text *Financial Accounting Workbook*.

1.1 Write out and complete the following sentences.

(a) The set of double-entry accounts of a business is called the ....

(b) A .... is a person who owes you money when you sell on credit.

(c) A .... is a person to whom you owe money when you buy on credit.

(d) The .... is a list of sales made, compiled from invoices issued.

(e) The business' record of bank account and amount of cash held is kept in the ....

(f) Accounts such as sales, purchases, expenses are kept in the ....

(g) The accounting equation is: .... minus .... equals ....

1.2 Distinguish between:

(a) assets and liabilities

(b) debtors and creditors

(c) purchases and sales

(d) credit purchases and cash purchases

1.3 Show the dual aspect, as it affects the accounting equation (assets – liabilities = capital), of the following transactions (which follow one another) for a particular business (ignore VAT):

(a) owner starts in business with capital of £8,000 in the bank

(b) buys a computer for £4,000, paying by cheque

(c) obtains a loan of £3,000 by cheque from a friend

(d) buys a van for £6,000, paying by cheque

1.4 Fill in the missing figures:

	Assets	*Liabilities*	*Capital*
	£	£	£
(a)	20,000	0	....
(b)	15,000	5,000	....
(c)	16,400	....	8,850
(d)	....	3,850	10,250
(e)	25,380	....	6,950
(f)	....	7,910	13,250

1.5 The table below sets out account balances from the books of a business. The columns (a) to (f) show the account balances resulting from a series of transactions that have taken place over time. You are to compare each set of adjacent columns, ie (a) with (b), (b) with (c), and so on and state, with figures, what accounting transactions have taken place in each case. (Ignore VAT).

	(a) £	(b) £	(c) £	(d) £	(e) £	(f) £
Assets						
Office equipment	–	2,000	2,000	2,000	2,000	2,000
Van	–	–	–	10,000	10,000	10,000
Bank	10,000	8,000	14,000	4,000	6,000	3,000
Liabilities						
Loan	–	–	6,000	6,000	6,000	3,000
Capital	10,000	10,000	10,000	10,000	12,000	12,000

2 DOUBLE-ENTRY BOOK-KEEPING

this chapter covers . . .

We saw in Chapter 1 that book-keeping is the basic recording of business transactions in financial terms. Before studying financial accounting in detail it is important to study the principles of double-entry book-keeping, as these form the basis of all that we shall be doing in the rest of the book.

In Chapter 1 we looked briefly at the dual aspect of accounting – each time there is a business transaction there are two effects on the accounting equation. This chapter shows how the dual aspect is used in the principles of book-keeping. In particular, we shall be looking at accounts used when:

- *starting a business*
- *dealing with cash and bank transactions*
- *paying expenses and receiving income*
- *buying and selling goods*
- *dealing with returned goods, carriage costs and discounts*
- *dealing with Value Added Tax*

NVQ PERFORMANCE CRITERIA COVERED

unit 4: MAINTAINING FINANCIAL RECORDS AND PREPARING ACCOUNTS

element 2

record income and expenditure

- ❏ *all income and expenditure is correctly identified and recorded in the appropriate accounts*
- ❏ *the organisation's policies, regulations, procedures and timescales in relation to recording income and expenditure are observed*

DOUBLE-ENTRY ACCOUNTS

In this book we will use a simple account layout shown as follows:

Dr		Bank Account		Cr
1998	£	1998		£
22 April Sales	450	23 April	Wages	7,900

This layout is often known in accounting jargon as a 'T' account; it separates in a simple way the two sides of the account – debit (Dr) and credit (Cr). Note that each side records three items – the date, the nature of the transaction and the money amount.

debits and credits

The principle of double-entry book-keeping is that for every business transaction:

- one account is *debited* with the money amount of the transaction, and
- one account is *credited* with the money amount of the transaction

Debit entries are on the left-hand side of the appropriate account, while credit entries are on the right. The rules for debits and credits are:

- *debit entry* – the account which gains value, or records an asset, or an expense
- *credit entry* – the account which gives value, or records a liability, or an income item

This is illustrated as follows:

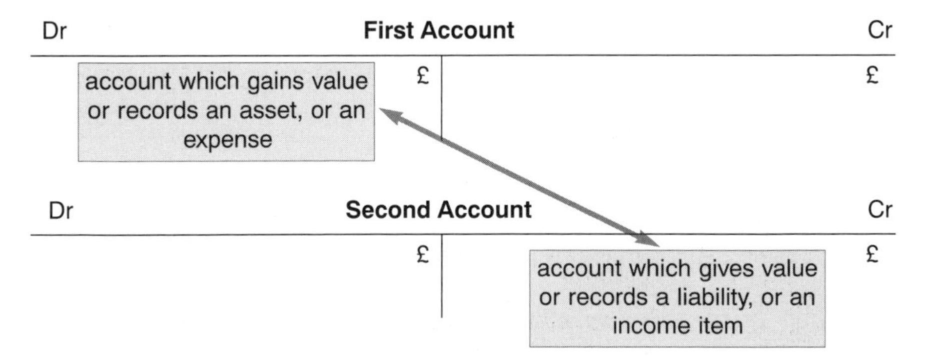

When one entry has been identified as a debit or credit, the other entry will be on the *opposite* side of the other account.

DOUBLE-ENTRY INVOLVING BANK ACCOUNT

In order to see how accounts are used, we will look at the business transactions undertaken by a new business which was set up by Jayne Hampson on 1 September 1998 (and is not registered for VAT):

1 Sep	Started in business with capital of £5,000: a cheque from Jayne Hampson paid into the business bank account
4 Sep	Bought office equipment £2,500, paying by cheque
7 Sep	Paid rent of office £500, by cheque
10 Sep	Received commission of £100, by cheque
14 Sep	Withdrew £250 from the bank for own use (drawings)
16 Sep	Received a loan of £1,000 from James Henderson by cheque

All of these transactions involve the bank, and the business will enter them in its *bank account*. The bank account records money in the form of bank receipts and payments, ie cheques, standing orders, direct debits, bank giro credits, credit card transactions, and debit card transactions. (Most businesses also use a *cash account* to record transactions which involve money in the form of cash.)

With both bank account and cash account, the rules for debit and credit are:

- *money in* is recorded on the debit side
- *money out* is recorded on the credit side

Using these rules, the bank account of Jayne Hampson's business, after entering the transactions listed above, appears as:

Dr **Bank Account** Cr

1998		£	1998		£
1 Sep	Capital	5,000	4 Sep	Office equipment	2,500
10 Sep	Commission	100	7 Sep	Rent paid	500
16 Sep	J Henderson: loan	1,000	14 Sep	Drawings	250
		Money in		Money out	

Note: the bank account shows the firm's record of how much has been paid into, and drawn out of, the bank – it is not exactly the same as the record of receipts and payments kept by the bank (the two are compared in the form of a *bank reconciliation statement* – see Chapter 11).

To complete the double-entry book-keeping transactions we need to:

- identify on which side of the bank account the transaction is recorded – debit (money in), or credit (money out)
- record the other double-entry transaction on the *opposite side* of the appropriate account
- note that business transactions involving cash will be entered in the cash account

The other accounts involved can now be recorded, and we shall look at the principles involved for each transaction.

CAPITAL ACCOUNT

Capital is the amount of money invested in the business by the owner (or owners). The amount is *owed* by the business back to the owner, although it is unlikely to be repaid immediately as the business would cease to exist. A *capital account* is used to record the amount(s) paid into the business; the book-keeping entries are:

- **capital introduced**
  - *debit* bank account, as in the case of Jayne Hampson, or cash account (or a fixed asset account – see below – where these form part of the capital)
  - *credit* capital account

example transaction

1 Sep 1998 Started in business with capital of £5,000, a cheque paid into the bank.

Dr		Capital Account			Cr
1998		£	1998		£
			1 Sep	Bank	5,000

Note: The dual aspect is that bank account has gained value and has been debited already (see page 16); capital account records a liability (to the owner) and is credited. Note that the business is a *separate entity* from the owner, and this book-keeping entry looks at the transaction from the point of view of the business. The introduction of capital into a business is often the very first business transaction entered into the books of account.

FIXED ASSETS

Fixed assets are items purchased by a business for use on a semi-permanent basis. Examples are premises, motor vehicles, machinery and office equipment. All of these are bought by a business with the intention that they will be used for some time. Without fixed assets, it would be difficult to continue in business, eg without machinery it would prove difficult to run a factory; without delivery vans and lorries it would be difficult to transport the firm's products to its customers.

When a business buys fixed assets, the expenditure is referred to as *capital expenditure.* This means that items have been bought for use in the business for some years to come. By contrast, *revenue expenditure* is where the items bought will be used by the business quite quickly. For example, the purchase of a car is capital expenditure, while the cost of repair of the car is revenue expenditure.

The importance of the difference between capital expenditure and revenue expenditure is covered in Chapter 8.

fixed assets and double-entry book-keeping

When fixed assets are bought, a separate account for each type of fixed asset is used, eg premises account, motor vehicles account, machinery account, etc. The book-keeping entries are:

- **purchase of a fixed asset**
  - *debit* fixed asset account (using the appropriate account)
  - *credit* bank account (or cash account)

example transaction

4 Sep 1998 Bought office equipment £2,500, paying by cheque.

Dr		**Office Equipment Account**		Cr
1998		£	1998	£
4 Sep	Bank	2,500		

The other part of the dual aspect of this transaction is a credit to bank account: this has been entered already (see account on page 16). Notice how the name of the other account involved in the double-entry transaction is always used in the details column as a description – this helps to cross-reference transactions.

EXPENSES

Businesses pay various running expenses, such as rent, wages, electricity, telephone, vehicle running expenses, etc. These day-to-day expenses of running the business are termed revenue expenditure. A separate account is used in the accounting system for each main class of revenue expenditure, eg rent paid account, wages account, etc.

The book-keeping entries are:

- **payment of an expense**
  - *debit* expense account (using the appropriate account)
  - *credit* bank account (or cash account)

example transaction

7 Sep 1998 Paid rent of office £500, by cheque.

Dr	Rent Paid Account				Cr
1998		£	1998		£
7 Sep	Bank	500			

Note: The accounting rules followed are that we have debited the account which has gained value (rent – the business has had the use of the office for a certain time). The account which has given value (bank) has already been credited (see page 16).

INCOME

From time-to-time a business may receive amounts of income, such as rent received, commission received, or fees received. These are recorded in separate accounts for each category of income, eg rent received account, commission received account. The book-keeping entries are:

- **receipt of income**
  - *debit* bank account (or cash account)
  - *credit* income account (using the appropriate account)

example transaction

10 Sep 1998 Received commission of £100, by cheque.

Dr		Commission Received Account		Cr
1998	£	1998		£
		10 Sep	Bank	100

Note: We have already debited the account which has gained value (bank – see page 16) and credited the account which has given value (commission received).

OWNER'S DRAWINGS

Drawings is the term used when the owner takes money, in cash or by cheque (or sometimes goods), from the business for personal use. A drawings account is used to record such amounts; the book-keeping entries for withdrawal of money are:

- **owner's drawings**
  - *debit* drawings account
  - *credit* bank account (or cash account)

example transaction

14 Sep 1998 Withdrew £250 from the bank for own use.

Dr		Drawings Account		Cr
1998		£	1998	£
14 Sep	Bank	250		

The other part of the dual aspect of this transaction is a credit to bank account: this entry has been made already (see page 16).

LOANS

When a business or organisation receives a loan, eg from a relative or from the bank, it is the cash account or bank account which gains value, while a loan account (in the name of the lender) records the liability.

- **loan received**
  - *debit* bank account (or cash account)
  - *credit* loan account (in name of the lender)

example transaction

16 Sep 1998 Received a loan of £1,000 from James Henderson by cheque

Dr	James Henderson: Loan Account				Cr
1998		£	1998		£
			16 Sep	Bank	1,000

The debit entry has already been made in bank account (see page 16).

FURTHER TRANSACTIONS

Using the accounts which we have seen already, here are some further transactions:

- **loan repayment**
  - *debit* loan account
  - *credit* bank account (or cash account)
- **sale of a fixed asset, or return of an unsuitable fixed asset**
  - debit bank account (or cash account)
  - credit fixed asset account
- **withdrawal of cash from the bank for use in the business**
  - *debit* cash account
  - *credit* bank account
- **payment of cash held by the business into the bank**
  - *debit* bank account
  - *credit* cash account

PURCHASES AND SALES

purchases account and sales account

Buying and selling goods or services are common business transactions. They are recorded in *purchases account* and *sales account* respectively. These two accounts are used to record the purchase and sale of the goods or services in which the business trades. For example, a shoe shop will buy shoes from the manufacturer and will record this in purchases account; as shoes are sold, the transactions will be recorded in sales account.

The normal entry on a purchases account is on the debit side – the account has gained value, ie the business has bought goods for resale. The normal entry on a sales account is on the credit side – the account has given value, ie the business has sold goods.

When a business buys an item for use in the business, eg a computer, this is debited to a separate account, because a fixed asset (see page 18) has been purchased. Likewise, when a fixed asset is sold, it is not entered in the sales account.

CASE STUDY

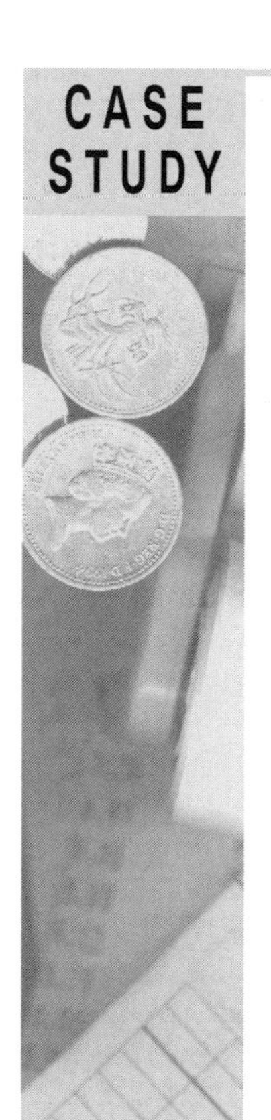

TEMESIDE TRADERS - PURCHASES AND SALES

situation

To show the double-entry book-keeping for purchases and sales, we will look at some financial transactions undertaken by Temeside Traders, a business which started trading on 1 October 1998:

1 Oct	Started in business with capital of £7,000 paid into the bank
2 Oct	Bought goods for £5,000, paying by cheque
5 Oct	Sold some of the goods for £3,000, a cheque being received
6 Oct	Bought equipment for use in the business, £700, paying by cheque
12 Oct	Bought goods for £2,800, paying by cheque
13 Oct	Sold some of the goods for £5,000, a cheque being received
15 Oct	Paid rent £150, by cheque

Note: Temeside Traders is not yet registered for Value Added Tax

solution

The entries into the book-keeping system are shown on the next page.

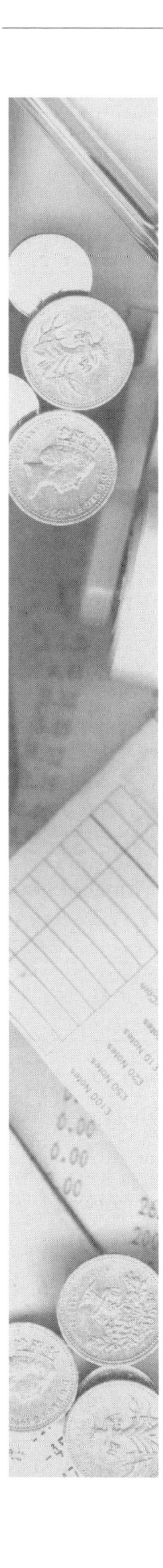

Dr		Bank Account			Cr
1998		£	1998		£
1 Oct	Capital	7,000	2 Oct	Purchases	5,000
5 Oct	Sales	3,000	6 Oct	Equipment	700
13 Oct	Sales	5,000	12 Oct	Purchases	2,800
			15 Oct	Rent paid	150

Dr		Capital Account			Cr
1998		£	1998		£
			1 Oct	Bank	7,000

Dr		Purchases Account			Cr
1998		£	1998		£
2 Oct	Bank	5,000			
12 Oct	Bank	2,800			

Dr		Sales Account			Cr
1998		£	1998		£
			5 Oct	Bank	3,000
			13 Oct	Bank	5,000

Dr		Equipment Account			Cr
1998		£	1998		£
6 Oct	Bank	700			

Dr		Rent Paid Account			Cr
1998		£	1998		£
15 Oct	Bank	150			

Notes:

- A purchases account and a sales account are used to record the two different movements of the goods or services in which a business trades.
- The equipment is a fixed asset, so its purchase is entered to a separate equipment account.
- The purchases and sales made in the transactions above are called cash purchases and cash sales, because payment is immediate.

CREDIT PURCHASES AND SALES

credit transactions

We have just looked at the book-keeping for cash purchases and cash sales, ie where payment is made immediately. However, in business, many transactions for purchases and sales are made on credit, ie the goods or services are bought or sold now, with payment to be made at a later date. It is an important aspect of double-entry book-keeping to record the credit transaction as a purchase or a sale, and then record the second entry in an account in the name of the creditor or debtor, ie to record the amount owing by the firm to a creditor, or to the firm by a debtor.

Businesses usually record credit transactions in appropriate primary accounting records:

- credit purchases are entered in the purchases day book
- credit sales are entered in the sales day book

At regular intervals – daily, weekly or monthly – the totals and amounts from the day books are transferred into the double-entry accounts. Day books are covered at level 2 of NVQ Accounting – see Osborne Books' *Cash & Credit Accounting Tutorial*, chapters 5 and 6.

credit purchases

Credit purchases are goods obtained from a supplier, with payment to take place at a later date. From the buyer's viewpoint, the supplier is a *creditor.*

The book-keeping entries are:

- **credit purchase**
  - *debit* purchases account
  - *credit* creditor's (supplier's) account

When payment is made to the creditor the book-keeping entries are:

- **payment made to creditor**
  - *debit* creditor's account
  - *credit* bank account or cash account

credit sales

With credit sales, goods or services are sold to a customer who is allowed to settle the account at a later date. From the seller's viewpoint, the customer is a *debtor.*

The book-keeping entries are:

- **credit sale**
  - *debit* debtor's (customer's) account
  - *credit* sales account

When payment is received from the debtor the book-keeping entries are:

- **payment received from debtor**
  - *debit* bank account or cash account
  - *credit* debtor's account

CASE STUDY

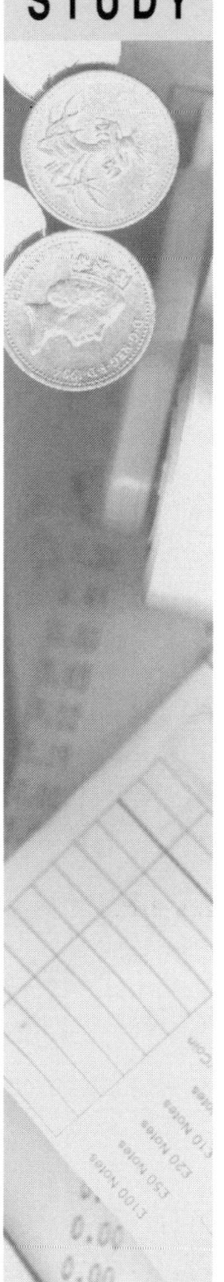

WYVERN WHOLESALERS - CREDIT TRANSACTIONS

situation

A local business, Wyvern Wholesalers, has the following transactions:

18 Sep	Bought goods, £250, on credit from Malvern Manufacturing, with payment to be made in 30 days' time
21 Sep	Sold goods, £175, on credit to Strensham Stores, payment to be made In 30 days' time
16 Oct	Paid £250 by cheque to Malvern Manufacturing
20 Oct	Received a cheque for £175 from Strensham Stores

Notes:

- *Wyvern Wholesalers is not registered for Value Added Tax*
- *day books are not used*

solution

These transactions will be recorded in the book-keeping system as follows (previous transactions on accounts, if there are any, are not shown here) :

Dr		**Purchases Account**			Cr
1998		£	1998		£
18 Sep	Malvern Manufacturing	250			

Dr		**Sales Account**			Cr
1998		£	1998		£
			21 Sep	Strensham Stores	175

Dr		Malvern Manufacturing			Cr
1998		£	1998		£
16 Oct	Bank	250	18 Sep	Purchases	250

Dr		Strensham Stores			Cr
1998		£	1998		£
21 Sep	Sales	175	20 Oct	Bank	175

Dr		Bank Account			Cr
1998		£	1998		£
20 Oct	Strensham Stores	175	16 Oct	Malvern Manufacturing	250

Note: the name of the other account involved has been used in the details column as a description.

balancing off accounts

In the case study above, after the transactions have been recorded in the books of Wyvern Wholesalers, the accounts of Malvern Manufacturing and Strensham Stores have the same amount entered on both debit and credit side. This means that nothing is owing to Wyvern Wholesalers, or is owed by it, ie the accounts have a 'nil' balance. In the course of trading, accounts will often *not* have a nil balance. We will explain in Chapter 3 how to 'balance' an account to show the 'total' of that account.

fixed assets bought on credit

Fixed assets are often purchased on credit terms. As with the purchase of goods for resale, an account is opened in the name of the creditor, as follows:

- **purchase of a fixed asset on credit**
  - *debit* fixed asset account
  - *credit* creditor's (supplier's) account

When payment is made to the creditor the book-keeping entries are:

- **payment made to creditor**
  - *debit* creditor's account
  - *credit* bank account or cash account

The primary accounting record for the purchase of fixed assets on credit is the journal – see Chapter 10.

PURCHASES RETURNS AND SALES RETURNS

From time-to-time goods bought or sold are returned, perhaps because the wrong items have been supplied (eg wrong type, size or colour), or because the goods are unsatisfactory. We will now explain the book-keeping entries for returned goods.

purchases returns

Purchases returns (or *returns out*) is where a business returns goods to a creditor (supplier).

The book-keeping entries are:

- *debit* creditor's (supplier's) account
- *credit* purchases returns (or returns outwards) account

Purchases returns are normally kept separate from purchases, ie they are entered in a separate purchases returns account rather than being credited to purchases account.

sales returns

Sales returns (or *returns in*) is where a debtor (customer) returns goods to the business.

The book-keeping entries are:

- *debit* sales returns (or returns in) account
- *credit* debtor's (customer's) account

Sales returns are normally kept separate from sales, ie they are entered in a separate sales returns account rather than being debited to sales account.

Businesses usually record returns transactions (of goods or services originally bought/sold on credit) in appropriate primary accounting records:

- purchases returns are entered in the purchases returns day book
- sales returns are entered in the sales returns day book

The totals and amounts from these day books are transferred into the double-entry accounts at regular intervals.

Now read the Case Study which follows on the next page. It shows how the double-entry book-keeping for purchases and sales returns is carried out.

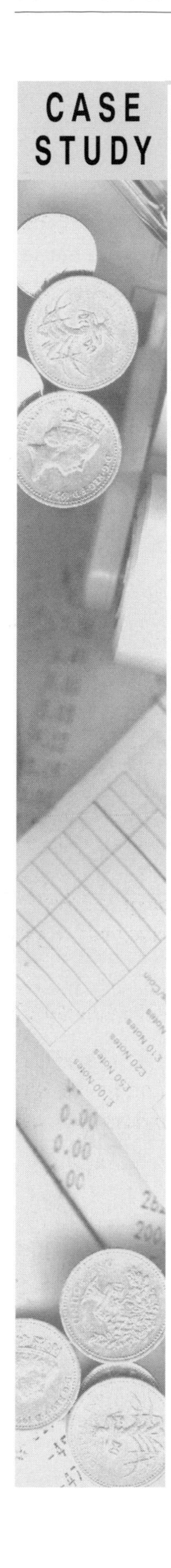

SUDBURY SUPPLIES - PURCHASES RETURNS AND SALES RETURNS

situation

Sudbury Suppliers, a builders' merchant, has the following transactions:

7 Oct	Bought goods, £280, on credit from B Lewis Limited
9 Oct	Returned unsatisfactory goods, £30, to B Lewis Limited
12 Oct	Sold goods, £125, on credit to A Holmes
19 Oct	A Holmes returned goods, £25
26 Oct	Paid the amount owing to B Lewis Limited by cheque
29 Oct	A Holmes paid the amount owing in cash

Notes:

- *Sudbury Suppliers is not registered for Value Added Tax*
- *day books are not used*

solution

The transactions will be recorded in the book-keeping system (previous transactions on accounts, if any, not shown) as follows:

Purchases Account

Dr					Cr
1998		£	1998		£
7 Oct	B Lewis Limited	280			

B Lewis Limited

Dr					Cr
1998		£	1998		£
9 Oct	Purchases Returns	30	7 Oct	Purchases	280
26 Oct	Bank	250			

Purchases Returns Account

Dr					Cr
1998		£	1998		£
			9 Oct	B Lewis Limited	30

Sales Account

Dr					Cr
1998		£	1998		£
			12 Oct	A Holmes	125

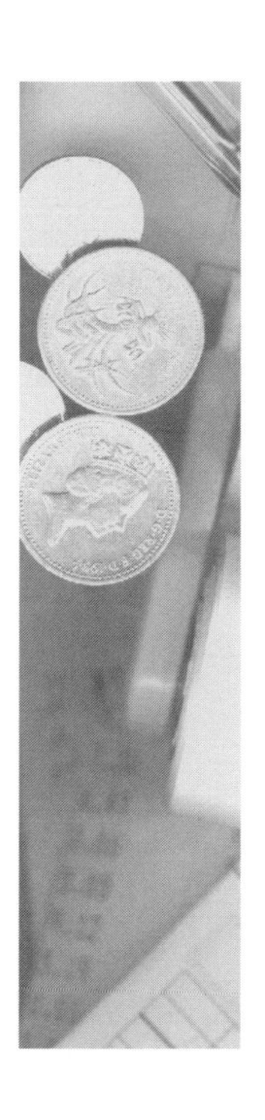

Dr		A Holmes			Cr
1998		£	1998		£
12 Oct	Sales	125	19 Oct	Sales Returns	25
			29 Oct	Cash	100

Dr		Sales Returns Account			Cr
1998		£	1998		£
19 Oct	A Holmes	25			

Dr		Bank Account			Cr
1998		£	1998		£
			26 Oct	B Lewis Limited	250

Dr		Cash Account			Cr
1998		£	1998		£
29 Oct	A Holmes	100			

CARRIAGE INWARDS AND CARRIAGE OUTWARDS

Carriage inwards is where the buyer pays the carriage (transport) cost of purchases, eg an item is purchased by mail order, and the buyer has to pay the additional cost of delivery (and possibly packing also).

*Carriage outward*s is where the seller pays the carriage charge, eg an item is sold to the customer and described as 'post free'.

Both carriage inwards and carriage outwards are expenses and their cost should be debited to two separate expenses accounts, *carriage inwards account* and *carriage outwards account* respectively:

- **carriage inwards**
  - *debit* carriage inwards account (alternatively, purchases account could be debited)
  - *credit* creditor's account, or bank account/cash account
- **carriage outwards**
  - *debit* carriage outwards account
  - *credit* bank account/cash account

CASH DISCOUNT IN THE BOOK-KEEPING SYSTEM

Cash discount is an allowance off the invoice amount for quick settlement, eg 2% cash discount for settlement within seven days. (Do not confuse cash discount with *trade* discount – an amount sometimes allowed as a reduction in price when goods are supplied to other businesses.) A business can be involved with cash discount in two ways:

- discount allowed to debtors
- discount received from creditors

CASE STUDY

R PATEL – DISCOUNTS ALLOWED AND RECEIVED

situation - discount allowed

R Patel sells TV and video equipment. When cash discount allowed is taken by one of his customers it is entered into the accounts as shown by the following transactions:

12 Oct Sold goods, £100, on credit to P Henry, allowing her a cash discount of 2% for settlement within 7 days (note: the seller of the goods is not VAT- registered)

16 Oct P Henry pays £98 by cheque

solution

Dr **Sales Account** Cr

1998		£	1998		£
			12 Oct	P Henry	100

Dr **P Henry** Cr

1998		£	1998		£
12 Oct	Sales	100	16 Oct	Bank	98
			16 Oct	Discount Allowed	2
		100			100

Dr **Bank Account** Cr

1998		£	1998		£
16 Oct	P Henry	98			

Dr **Discount Allowed Account** Cr

1998		£	1998		£
16 Oct	P Henry	2			

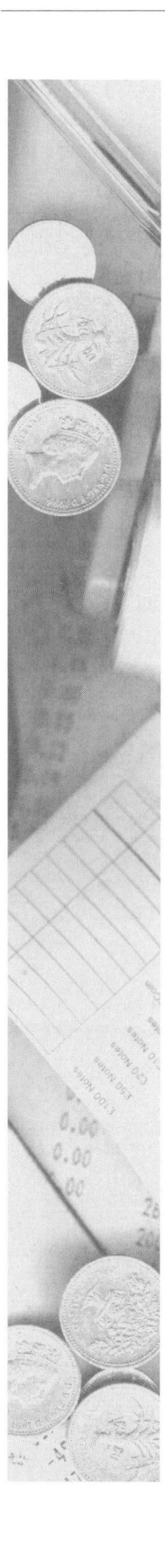

notes

- *The amount of the payment received from the debtor (P Henry) is debited to the bank account and credited to the debtor's account.*
- *The amount of discount allowed – an expense to the business – is debited to discount allowed account and credited to the debtor's account.*

situation – discount received

R Patel is allowed cash discount for quick settlement by his creditors. The following transactions show how discount received is entered into the accounts.

20 Oct Bought goods, £200, on credit from H Singh Limited; 2.5% cash discount is offered for settlement by the end of October (note: the seller of the goods is not registered for VAT)

30 Oct Paid H Singh Limited £195 by cheque

solution

Purchases Account

Dr					Cr
1998		£	1998		£
20 Oct	H Singh Limited	200			

H Singh Limited

Dr					Cr
1998		£	1998		£
30 Oct	Bank	195	20 Oct	Purchases	200
30 Oct	Discount Received	5			
		200			200

Bank Account

Dr					Cr
1998		£	1998		£
			30 Oct	H Singh Limited	195

Discount Received Account

Dr					Cr
1998		£	1998		£
			30 Oct	H Singh Limited	5

notes

- *The business is receiving cash discount from its creditor, and the amount is entered as: debit creditor's account, credit discount received account.*
- *Discount received account is an income account, because it represents a benefit given to the business by creditors.*

VAT AND DOUBLE-ENTRY ACCOUNTS

When a business is registered for Value Added Tax it is normally able to claim back VAT paid on purchases of goods, fixed assets and expenses – this is known as *input tax*. A VAT-registered business must also charge VAT – *output tax* – whenever it supplies goods and services (except for zero-rated and exempt goods and services). A separate account is opened for VAT.

When a VAT-registered business buys, for example, fixed assets it will enter the amount of input VAT direct to the debit side of VAT account.

example transaction

On 16 April 1998, Osborne Paints Limited, a company which is registered for Value Added Tax, buys a new computer at a cost of £1,000 + VAT of £175, paying by a cheque for £1,175.

This is recorded in the double-entry accounts as:

Computer Account

Dr					Cr
1998		£	1998		£
16 Apr	Bank	1,000			

Value Added Tax Account

Dr					Cr
1998		£	1998		£
16 Apr	Bank	175			

Bank Account

Dr					Cr
1998		£	1998		£
			16 Apr	Computer	1,175

Similarly when the business sells its paints to a customer it will charge *output VAT* on the goods. The entries for a sale of £705 (£600 + VAT) will be:

- *debit* customer's account £705 – this is the amount owed
- *credit* VAT account £105 – this is the VAT charged on the sale
- *credit* sales account £600 – this is the value of the goods sold

For more detail on Value Added Tax, please see Chapter 8 (page 121 of this book) and Osborne Books' *Costing, Reports & Returns Tutorial.*

CHAPTER SUMMARY

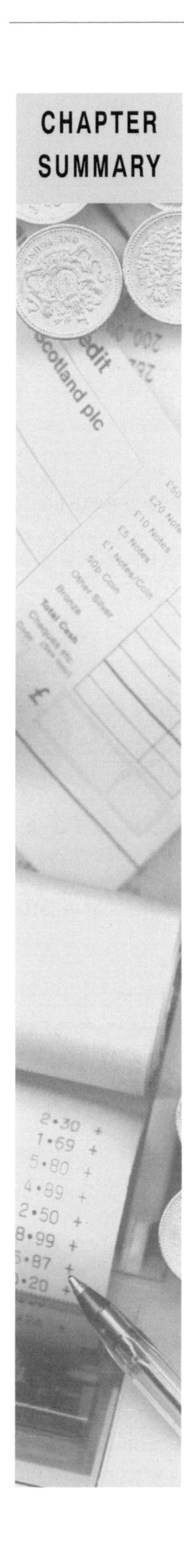

- Business transactions are recorded in ledger accounts using double-entry book-keeping principles.
- Each double-entry book-keeping transaction involves a debit entry and a credit entry.
- Entries in the bank account and cash account are:
  - *debit* money in
  - *credit* money out
- Fixed assets are items purchased by a business for use on a semi-permanent basis, eg premises, motor vehicles, machinery and office equipment. The purchase of such items is called *capital expenditure*.
- Running expenses of a business, such as rent paid, wages, electricity, etc are called *revenue expenditure*.
- Other accounts are opened in the book-keeping system for: capital, fixed assets, expenses, income, drawings and loans.
- Purchases account is used to record the purchase of goods in which the business trades: the normal entry is on the debit side.
- Sales account is used to record the sale of goods or services in which the business trades: the normal entry is on the credit side.
- The purchase of goods is recorded as:
  - *debit* purchases account
  - *credit* bank/cash account or, if bought on credit, creditor's account
- The sale of goods or services is recorded as:
  - *debit* bank/cash account or, if sold on credit, debtor's account
  - *credit* sales account
- Purchases returns (or returns out) are recorded as:
  - *debit* creditor's account
  - *credit* purchases returns account
- Sales returns (or returns in) are recorded as:
  - *debit* sales returns account
  - *credit* debtor's account
- 'Carriage' is the expense of transporting goods:
  - *carriage inwards* is the cost of carriage paid on purchases
  - *carriage outwards* is the cost of carriage paid on sales
- Cash discount allowed (for quick settlement) is entered in the accounts as:
  - *debit* discount allowed account
  - *credit* debtor's account
- Cash discount received is entered as:
  - *debit* creditor's account
  - *credit* discount received account
- VAT account will record the amounts of input VAT (VAT on purchases and expenses) and output VAT (VAT on sales of goods and services).

KEY TERMS

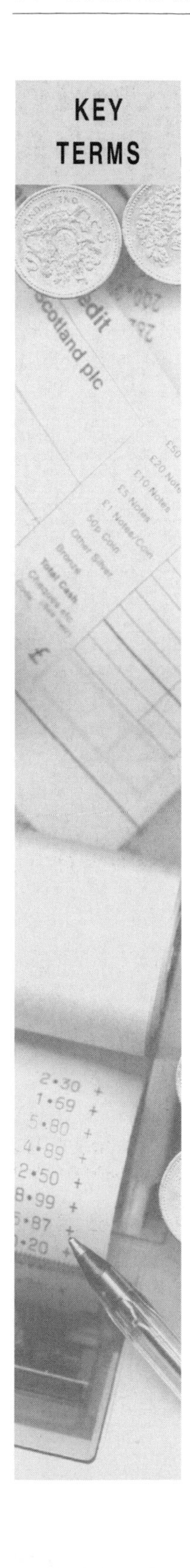

ledger accounts	where double-entry book-keeping transactions are recorded
debit entry	the account which gains value, or records an asset or an expense
credit entry	the account which gives value, or records a liability, or an income item
capital	the amount of money invested in the business by the owner (or owners)
fixed asset	item purchased by a business for use on a semi-permanent basis
capital expenditure	the purchase of fixed assets for use by the business
revenue expenditure	the expenses incurred in the day-to-day running of the business
drawings	money taken from the business by the owner, in the form of cash or cheque (or sometimes goods) for personal use
purchases account	used to record the purchase – whether on credit or for cash – of the goods in which the business trades
sales account	used to record the sale – whether on credit or for cash – of the goods in which the business trades
credit purchases	goods bought, with payment to be made at a later date
credit sales	goods sold, with payment to be received at an agreed date in the future
purchases returns	where a business returns goods to a creditor (supplier)
sales returns	where a debtor (customer) returns goods to the business
carriage inwards	the cost of carriage paid on purchases
carriage outwards	the cost of carriage paid on sales
cash discount	an allowance off the invoice amount for quick settlement
discount allowed	cash discount allowed to debtors
discount received	cash discount received from creditors

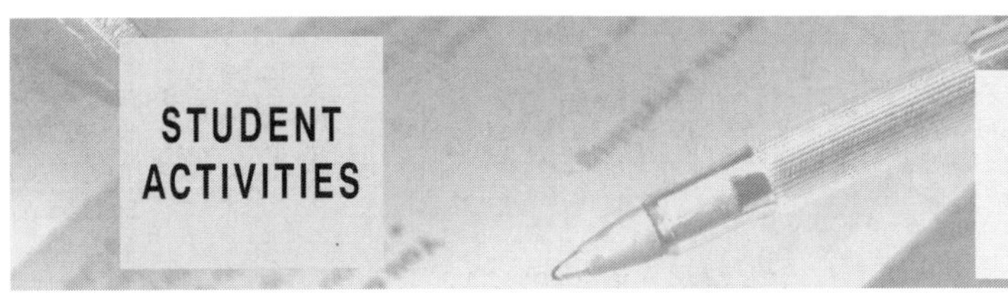

The answers to these Student Activities are printed in the back of this book. Further questions and more fully extended Student Activities and Assessments are to be found in the accompanying Osborne Books' text *Financial Accounting Workbook*.

2.1 The payment of wages in cash is recorded in the accounts as:

	Debit	*Credit*
(a)	wages account	drawings account
(b)	cash account	wages account
(c)	capital account	wages account
(d)	wages account	cash account

Answer (a) or (b) or (c) or (d)

2.2 A loan is received by cheque from John Box. This is recorded in the accounts as:

	Debit	*Credit*
(a)	bank account	capital account
(b)	bank account	John Box: loan account
(c)	drawings account	John Box: loan account
(d)	John Box: loan account	bank account

Answer (a) or (b) or (c) or (d)

2.3 The owner of a business withdraws cash for her own use. This is recorded in the accounts as:

	Debit	*Credit*
(a)	drawings account	bank account
(b)	bank account	cash account
(c)	wages account	cash account
(d)	drawings account	cash account

Answer (a) or (b) or (c) or (d)

2.4 James Anderson has kept his bank account up-to-date, but has not got around to the other double-entry book-keeping entries. Rule up the other accounts for him, and make the appropriate entries.

Dr **Bank Account** Cr

1998		£	1998		£
2 Feb	Capital	7,500	6 Feb	Computer	2,000
13 Feb	Bank loan	2,500	9 Feb	Rent paid	750
20 Feb	Commission received	145	12 Feb	Wages	425
			23 Feb	Drawings	200
			25 Feb	Wages	380
			27 Feb	Van	6,000

Note: James Anderson is not registered for Value Added Tax

3 BALANCING ACCOUNTS AND THE TRIAL BALANCE

this chapter covers . . .

With the 'traditional' form of account (the 'T' account) that we have used so far, it is necessary to calculate the balance of each account from time-to-time, according to the needs of the business, and at the end of each financial year.

The balance of an account is the total of that account to date, eg the amount of wages paid, the amount of sales made. In this chapter we shall see how this balancing of accounts is carried out.

We shall then use the balances from each account in order to check the double-entry book-keeping by extracting a trial balance, which is a list of the balances of all the ledger accounts.

NVQ PERFORMANCE CRITERIA COVERED

unit 4: MAINTAINING FINANCIAL RECORDS AND PREPARING ACCOUNTS

element 3

collect and collate information for the preparation of final accounts

- ❑ *the trial balance is accurately prepared and, where necessary, a suspense account* is opened and reconciled*

**see Chapter 10 for coverage of suspense accounts*

TARA SMITH, TRADING AS "THE FASHION SHOP"

Trial balance as at 31 December 1998

	Dr	*Cr*
	£	£
Stock at 1 January 1998	12,500	
Purchases	105,000	
Sales		155,000
Administration expenses	6,200	
Wages	23,500	
Rent paid	750	
Telephone	500	
Interest paid	4,500	
Travel expenses	550	
Premises	100,000	
Shop fittings	20,000	
Debtors	10,500	
Bank	5,450	
Cash	50	
Capital		75,000
Drawings	7,000	
Loan from bank		50,000
Creditors		14,500
Value Added Tax		2,000
	296,500	296,500

DEBIT AND CREDIT BALANCES – GUIDELINES

Certain accounts always have a debit balance, while others always have a credit balance. You should already know these, but the lists set out below will act as a revision guide, and will also help in your understanding of trial balances.

debit balances

- cash account
- purchases account
- sales returns account (returns in)
- fixed asset accounts, eg computers, motor vehicles, machinery, etc

- expenses accounts, eg wages, telephone, rent paid, etc
- drawings account
- debtors' accounts (many businesses use a *sales ledger control account* – see Chapter 9 – the balance of which gives the total of debtors: this balance is entered in the trial balance as 'debtors')

credit balances

- sales account
- purchases returns account (returns out)
- income accounts, eg rent received, commission received, fees received, etc
- capital account
- loan account, eg loan from bank
- creditors' accounts (many businesses use a *purchases ledger control account* – see Chapter 9 – the balance of which gives the total of creditors: this balance is entered in the trial balance as 'creditors')

Note that:

- *Bank account* can be either debit or credit – it will be debit when the business has money in the bank, and credit when it is overdrawn.
- *Value Added Tax account* can be either debit or credit – it will be debit when VAT is due to the business and credit when the business owes VAT to HM Customs & Excise.

IF THE TRIAL BALANCE DOESN'T BALANCE . . .

If the trial balance fails to balance, ie the two totals are different, there is an error (or errors):

- *either* in the addition of the trial balance
- *and/or* in the double-entry book-keeping

The procedure for finding the error(s) is as follows:

- check the addition of the trial balance
- check that the balance of each account has been correctly entered in the trial balance, and under the correct heading, ie debit or credit
- check that the balance of every account in the ledger has been included in the trial balance
- check the calculation of the balance on each account
- calculate the amount that the trial balance is wrong, and then look in the accounts for a transaction for this amount: if one is found, check that the double-entry book-keeping has been carried out correctly

- halve the amount by which the trial balance is wrong, and look for a transaction for this amount: if it is found, check the double-entry book-keeping
- if the amount by which the trial balance is wrong is divisible by nine, then the error may be a reversal of figures, eg £65 entered as £56, or £45 entered as £54
- if the trial balance is wrong by a round amount, eg £10, £100, £1,000, the error is likely to be in the calculation of the account balances
- if the error(s) is still not found, it is necessary to check the book-keeping transactions since the date of the last trial balance, by going back to the prime documents (invoices, cheques, etc) and the primary accounting records (day books and cash books)

ERRORS NOT SHOWN BY A TRIAL BALANCE

As mentioned earlier, a trial balance does not prove the complete accuracy of the accounting records. There are six types of errors that are not shown by a trial balance.

error of omission

Here a business transaction has been completely omitted from the accounting records, ie both the debit and credit entries have not been made.

reversal of entries

With this error, the debit and credit entries have been made in the accounts but on the wrong side of the two accounts concerned. For example, a cash sale has been entered wrongly as a debit to sales account, and as a credit to cash account. (This should have been entered as a debit to cash account, and a credit to sales account.)

mispost/error of commission

Here, a transaction is entered to the wrong person's account. For example, a sale of goods on credit to A T Hughes has been entered as a debit to A J Hughes' account and as a credit to sales account. Here, double-entry book-keeping has been completed but, when A J Hughes receives a statement of account, he or she will soon complain about being debited with goods not ordered or received.

error of principle

This is when a transaction has been entered in the wrong type of account. For example, the cost of fuel for vehicles has been entered as a debit to motor vehicles account, and as a credit to bank account. The error is that motor vehicles account represents fixed assets – the transaction should have been debited to the expense account for motor vehicle running expenses.

error of original entry (or transcription)

Here, the correct accounts have been used, and the correct sides: what is wrong is that the amount has been entered incorrectly in *both* accounts. This could be caused by a 'bad figure' on an invoice or a cheque, or it could be caused by a 'reversal of figures', eg an amount of £45 being entered in both accounts as £54. Note that where both debit and credit entries have been made incorrectly the trial balance will still balance; if one entry has been made incorrectly and the other is correct, then the error will be shown.

compensating error

This is where two errors cancel each other out. For example, if the balance of purchases account is calculated wrongly at £10 too much, and a similar error has occurred in calculating the balance of sales account, then the two errors will compensate each other, and the trial balance will not show the errors.

Correction of errors is covered fully in Chapter 10.

IMPORTANCE OF THE TRIAL BALANCE

A business will extract a trial balance on a regular basis to check the arithmetical accuracy of the book-keeping. More importantly, the trial balance is used as a basis for the production of the *final accounts* of a business. These final accounts, which are prepared once a year (often more frequently) comprise:

- profit and loss account
- balance sheet

The final accounts show the owner(s) how profitable the business has been, what the business owns, and how the business is financed. The preparation of final accounts is an important aspect of accounting and one which we shall be expanding in the remainder of this book.

In the next chapter we will see how the two-column trial balance is 'extended' and the figures entered into further columns in preparation for the production of the final accounts.

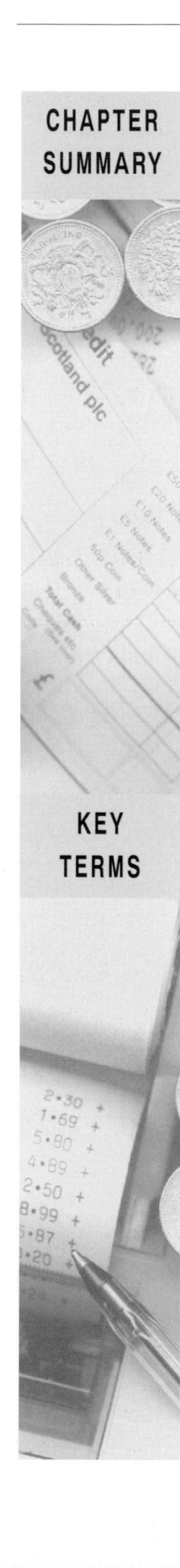

CHAPTER SUMMARY

- The traditional 'T' account needs to be balanced at regular intervals – often at the month-end.
- When balancing accounts, the book-keeper must adhere strictly to the rules of double-entry book-keeping.
- When each account in the ledger has been balanced, a trial balance can be extracted.
- A trial balance does not prove the complete accuracy of the accounting records; errors not shown by a trial balance are:
  - error of omission
  - reversal of entries
  - mispost/error of commission
  - error of principle
  - error of original entry
  - compensating error
- The trial balance is used as the starting point for the preparation of a business' final accounts.

KEY TERMS

balance of account	the total of the account to date
trial balance	list of the balances of every account forming the ledger, distinguishing between those accounts which have debit balances and those which have credit balances
error of omission	business transaction completely omitted from the accounting records
reversal of entries	debit and credit entries made on the wrong side of the accounts
mispost/error of commission	transaction entered to the wrong person's account
error of principle	transaction entered in the wrong type of account
error of original entry	wrong amount entered incorrectly in accounts
compensating error	where two errors cancel each other out

STUDENT ACTIVITIES

The answers to these Student Activities are printed in the back of this book. Further questions and more fully extended Student Activities and Assessments are to be found in the accompanying Osborne Books' text *Financial Accounting Workbook*.

3.1 A firm's bank account is as follows:

Dr		Bank Account			Cr
1999		£	1999		£
1 Jan	Capital	1,000	9 Jan	Computer	500
19 Jan	Sales	650	12 Jan	Purchases	400
			27 Jan	Purchases	350
			29 Jan	Electricity	75

At 31 January 1999, the balance of the account is:

(a) credit £325

(b) debit £1,650

(c) debit £325

(d) credit £1,325

Answer (a) or (b) or (c) or (d)

3.2 Which one of the following accounts normally has a debit balance?

(a) capital account

(b) purchases account

(c) sales account

(d) purchases returns account

Answer (a) or (b) or (c) or (d)

3.3 Which one of the following accounts normally has a credit balance?

(a) purchases account

(b) premises account

(c) capital account

(d) wages account

Answer (a) or (b) or (c) or (d)

3.4 The following are the business transactions of Andrew Johnstone, a retailer of computer software, for the months of January and February 1999:

Transactions for January

1 Jan	Started in business with £10,000 in the bank
4 Jan	Paid rent on premises £500, by cheque
5 Jan	Bought shop fittings £1,500, by cheque
7 Jan	Bought stock of computer software £5,000, on credit from Comp Supplies Limited
11 Jan	Software sales £1,000 paid into bank
12 Jan	Software sales £1,250 paid into bank
16 Jan	Software sales £850 on credit to Rowcester College
20 Jan	Paid Comp Supplies Limited £5,000 by cheque
22 Jan	Software sales £1,450 paid into bank
25 Jan	Bought software £6,500 on credit from Comp Supplies Limited
27 Jan	Rowcester College returns software £100

Transactions for February

2 Feb	Paid rent on premises £500 by cheque
4 Feb	Software sales £1,550 paid into bank
5 Feb	Returned faulty software, £150 to Comp Supplies Limited
10 Feb	Software sales £1,300 paid into bank
12 Feb	Rowcester College pays the amount owing by cheque
15 Feb	Bought shop fittings £850 by cheque
19 Feb	Software sales £1,600 paid into bank
22 Feb	Paid Comp Supplies Limited the amount owing by cheque
24 Feb	Bought software £5,500 on credit from Comp Supplies Limited
25 Feb	Software sales £1,100 paid into bank
26 Feb	Software sales £1,050 on credit to Rowcester College

You are to:

(a) record the January transactions in the books of account, and balance each account at 31 January 1999

(b) draw up a trial balance at 31 January 1999

(c) record the February transactions in the books of account, and balance each account at 28 February 1999

(d) draw up a trial balance at 28 February 1999

Notes

- *Andrew Johnstone is not registered for Value Added Tax*
- *day books are not required*
- *make sure that you leave plenty of space for each account – particularly sales, purchases and bank*

4 FINAL ACCOUNTS – THE EXTENDED TRIAL BALANCE

this chapter covers . . .

So far we have looked at the techniques of recording different types of financial transactions in the books of account. The financial accountant will use the information from the accounting system, summarised in the two-column trial balance, to produce the final accounts of the business: profit and loss account and balance sheet.

These financial statements can be produced from a more elaborate form of trial balance known as the extended trial balance. This sets out debit and credit columns for:

- *the ledger balances*
- *adjustments to the figures*
- *the financial statements where the figures are used: profit and loss account and balance sheet*

NVQ PERFORMANCE CRITERIA COVERED

unit 4: MAINTAINING FINANCIAL RECORDS AND PREPARING ACCOUNTS

element 3

collect and collate information for the preparation of final accounts

- ❑ *the organisation's policies, regulations, procedures and timescales relating to preparing final accounts are observed*

element 4

prepare the extended trial balance

- ❑ *totals from the general ledger or other records are correctly entered on the extended trial balance*
- ❑ *the extended trial balance is accurately extended and totalled*

THE FINAL ACCOUNTS

At regular intervals the owner of a business and other interested parties need to know how the business is progressing. To meet this need, final accounts are prepared which comprise the accounting statements of:

- *profit and loss account* – showing the profitability and performance of the business during the accounting period
- *balance sheet* – showing what the business is worth (in terms of assets, liabilities, and capital) at the end of the accounting period

In this chapter we will see how the figures for the final accounts are prepared by means of the *extended trial balance* which takes the figures from the two-column trial balance explained in the last chapter and sets them out in columns ready for the preparation of the profit and loss account and balance sheet. To illustrate this process we will look at the accounts of a sole trader boutique owner, Tara Smith.

important study note

You do not need at this stage of your course to study the final accounts in depth, but you should know how they are structured and where the figures from the extended trial balance are entered. When working through this book you will find it useful to refer to the Appendix (page 303); this sets out the format of final accounts and explains the individual items which appear in them.

THE PROFIT AND LOSS ACCOUNT

income minus **expenses** equals **net profit (or loss)**

The profit and loss account shows the income a business has received over a given period for goods sold or services provided (together with any small amounts of other income, eg rent received). It also sets out the expenses incurred – the cost of the product, and the overheads (eg wages, administration expenses, rent, and so on). The difference between income and expenses is the *net profit* of the business. If expenses are greater than income, then a loss has been made. The net profit (or loss) belongs to the owner(s) of the business. If the business trades in goods (as Tara Smith's does) a figure for *gross profit* shows the profit made before overheads are deducted.

The illustration on page 50 shows Tara Smith's profit and loss account. Study it carefully and see how the figures can be identified on Tara Smith's trial balance (shown on page 53).

TARA SMITH, TRADING AS "THE FASHION SHOP"

PROFIT AND LOSS ACCOUNT
for the year ended 31 December 1998

	£	£
Sales		155,000
Opening stock (1 January 1998)	12,500	
Purchases	105,000	
	117,500	
Less Closing stock (31 December 1998)	10,500	
Cost of sales		107,000
Gross profit		48,000
Less overheads:		
Administration expenses	6,200	
Wages	23,500	
Rent paid	750	
Telephone	500	
Interest paid	4,500	
Travel expenses	550	
		36,000
Net profit		12,000

THE BALANCE SHEET

assets minus **liabilities** equals **capital**

Tara's balance sheet (shown opposite) gives a 'snapshot' of her business at a particular date – the end of the shop's financial year. Study the format and see how the figures have been taken from her trial balance on page 53. A typical business balance sheet will show:

assets What the business owns:

- fixed assets, eg premises, vehicles, computers
- current assets, eg stock of goods for resale, debtors, bank and cash balances

liabilities What the business owes:

- current liabilities, eg creditors, overdrafts, VAT due
- long-term liabilities, eg long-term bank loans

net assets The total of fixed and current assets, less current and long-term liabilities. The net assets are financed by the owner(s) of the business, in the form of capital. Net assets therefore equals the total of the 'financed by' section – the balance sheet 'balances'.

capital Where the money to finance the business has come from, eg the owner's investment, business profits.

TARA SMITH, TRADING AS "THE FASHION SHOP"

BALANCE SHEET
as at 31 December 1998

	£	£	£
Fixed assets			
Premises			100,000
Shop fittings			20,000
			120,000
Current assets			
Stock		10,500	
Debtors		10,500	
Bank		5,450	
Cash		50	
		26,500	
Less Current liabilities			
Creditors	14,500		
Value Added Tax	2,000		
		16,500	
Working capital			10,000
			130,000
Less Long-term liabilities			
Loan from bank			50,000
NET ASSETS			80,000
FINANCED BY			
Capital			
Opening capital			75,000
Add net profit			12,000
			87,000
Less drawings			7,000
Closing capital			80,000

ACCOUNTING PERIODS

The final accounts are linked: a profit and loss account covers a specific time period, and a balance sheet shows the state of the business on the last day of that time period. For example:

- profit and loss account **for the year ended** 31 December 1998
- balance sheet **as at** 31 December 1998

The time period covered by the profit and loss account is known as an *accounting period*. Generally, for each business, an accounting period covers the same length of time, for example the year ended 31 December 1998, year ended 31 December 1999, and so on. The last day of one accounting period is immediately followed by the first day of the next accounting period. While accounting periods can cover any length of time, the most common are:

- *monthly or quarterly* – used within a business to monitor activity and profitability in the accounting period, and the state of the business, in terms of assets and liabilities, at the end of the period
- *half-yearly* – often produced by public limited companies as information for their shareholders
- *annually* – the most common accounting period, used by virtually every business from sole traders through to the largest public limited companies

FINAL ACCOUNTS AND THE TRIAL BALANCE

As we have seen in earlier chapters, the book-keeping system records day-to-day financial transactions. At regular intervals a trial balance is extracted to prove the arithmetical accuracy of the book-keeping. It is the trial balance that provides the starting point in the preparation of final accounts. As noted earlier there are two trial balance formats:

- the two-column trial balance (shown opposite)
- the trial balance *extended* into a number of columns (see page 55)

Note that the profit and loss account is an 'account' in terms of double-entry book-keeping. This means that an amount recorded in this account must be recorded elsewhere in the book-keeping system, eg a debit to profit and loss is recorded as a credit to another account, in order to complete double-entry. By contrast, the balance sheet is not an account, but is a statement of account balances remaining after the profit and loss account has been prepared.

To understand the preparation of the extended trial balance you should now read the Tara Smith Case Study which starts on the next page.

- net profit
  - *debit* profit and loss account
  - *credit* capital account
- net loss
  - *debit* capital account
  - *credit* profit and loss account

A net profit increases the owner's stake in the business by adding to capital account, while a net loss decreases the owner's stake.

At the same time the account for drawings, which has been storing up the amount of drawings during the year is also transferred to capital account:

- *debit* capital account
- *credit* drawings account

Thus the total of drawings for the year is debited to capital account.

When these transactions are completed, the capital account for Tara Smith appears as:

Capital Account

Dr			Cr		
1998		£	1998		£
31 Dec	Drawings for year	7,000	31 Dec	Balance b/d	75,000
31 Dec	Balance c/d	80,000	31 Dec	Profit and loss account (net profit for year)	12,000
		87,000			87,000
1999			1999		
			1 Jan	Balance b/d	80,000

Note: Although the balance of capital account at the end of the year, £80,000, does not appear on the extended trial balance, the constituent figures are shown, ie capital £75,000, net profit £12,000, drawings £7,000. The balance sheet of Tara Smith on page 51 shows the changes to capital account during the year, and closes with a balance of £80,000.

balance sheet

Unlike profit and loss account, the balance sheet is not part of the double-entry accounts. The balance sheet is made up of those accounts which remain with balances at the end of the financial year, after the profit and loss account transfers have been made. Thus it consists of asset and liability accounts, not forgetting the asset of closing stock, together with the owner's capital and drawings.

CHAPTER SUMMARY

- The final accounts of a business comprise:
  - profit and loss account
  - balance sheet

- The extended trial balance method of preparing final accounts starts with the trial balance and then transfers each account balance to one of the final accounts.

- Each account balance from the trial balance is entered into the final accounts once only; the additional items of closing stock and net profit or loss are entered into both final accounts – this ensures that the double-entry rules of one debit and one credit entry for each transaction are maintained.

- The profit and loss account forms part of the double-entry system; amounts entered must have the opposite entry recorded in the appropriate general (or nominal) ledger account.

- The balance sheet is not part of the double-entry system; it lists the balances of accounts for assets, liabilities and capital at a particular date.

- The extended trial balance gives an understanding of the principles of final accounts. It is often used by accountancy firms as a first step towards preparing year-end accounts for their clients.

KEY TERMS

final accounts — accounting statements, comprising the profit and loss account and balance sheet, produced at least once a year, which give information to the owner(s) and other interested parties on how the business is progressing

profit and loss account — shows the net profit (or net loss) of the business for the accounting period

balance sheet — shows the assets, liabilities and capital of the business at the end of the accounting period

extended trial balance — a spreadsheet format used to produce the final accounts

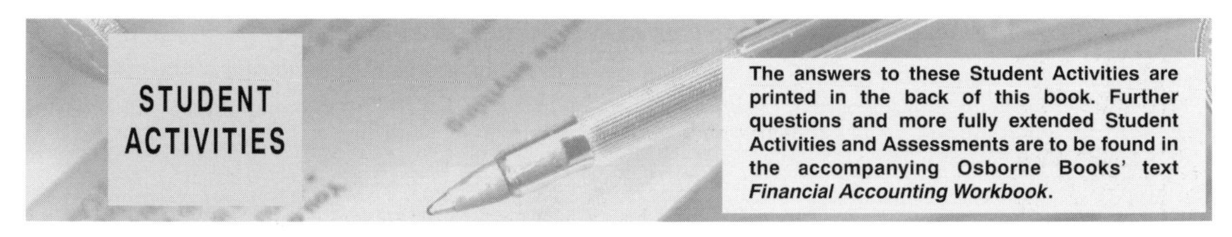

Extended trial balance format: *a blank photocopiable pro-forma of the extended trial balance is included in the Appendix (page 308)– it is advisable to enlarge it up to full A4 size. Alternatively you can set up a computer spreadsheet – but remember to allow for all the rows shown on the pro-forma – they will be needed in later chapters.*

Optional activities: *the figures from the extended trial balance columns can, in addition, be extracted to set out statements of income and expenditure (to determine net profit) and totalled lists of assets, liabilities and capital. You may also wish to set out the final accounts in full as preparation for NVQ Level 4 work .*

4.1 Which one of the following does not appear in the profit and loss account?

(a) salaries

(b) vehicles

(c) fuel for vehicles

(d) net profit

Answer (a) or (b) or (c) or (d)

4.2 Net profit is:

(a) assets minus liabilities

(b) debtors minus creditors

(c) closing bank balance minus opening bank balance

(d) income minus expenses

Answer (a) or (b) or (c) or (d)

4.3 You are to fill in the missing figures for the following businesses:

	Income	Expenses	Net profit or loss*	Assets	Liabilities	Capital
	£	£	£	£	£	£
Business A	100,000	60,000	....	250,000	150,000	....
Business B	80,000	....	10,000	200,000	....	100,000
Business C	....	50,000	20,000	....	40,000	50,000
Business D	60,000	....	(15,000)	130,000	....	70,000
Business E	90,000	100,000	....	....	60,000	40,000

* Note: net loss is indicated by brackets

4.4 Complete the table below for each item (a) to (g) indicating with a tick:

- whether the item would normally appear in the debit or credit column of the trial balance
- in which final account the item would appear at the end of the accounting period and whether as a debit or credit

	TRIAL BALANCE		FINAL ACCOUNTS			
			PROFIT & LOSS		BALANCE SHEET	
	Debit	Credit	Debit	Credit	Debit	Credit
(a) Salaries						
(b) Purchases						
(c) Debtors						
(d) Sales returns						
(e) Discount received						
(f) Motor vehicle						
(g) Capital						

4.5 The following trial balance has been extracted by Nick Johnson on 31 December 1998:

	Dr £	*Cr* £
Stock at 1 January 1998	25,000	
Purchases	210,000	
Sales		310,000
Administration expenses	12,400	
Wages	41,000	
Rent paid	7,500	
Telephone	1,000	
Interest paid	9,000	
Travel expenses	1,100	
Premises	200,000	
Machinery	40,000	
Debtors	31,000	
Bank	900	
Cash	100	
Capital		150,000
Drawings	14,000	
Loan from bank		100,000
Creditors		29,000
Value Added Tax		4,000
	593,000	593,000

Note: stock at 31 December 1998 was valued at £21,000

You are to prepare the figures for the final accounts of Nick Johnson for the year ended 31 December 1998, using the extended trial balance method.

4.6 The following trial balance has been extracted by the book-keeper of Alan Harris at 30 June 1998:

	Dr	*Cr*
	£	£
Stock at 1 July 1997	13,250	
Capital		70,000
Premises	65,000	
Motor vehicle	5,250	
Purchases	55,000	
Sales		85,500
Administration expenses	850	
Wages	9,220	
Rent paid	1,200	
Telephone	680	
Interest paid	120	
Travel expenses	330	
Debtors	1,350	
Creditors		6,400
Value Added Tax		1,150
Bank	2,100	
Cash	600	
Drawings	8,100	
	163,050	163,050

Note: stock at 30 June 1998 was valued at £18,100

You are to prepare the figures for the final accounts of Alan Harris for the year ended 30 June 1998, using the extended trial balance method.

5 ACCRUALS AND PREPAYMENTS

this chapter covers . . .

In the last chapter we looked at the preparation of final accounts

- *using the extended trial balance, or spreadsheet, approach*
- *in the conventional format with profit and loss account and balance sheet*

There are a number of adjustments which are made to the final accounts at the year-end in order to show a more realistic view of the state of the business. This chapter is concerned with the adjustments to be made for accruals and prepayments of expenses and income.

To illustrate the effect of adjustments for accruals and prepayments on final accounts we shall be referring to the final accounts of Tara Smith seen in the previous chapter.

NVQ PERFORMANCE CRITERIA COVERED

unit 4: MAINTAINING FINANCIAL RECORDS AND PREPARING ACCOUNTS

element 2

record income and expenditure

- ❑ *relevant accrued and prepaid income and expenditure is correctly identified and adjustments are made*
- ❑ *the organisation's policies, regulations, procedures and timescales in relation to recording income and expenditure are observed*

element 4

prepare the extended trial balance

- ❑ *adjustments not dealt with in the ledger accounts are correctly entered on the extended trial balance*

ACCRUAL OF EXPENSES

An accrual is an amount due in an accounting period which is unpaid at the end of that period, eg an insurance premium or an auditor's bill not yet paid.

In the final accounts, accrued expenses are:

- added to the expense account (eg insurance account, audit account) shown in the trial balance, before it is listed in the profit and loss account
- shown as a current liability in the year-end balance sheet

The reason for dealing with accruals in this way is to ensure that the profit and loss account records the cost that has been incurred for the year, instead of simply the amount that has been paid. In other words, the expense is adjusted to relate to the time period covered by the profit and loss account. The year-end balance sheet shows a liability for the amount that is due, but unpaid.

CASE STUDY

TARA SMITH: ACCRUAL OF AN EXPENSE

The trial balance of Tara Smith (see page 53) shows a debit balance for telephone expenses of £500. Before preparing the final accounts, a telephone bill for £100 is received on 4 January 1999, ie early in the new financial year. An examination of the bill shows that it is for costs incurred in 1998, therefore an adjustment needs to be made in the final accounts for 1998 to record this accrued expense.

accruals – the extended trial balance

The accrual is shown in the extended trial balance as follows:

- in the adjustments column
  - record £100 on the debit side of the telephone row
  - record £100 on the credit side of the accruals row
- on the debit side of the profit and loss column the total cost of the telephone row is now £600 (ie £500 from the trial balance, plus £100 accrual)
- on the credit side of the balance sheet column £100 from the accruals row is shown as a liability of the business

This adjustment is shown on Tara Smith's extended trial balance (page 70): the figures affected by the accrual (and also the prepayment – see below) are shaded for ease of reference.

accruals – the book-keeping records

In the double-entry records, a separate accruals account is opened which shows the amount owing at the end of the financial year. Thus telephone account and accruals account in the records of Tara Smith will appear as follows:

Dr	Telephone Account		Cr		
1998		£	1998		£
31 Dec	Balance b/d	500	31 Dec	Profit and loss account	600
31 Dec	Accruals account	100			
		600			600

Dr	Accruals Account		Cr		
1998		£	1998		£
31 Dec	Balance c/d	100	31 Dec	Telephone account	100
1999		£	1999		£
			1 Jan	Balance b/d	100

Notes:

- The book-keeper's trial balance showed the debit side balance brought down of £500 on telephone account
- As £100 is owing for telephone expenses at the end of the year, the transfer to profit and loss account is the cost that has been incurred for the year of £600
- The amount of the accrual is transferred to the credit side of accruals account; it is listed on the balance sheet at 31 December 1998 as a liability

Later on, for example on 15 January 1999, the telephone bill is paid by cheque and the accruals account now appears as:

Dr	Accruals Account		Cr		
1999		£	1999		£
15 Jan	Bank	100	1 Jan	Balance b/d	100

The effect of the payment on 15 January is that accruals account now has a 'nil' balance and the bill received on 4 January will not be recorded as an expense in the profit and loss account drawn up at the end of 1999. Where the accruals account contains a number of separate accruals – eg telephone, wages, rates, vehicle expenses – it is essential to keep a note of the amount of each. In this way, we can ensure that each is cleared during the new financial year.

the effect of an accrual on profit

Taking note of the accrual of an expense has the effect of reducing net profit for the accounting period in question. As the expenses have been increased, net profit is reduced. In this case the telephone bill due for the period reduces the net profit of Tara Smith by £100 from £12,000 to £11,900.

PREPAYMENT OF EXPENSES

A prepayment is a payment made in advance of the accounting period to which it relates.

A prepayment is, therefore, the opposite of an accrual: with a prepayment of expenses, some part of the expense has been paid in advance.

In the final accounts, prepaid expenses are:

- deducted from the expense account shown in the trial balance before it is listed in the profit and loss account
- shown as a current asset in the year-end balance sheet

As with accruals, the reason for dealing with prepaid expenses in this way is to ensure that the profit and loss account records the cost incurred for the year, and not the amount that has been paid – the profit and loss account expense relates to the time period covered by the profit and loss account. The year-end balance sheet shows an asset for the amount that has been prepaid.

CASE STUDY

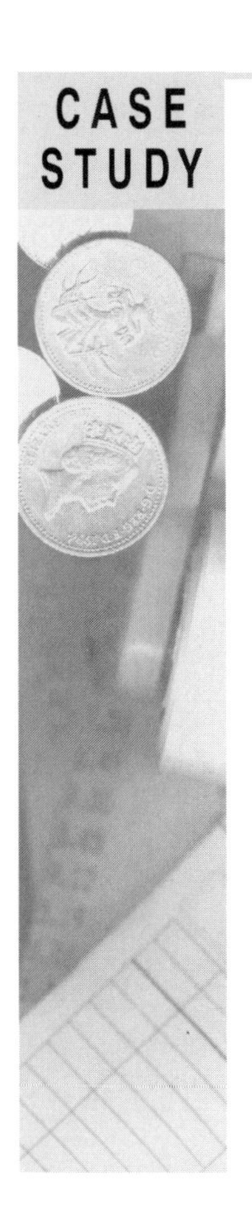

TARA SMITH: PREPAID EXPENSES

Tara Smith tells you that the trial balance figure for rent paid of £750 includes £75 of rent for January 1999 paid in advance. An adjustment needs to be made in the final accounts for 1998 to record this prepaid expense.

prepayments – the extended trial balance

The prepayment is shown in the extended trial balance as follows:

- in the adjustments column
  - record £75 on the credit side of the rent paid row
  - record £75 on the debit side of the prepayments row
- on the credit side of the profit and loss column the total cost of rent paid is now £675 (ie £750 from the trial balance, less £75 prepaid)
- on the debit side of the balance sheet column £75 from the prepayments row is shown as an asset of the business

The prepayment adjustment is shown on Tara Smith's extended trial balance (page 70), together with the accrual we have just dealt with – both are shaded for ease of reference.

prepayments – the book-keeping records

In the double-entry records, prepayments must be recorded in an asset account at the end of the financial year.

The expense account for 'rent paid' in the records of Tara Smith will appear as follows:

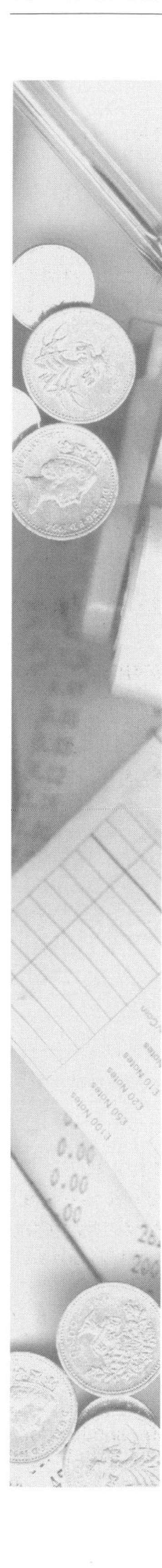

Dr	Rent Paid Account				Cr
1998		£	1998		£
31 Dec	Balance b/d	750	31 Dec	Profit and loss account	675
			31 Dec	Prepayments account	75
		750			750
1999		£	1999		£
1 Jan	Prepayments account	75			

Dr	**Prepayments Account**				**Cr**
1998		£	1998		£
31 Dec	Rent paid account	75	31 Dec	Balance c/d	75
1999		£	1999		£
1 Jan	Balance b/d	75	1 Jan	Rent paid account	75

Notes:

- The trial balance total for rent paid is £750
- As £75 is prepaid at the end of the year, the transfer to profit and loss account is the cost that has been incurred for the year of £675
- The amount of the prepayment is transferred to the debit side of prepayments account; it is listed on the balance sheet at 31 December 1998 as an asset
- At the beginning of the new financial year, amounts held in prepayments account are transferred back to the expense accounts. Thus, for the rent prepaid, the book-keeping entries on 1 January 1999 are:
  - *debit* rent paid account
  - *credit* prepayments account

  This now gives rent paid account a debit balance which will be included in the expense for rent paid for the year and will be transferred to profit and loss account on 31 December 1999.

effect on profit

Taking note of the prepayment of an expense has the effect of increasing a previously reported net profit – expenses have been reduced, so net profit is greater.

TARA SMITH: ACCRUALS AND PREPAYMENTS IN THE FINAL ACCOUNTS

We will now focus on how the adjustments for accruals and prepayments are shown in the profit and loss account and balance sheet of Tara Smith. Remember that we are taking note of the following items at 31 December 1998:

- telephone accrued £100
- rent prepaid £75

extended trial balance (page 70)

The layout for the extended trial balance includes rows for accruals and prepayments. The columns which are affected are adjustments, profit and loss, and balance sheet – the altered figures are shaded for illustrative purposes. Note that:

- the profit and loss column shows the net figure for each expense after allowing for the accrual or prepayment
- the balance sheet column shows the accrual as a liability and the prepayment as an asset

The effect of taking note of accruals and prepayments is to alter net profit from that shown by the extended trial balance for Tara Smith, seen earlier (page 55):

	£
Net profit (before adjustments)	12,000
Less telephone accrued	100
	11,900
Add rent prepaid	75
Net profit after adjustments	11,975

final accounts: conventional format (pages 71 – 72)

There is no effect on the gross profit; net profit is changed to £11,975 because of the amounts of the accrual and prepayment. In conventional format final accounts, there is no need to show the calculations – they are presented here for illustrative purposes.

In the conventional format balance sheet

- prepayments are included amongst the current assets
- accruals are included amongst the current liabilities

In Tara Smith's balance sheet, the accruals and prepayments are shaded for illustrative purposes.

EXTENDED TRIAL BALANCE **TARA SMITH TRADING AS "THE FASHION SHOP"** **31 DECEMBER 1998**

Description	Ledger balances		Adjustments		Profit and loss		Balance sheet	
	Dr £	*Cr* £	*Dr* £	*Cr* £	*Dr* £	*Cr* £	*Dr* £	*Cr* £
Stocks at 1 Jan 1998	12,500				12,500			
Purchases	105,000				105,000			
Sales		155,000				155,000		
Administration expenses	6,200				6,200			
Wages	23,500				23,500			
Rent paid	750			75	675			
Telephone	500		100		600			
Interest paid	4,500				4,500			
Travel expenses	550				550			
Premises	100,000						100,000	
Shop fittings	20,000						20,000	
Debtors	10,500						10,500	
Bank	5,450						5,450	
Cash	50						50	
Capital		75,000						75,000
Drawings	7,000						7,000	
Loan from bank		50,000						50,000
Creditors		14,500						14,500
Value Added Tax		2,000						2,000
Closing stock: Profit and loss				10,500		10,500		
Closing stock: Balance sheet			10,500				10,500	
Accruals				100				100
Prepayments			75				75	
Depreciation								
Bad debts								
Provision for bad debts:adjustment								
Net profit/loss					11,975			11,975
	296,500	296,500	10,675	10,675	165,500	165,500	153,575	153,575

TARA SMITH, TRADING AS "THE FASHION SHOP"

PROFIT AND LOSS ACCOUNT
for the year ended 31 December 1998

		£	£
Sales			155,000
Opening stock (1 January 1998)		12,500	
Purchases		105,000	
		117,500	
Less Closing stock (31 December 1998)		10,500	
Cost of sales			107,000
Gross profit			48,000
Less overheads:			
Administration expenses		6,200	
Wages		23,500	
Rent paid	750 – 75 =	675	
Telephone	500 + 100 =	600	
Interest paid		4,500	
Travel expenses		550	
			36,025
Net profit			11,975

note
The calculations in the grey box relate to accrued and prepaid expenses. They are shown here for illustrative purposes. The actual profit and loss account produced would not show these workings, but just the final expense figures.

TARA SMITH, TRADING AS "THE FASHION SHOP"

BALANCE SHEET
as at 31 December 1998

	£	£	£
Fixed assets			
Premises			100,000
Shop fittings			20,000
			120,000
Current assets			
Stock		10,500	
Debtors		10,500	
Prepayment		75	
Bank		5,450	
Cash		50	
		26,575	
Less Current liabilities			
Creditors	14,500		
Value Added Tax	2,000		
Accrual	100		
		16,600	
Working capital			9,975
			129,975
Less Long-term liabilities			
Loan from bank			50,000
NET ASSETS			79,975
FINANCED BY			
Capital			
Opening capital			75,000
Add net profit			11,975
			86,975
Less drawings			7,000
Closing capital			79,975

note
The figures in the grey boxes relate to the prepayment and the accrual as they appear on the balance sheet. The accrual is a current liability because it is still owing and due at the balance sheet date; the prepayment is a current asset as it represents an expense which has already been paid for at the balance sheet date – it is an item of value to the business.

ACCRUALS AND PREPAYMENTS OF INCOME

Just as expenses can be accrued or prepaid at the end of a financial year, income amounts can also be accrued or prepaid.

accrual of income

Here, income of a business is due but unpaid at the end of the financial year. For example, commission might have been earned, but the payment is received after the end of the financial year to which it relates. In the extended trial balance and final accounts, accrual of income is:

- added to the income amount in the trial balance before it is listed in the profit and loss account
- shown as a current asset (eg commission receivable) in the year-end balance sheet

prepayment of income

Here, the income of a business has been paid in advance by the payer. For example, the rent received account for this financial year could include an advance payment received from a tenant in respect of the next financial year. In the extended trial balance and final accounts, prepayment of income is:

- deducted from the income amount in the trial balance before it is listed in the profit and loss account
- shown as a current liability (eg rent received in advance) in the year-end balance sheet

As with expenses, the objective of taking note of accruals and prepayments of income is to ensure that the money amount listed in the profit and loss account relates to the period covered by that account.

PRIVATE EXPENSES AND GOODS FOR OWN USE

Adjustments also have to be made in the final accounts for the amount of any business facilities that are used by the owner for private purposes. These adjustments are for private expenses and goods for own use.

private expenses

Sometimes the owner of a business uses business facilities for private purposes, eg telephone, or car. The owner will agree that part of the expense shall be charged to him or her as drawings, while the other part represents a business expense.

For example, the balance of the telephone account is £600 at the year-end, and the owner agrees that this should be split as one-quarter private use, and three-quarters to the business. The book-keeping entries to record such adjustments are:

- *debit* drawings account
- *credit* telephone account
- *debit* profit and loss account
- *credit* telephone account

The telephone account will be completed at the end of the year as follows:

Dr		Telephone Account			Cr
1998		£	1998		£
31 Dec	Balance b/d	600	31 Dec	Drawings	150
			31 Dec	Profit and loss account	450
		600			600

When using a trial balance to produce the final accounts, private expenses should be adjusted by deducting from the expense account and adding to drawings.

goods for own use

When the owner of a business takes some of the goods in which the business trades for his or her own use, the double-entry book-keeping is:

- *debit* drawings account
- *credit* purchases account

Note that:

- Where a business is VAT-registered, VAT must be accounted for on goods taken by the owner.
- An alternative method of accounting for goods for own use is:
  - *debit* drawings account
  - *credit* sales account

This method is preferred by the Inland Revenue for tax purposes; however, either is acceptable for the purpose of financial accounting – which method is used will depend on the custom and practice of the business.

When using a trial balance to produce the final accounts, goods for own use should be adjusted by adding to drawings and deducting from purchases (or adding to sales).

INSURANCE CLAIMS

When a business loses stock as a result of causes such as fire, theft, water damage, a claim is made to the insurance company for the cost of the insured stock. Once the amount of the claim has been agreed with the insurance company, the book-keeping entries are:

- *debit* insurance claims account
- *credit* purchases account

In this way, the figure for purchases is reduced for profit and loss account. If a balance sheet is prepared before payment is received from the insurance company, the insurance claims account will be shown as a current asset.

When payment is received from the insurance company, the book-keeping entries are:

- *debit* bank account
- *credit* insurance claims account

Thus insurance claims account now has a nil balance, and the business has received payment from the insurance company for loss of the stock.

INCOME AND EXPENDITURE ACCOUNTING

In this chapter we have made adjustments for accruals and prepayments to ensure that the profit and loss account shows the correct amount of income and expenses for the financial year, ie what should have been paid, instead of what has actually been paid. In doing this we are adopting the principle of *income and expenditure accounting*. If we simply used the trial balance figures, we would be following the principle of *receipts* and *payments accounting*, ie comparing money coming in, with money going out: this would usually give a false view of the net profit for the year.

The principle of income and expenditure accounting is applied in the same way to purchases and sales, although no adjustments are needed because of the way in which these two are handled in the accounting records. For purchases, the amount is entered into the accounts when the supplier's invoice is received, although the agreement to buy will be contained in the legal contract which exists between buyer and seller. From the accounting viewpoint, it is receipt of the supplier's invoice that causes an accounting entry to be made; the subsequent payment is handled as a different accounting transaction. A business could have bought goods, not paid for them yet, but will have a purchases figure to enter into the profit and loss account – the creditors will soon be wanting payment!

Sales are recorded in a similar way – when the invoice for the goods is sent, rather than when payment is made. This applies the principle of income and expenditure accounting. In this way, a business could have made a large amount of sales, which will be entered in the profit and loss account, but may not yet have received any payments.

The way in which accounts are adjusted to take note of accruals and prepayments is formally recognised in the accruals (or matching) concept, which is discussed in more detail in Chapter 8.

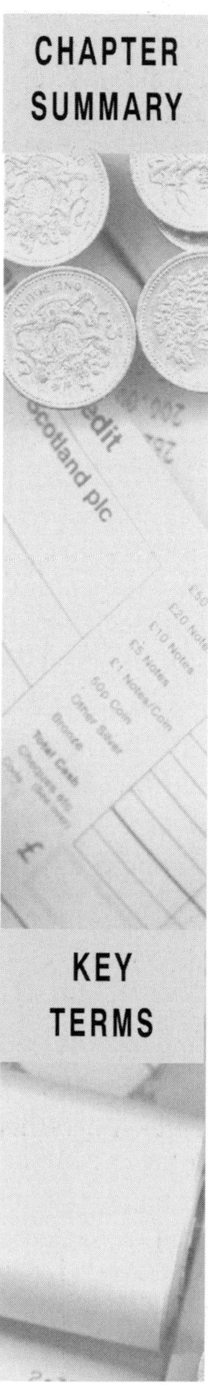

CHAPTER SUMMARY

- Final accounts are prepared on the income and expenditure basis, rather than the receipts and payments basis.
- An adjustment should be made at the end of the financial year in respect of accruals and prepayments.
- In the final accounts, accrued expenses are:
  - added to the expense from the trial balance
  - shown as a current liability in the balance sheet
- Prepaid expenses are:
  - deducted from the expense from the trial balance
  - shown as a current asset in the balance sheet
- An accrual of income is:
  - added to the income amount from the trial balance
  - shown as a current asset in the balance sheet
- A prepayment of income is:
  - deducted from the income amount from the trial balance
  - shown as a current liability in the balance sheet
- Adjustments also need to be made in the final accounts for:
  - private expenses
  - goods for own use

KEY TERMS

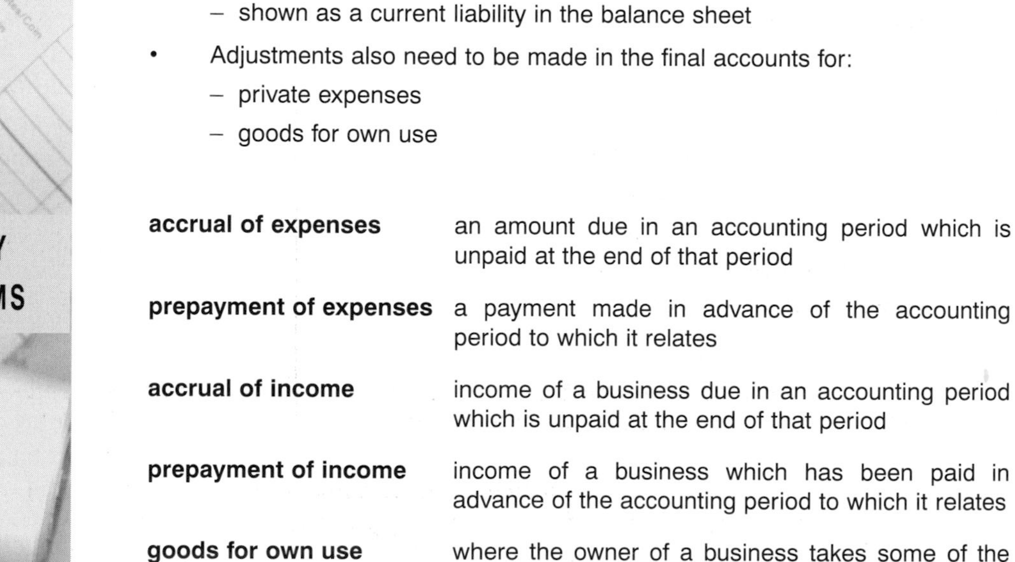

accrual of expenses — an amount due in an accounting period which is unpaid at the end of that period

prepayment of expenses — a payment made in advance of the accounting period to which it relates

accrual of income — income of a business due in an accounting period which is unpaid at the end of that period

prepayment of income — income of a business which has been paid in advance of the accounting period to which it relates

goods for own use — where the owner of a business takes some of the goods in which the business trades for his/her own use

income and expenditure accounting recording the amounts that should have been received and paid during an accounting period

receipts and payments accounting recording the actual amounts that have been received and paid during an accounting period, without taking note of accruals and prepayments

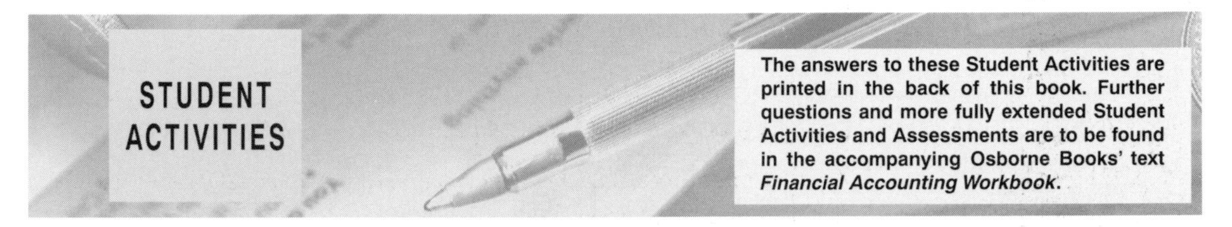

STUDENT ACTIVITIES

The answers to these Student Activities are printed in the back of this book. Further questions and more fully extended Student Activities and Assessments are to be found in the accompanying Osborne Books' text *Financial Accounting Workbook*.

Extended trial balance format: *a blank photocopiable pro-forma of the extended trial balance is included in the Appendix (page 308) – it is advisable to enlarge it up to full A4 size.*

Optional activities: *the figures from the extended trial balance columns can, in addition, be extracted to set out statements of income and expenditure (to determine net profit) and totalled lists of assets, liabilities and capital. You may also wish to set out the final accounts in full as preparation for NVQ Level 4 work .*

5.1 Wages accrued are shown as a:

(a) current asset in the balance sheet

(b) debit balance in accruals account

(c) fixed asset in the balance sheet

(d) credit balance in accruals account

Answer (a) or (b) or (c) or (d)

5.2 Rates prepaid are shown as a:

(a) current liability in the balance sheet

(b) fixed asset in the balance sheet

(c) debit balance in prepayments account

(d) credit balance in prepayments account

Answer (a) or (b) or (c) or (d)

5.3 John Harrington runs an import/export business. At the end of his financial year, on 31 December 1999, the vehicle expenses account is as follows:

Dr		**Vehicle Expenses Account**			Cr
1999		£	1999		£
31 Dec	Balance b/d	1,680			

John Harrington tells you that 25 per cent of vehicle expenses represent his private motoring expenses. He asks you to transfer the amount to his drawings account, before transferring the remainder to profit and loss account. Show the vehicle expenses account after these transactions have been entered.

5.4 Wyvern Stationery Limited has made a claim on its insurance policy for stock damaged by a burst water pipe. The amount of the claim has been agreed today, 17 December 1998, at £845. Show the book-keeping entries to record this and, if the amount is not paid by the end of the financial year on 31 December 1998, how it will be dealt with in the year-end balance sheet.

5.5 Explain how the following would be dealt with in the profit and loss account, and balance sheet of a business with a financial year end of 31 December 1999:

(a) Wages and salaries paid to 31 December 1999 amount to £55,640. However, at that date £1,120 is owing: this amount is paid on 4 January 2000.

(b) Rates totalling £3,565 have been paid to cover the period 1 January 1999 to 31 March 2000.

(c) A computer is rented at a cost of £150 per month. The rental for January 2000 was paid in December 1999 and is included in the total payments during 1999 which amount to £1,950.

5.6 The following trial balance has been extracted by the book-keeper of Don Smith, who runs a wholesale stationery business, at 31 December 1998:

	Dr	*Cr*
	£	£
Debtors	24,325	
Creditors		15,408
Value Added Tax		4,276
Capital		30,000
Bank		1,083
Rent and rates	10,862	
Electricity	2,054	
Telephone	1,695	
Salaries	55,891	
Motor vehicles	22,250	
Office equipment	7,500	
Motor vehicle expenses	10,855	
Drawings	15,275	
Discount allowed	478	
Discount received		591
Purchases	138,960	
Sales		257,258
Stock at 1 January 1998	18,471	
	308,616	308,616

Notes at 31 December 1998:

- stock was valued at £14,075
- rates are prepaid £250
- electricity owing £110
- salaries are owing £365

You are to prepare the figures for the final accounts of Don Smith for the year ended 31 December 1998, using the extended trial balance method.

5.7 The following trial balance has been extracted by the book-keeper of John Barclay at 30 June 1999:

	Dr	*Cr*
	£	£
Sales		864,321
Purchases	600,128	
Sales returns	2,746	
Purchases returns		3,894
Office expenses	33,947	
Salaries	122,611	
Motor vehicle expenses	36,894	
Discounts allowed	3,187	
Discounts received		4,951
Debtors and creditors	74,328	52,919
Value Added Tax		10,497
Stock at 1 July 1998	63,084	
Motor vehicles	83,500	
Office equipment	23,250	
Land and buildings	100,000	
Bank loan		75,000
Bank	1,197	
Capital		155,000
Drawings	21,710	
	1,166,582	1,166,582

Notes at 30 June 1999:

- stock was valued at £66,941
- motor vehicle expenses owing £1,250
- office expenses prepaid £346
- goods costing £250 were taken by John Barclay for his own use

You are to prepare the figures for the final accounts of John Barclay for the year ended 30 June 1999, using the extended trial balance method.

6 DEPRECIATION OF FIXED ASSETS

this chapter covers . . .

Fixed assets, such as machinery and vehicles, lose value as time goes by, largely as a result of wear and tear. This loss in value is known as depreciation. In financial accounting it is necessary to record an estimate of depreciation in the accounting records. In this chapter we will:

- *define depreciation*
- *consider the main methods of calculating depreciation*
- *study the book-keeping entries for depreciation*
- *apply depreciation to the extended trial balance*
- *investigate the book-keeping entries involved when a fixed asset is sold*

NVQ PERFORMANCE CRITERIA COVERED

unit 4: MAINTAINING FINANCIAL RECORDS AND PREPARING ACCOUNTS

element 2

record income and expenditure

- ❏ *the organisation's policies, regulations, procedures and timescales in relation to recording income and expenditure are observed*

element 4

prepare the extended trial balance

- ❏ *the organisation's policies, regulations, procedures and timescales in relation to preparing extended trial balances are observed*
- ❏ *the extended trial balance is accurately extended and totalled*

WHAT IS DEPRECIATION?

Depreciation is the estimate of the amount of the loss in value of fixed assets over an estimated time period.

Most fixed assets lose value over time and it is necessary, in order to present a realistic view of the business, to record the amount of the loss in value. This is done by

- showing an expense – called 'depreciation of fixed assets' – in the profit and loss account
- showing the fixed asset at cost price less depreciation to date – called 'provision for depreciation' – in the balance sheet

Depreciation – which is linked to the cost price of the asset – *estimates* the loss in value and the time period over which the loss occurs.

The main factors which cause fixed assets to depreciate are:

- *wear and tear through use*, eg motor vehicles, machinery, etc
- *passage of time*, eg the lease on a building
- *depletion,* eg extraction of stone from a quarry
- *economic reasons*
  - obsolescence, eg a new design of machine which does the job better and faster, making the old machine obsolete
  - inadequacy, eg a machine such as a photocopier no longer has the volume capacity to meet the needs of the business

Fixed assets – including buildings – are depreciated over their useful economic life. The only exception is land, which does not normally depreciate (unless it is a quarry or a mine, when it will have a known useful economic life).

CALCULATING DEPRECIATION

There are several different ways in which we can allow for the loss in value of fixed assets. All of these are *estimates,* and it is only when the asset is sold or scrapped that we will know the accuracy of the estimate. A business can use any acceptable depreciation method; however, once selected, the method would not be changed from one year to the next without good reason.

The two most common methods of calculating depreciation are:

- straight-line method
- reducing balance method

For the calculations of depreciation amounts we will use the following data:

DATA FOR DEPRECIATION OF MACHINE	
Cost price (net of VAT)	£2,000
Estimated life	4 years
Estimated scrap value (net of VAT) at end of four years	£400

straight-line method of depreciation

With this method, a fixed percentage is written off the *original cost* of the asset each year. For this example, twenty-five per cent will be written off each year by the straight-line method. The depreciation amount (ignoring for the moment any residual or scrap value) for *each year* is:

£2,000 x 25% = £500 per year

The depreciation percentage will be decided by a business on the basis of what it considers to be the useful economic life of the asset. Thus, twenty-five per cent each year gives a useful economic life of four years (assuming a nil residual value at the end of its life).

Different classes of fixed assets are often depreciated at different rates, eg motor vehicles may be depreciated at a different rate to office equipment. It is important that, once a particular method and rate of depreciation has been selected, depreciation should be applied consistently, ie methods and rates are not changed from year-to-year without good reason.

The method of calculating straight-line depreciation, taking into account the asset's estimated sale proceeds at the end of its useful economic life, is:

$$\frac{\text{cost of asset} - \text{estimated residual (scrap or salvage) sale proceeds}}{\text{number of years' expected use of asset}}$$

For example, the machine is expected to have a residual (scrap or salvage) value of £400, so the depreciation amount will be:

$$\frac{\pounds 2{,}000 - \pounds 400}{\text{4 years}} = \pounds 400 \text{ per year (ie 20\% per annum on cost)}$$

reducing balance method

With this method, a fixed percentage is written off the reduced balance of the asset each year. The reduced balance is the cost of the asset less the provision for depreciation. For example, the machine is to be depreciated by 33.3% (one-third) each year, using the reducing balance method. The depreciation amounts for the four years of ownership are:

Original cost	£2,000
Year 1 depreciation: 33.3% of £2,000	£667
Value at end of year 1	£1,333
Year 2 depreciation: 33.3% of £1,333	£444
Value at end of year 2	£889
Year 3 depreciation: 33.3% of £889	£296
Value at end of year 3	£593
Year 4 depreciation: 33.3% of £593	£193
Value at end of year 4	£400

Note: the figures have been rounded to the nearest £, and year 4 depreciation has been adjusted by £5 to leave a residual value of £400.

The formula to calculate the percentage of reducing balance depreciation is:

$$r = 1 - \sqrt[n]{\frac{s}{c}}$$

where:

r = percentage rate of depreciation

n = number of years

s = salvage (residual) value

c = cost of asset

In the example above the 33.3% is calculated as:

$$r = 1 - \sqrt[4]{\frac{400}{2,000}}$$

$$r = 1 - \sqrt[4]{0.2}$$

(to find the fourth root press the square root key on the calculator twice)

$$r = 1 - 0.669$$

r = 0.331 or 33.1% (which is close to the 33.3% used above)

straight-line and reducing balance methods compared

The following tables use the depreciation amounts calculated above.

straight-line depreciation				
	1	*2*	*3*	*4*
Year	Original cost	Depreciation for year	Provision for depreciation	Net book value (ie column 1-3)
	£	£	£	£
1	2,000	400	400	1,600
2	2,000	400	800	1,200
3	2,000	400	1,200	800
4	2,000	400	1,600	400

Note: Net book value is cost, less provision for depreciation, ie column 1, less column 3.

These calculations will be used in the final accounts (see page 88) as follows: taking year 2 as an example, the profit and loss account will show £400 (column 2) as an expense, while the balance sheet will record £1,200 (column 4) as the net book value.

reducing balance depreciation				
	1	*2*	*3*	*4*
Year	Original cost	Depreciation for year	Provision for depreciation	Net book value (ie column 1-3)
	£	£	£	£
1	2,000	667	667	1,333
2	2,000	444	1,111	889
3	2,000	296	1,407	593
4	2,000	193	1,600	400

In the final accounts, using year 3 as an example, £296 (column 2) will be shown as an expense in profit and loss account, while £593 (column 4) is the net book value that will be recorded in the balance sheet. We shall look in more detail at how depreciation is shown in the final accounts later in the chapter.

Using these tables, we will now see how the two methods compare:

	straight-line method	reducing balance method
depreciation amount	Same money amount each year – see chart below	Different money amounts each year: more than straight-line in early years, less in later years – see chart below
depreciation percentage	Lower depreciation percentage required to achieve same residual value	Higher depreciation percentage required to achieve same residual value – but can never reach a nil value
suitability	Best used for fixed assets likely to be kept for the whole of their expected lives, eg machinery, office equipment, fixtures and fittings	Best used for fixed assets which depreciate more in early years and which are not kept for the whole of expected lives, eg vehicles

The year-by-year depreciation amounts of the machine in the example are shown on the following bar chart:

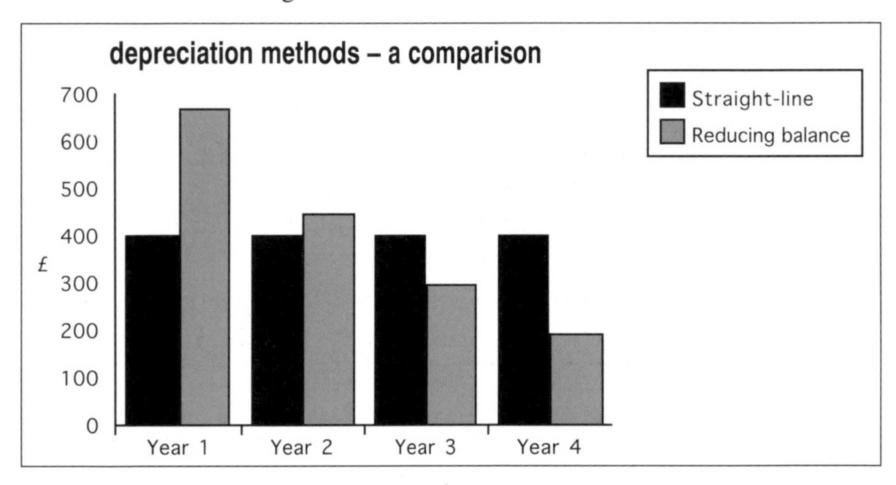

BOOK-KEEPING ENTRIES FOR DEPRECIATION

Once the amounts of depreciation have been calculated using the methods described in the previous section, they can be recorded in the book-keeping system. The usual procedure is to have three accounts:

- *fixed asset account*, which records the cost price of the asset (note that the value of the asset can include certain other capital costs, eg installation costs – see page 128)
- *depreciation account*, which records the amount of depreciation for the asset for the year
- *provision for depreciation account*, which records the amount of depreciation to date for each class of fixed asset in separate provision for depreciation accounts

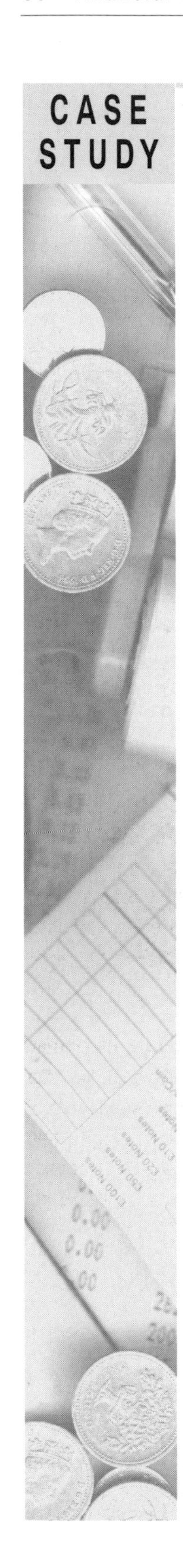

BOOK-KEEPING ENTRIES FOR DEPRECIATION

A machine is purchased for £2,000 net of VAT on 1 January 1998. It is decided to depreciate it at twenty per cent each year, using the straight-line method. The firm's financial year runs from 1 January to 31 December. The accounting records for the first four years will be:

Dr		**Machinery Account**			Cr
1998		£	1998		£
1 Jan	Bank	2,000			

This account remains with the balance of £2,000, which is the cost price of the machine. (The other transactions on 1 January 1998 are to bank account and VAT account – these have not been shown.)

Dr		**Depreciation Account**			Cr
1998		£	1998		£
31 Dec	Provision for depreciation	400	31 Dec	Profit and loss account	400
1999			1999		
31 Dec	Provision for depreciation	400	31 Dec	Profit and loss account	400
2000			2000		
31 Dec	Provision for depreciation	400	31 Dec	Profit and loss account	400
2001			2001		
31 Dec	Provision for depreciation	400	31 Dec	Profit and loss account	400

The depreciation account acts as a 'holding' account for the year's depreciation. The amount is

- credited to depreciation account (and debited to profit and loss account – see later)
- debited to depreciation account (and credited to provision for depreciation account – see next page)

Note that depreciation account may be credited with depreciation amounts for various classes of fixed assets (eg buildings, machinery, vehicles); the amounts are then debited out and credited to the provision for depreciation account for each class of fixed asset.

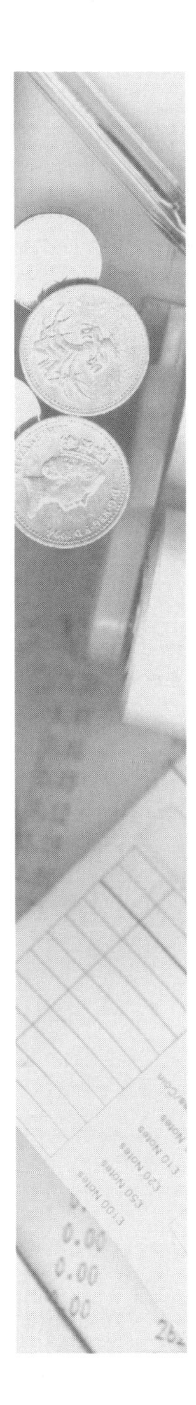

Dr		Provision for Depreciation Account – Machinery			Cr
1998		£	1998		£
31 Dec	Balance c/d	400	31 Dec	Depreciation account	400
1999			1999		
31 Dec	Balance c/d	800	1 Jan	Balance b/d	400
			31 Dec	Depreciation account	400
		800			800
2000			2000		
31 Dec	Balance c/d	1,200	1 Jan	Balance b/d	800
			31 Dec	Depreciation account	400
		1,200			1,200
2001			2001		
31 Dec	Balance c/d	1,600	1 Jan	Balance b/d	1,200
			31 Dec	Depreciation account	400
		1,600			1,600
2002			2002		
			1 Jan	Balance b/d	1,600

The provision for depreciation account – which is specific to each class of fixed asset – stores up the amounts of depreciation year by year. Notice that, while the asset account of machinery has a debit balance, provision for depreciation account has a credit balance. The difference between the two balances at any time will tell us the net book value of the asset, ie what it is worth according to our accounting records. For example, at 31 December 2000, the net book value of the machine is £800 (£2,000 cost, less £1,200 provision for depreciation).

When a business owns several fixed assets of the same class, eg several machines, it is usual practice to maintain only one asset account and one provision for depreciation account for that class. This does mean that the calculation of amounts of depreciation can become quite complex – particularly when assets are bought and sold during the year. It is good practice to calculate the separate depreciation amount for each machine, or asset, before amalgamating the figures as the year's depreciation charge.

DEPRECIATION AND FINAL ACCOUNTS

profit and loss account

The depreciation amount calculated for each class of asset is listed amongst the expenses in profit and loss account. For example, to consider the machine depreciated in the previous sections, the profit and loss account will show 'depreciation: machinery £400' amongst the expenses. The double-entry book-keeping records the annual amount for depreciation as follows:

- *debit* profit and loss account
- *credit* depreciation account

As we have seen earlier, amounts held in depreciation account are then debited out and credited to the appropriate provision for depreciation accounts.

balance sheet

Each class of fixed asset is shown at cost price, less provision for depreciation (ie accumulated depreciation to date). The resulting figure is the net book value of the fixed asset. The usual way of setting these out in a balance sheet (using figures for the machine in the previous section) is:

Balance sheet (extract) .... as at 31 December 1998

	£	£	£
	Cost	Provision for dep'n	Net
Fixed assets			
Machinery	2,000	400	1,600
Vehicles, etc	x	x	x
	x	x	x

Balance sheet (extract) .... as at 31 December 1999

	£	£	£
	Cost	Provision for dep'n	Net
Fixed assets			
Machinery	2,000	800	1,200
Vehicles, etc	x	x	x
	x	x	x

Notice, from the above, how provision for depreciation increases with the addition of each further year's depreciation. At the same time, the net figure reduces – it is this net figure which is added to the other fixed assets to give a sub-total for this section of the balance sheet.

trial balance figures

When preparing final accounts from a trial balance, the trial balance often gives separate figures for the cost of an asset and its provision for depreciation at the start of the year. For example:

Trial balance of .... as at 31 December 2000

	Dr	Cr
	£	£
Machinery at cost	2,000	
Provision for depreciation: machinery		800

If a note to the trial balance then says, for example, to "depreciate machinery for the year at twenty per cent on cost", depreciation of £400 for the year 2000 must be calculated and shown as an expense in profit and loss account. The balance sheet will then show:

Balance sheet (extract) .... as at 31 December 2000

	£	£	£
	Cost	Provision for dep'n	Net
Fixed assets			
Machinery	2,000	1,200	800
Vehicles, etc	x	x	x
	x	x	x

depreciation policies of a business

In a Student Activity or in an Assessment, information will be given – where it is needed – on the accounting policy for depreciation of the business whose accounts are being prepared. In particular, information will be given on what to do when a fixed asset is bought part of the way through a firm's financial year. The choices here will be to allocate depreciation for the part of the year that it is owned; alternatively the firm may choose to provide for depreciation for the whole year on assets held at the end of the year.

CASE STUDY

DEPRECIATION IN THE EXTENDED TRIAL BALANCE

The extended trial balance format includes a pre-printed row allocated for depreciation. We will adopt the extended trial balance of Tara Smith (see next page) to include depreciation for the year of

- premises: 2 per cent straight-line, ie £2,000
- shop fittings: 25 per cent reducing balance, ie £5,000

Study the extended trial balance on the next page and read the notes that follow. The depreciation is shown in the extended trial balance as follows:

- in the description column
  - on the blank line below premises write in 'provision for depreciation: premises'
  - on the blank line below shop fittings write in 'provision for depreciation: shop fittings'

EXTENDED TRIAL BALANCE — TARA SMITH TRADING AS "THE FASHION SHOP" — 31 DECEMBER 1998

Description	Ledger balances		Adjustments		Profit and loss		Balance sheet	
	Dr £	*Cr* £	*Dr* £	*Cr* £	*Dr* £	*Cr* £	*Dr* £	*Cr* £
Stocks at 1 Jan 1998	12,500				12,500			
Purchases	105,000				105,000			
Sales		155,000				155,000		
Administration expenses	6,200				6,200			
Wages	23,500				23,500			
Rent paid	750			75	675			
Telephone	500		100		600			
Interest paid	4,500				4,500			
Travel expenses	550				550			
Premises	100,000						100,000	
Provision for depreciation: premises				2,000				2,000
Shop fittings	20,000						20,000	
Provision for depreciation: shop fittings				5,000				5,000
Debtors	10,500						10,500	
Bank	5,450						5,450	
Cash	50						50	
Capital		75,000						75,000
Drawings	7,000						7,000	
Loan from bank		50,000						50,000
Creditors		14,500						14,500
Value Added Tax		2,000						2,000
Closing stock: Profit & loss				10,500		10,500		
Closing stock: Balance sheet			10,500				10,500	
Accruals				100				100
Prepayments			75				75	
Depreciation			7,000		7,000			
Bad debts								
Provision for bad debts:adjustment								
Net profit/loss					4,975			4,975
	296,500	296,500	17,675	17,675	165,500	165,500	153,575	153,575

- in the adjustments column
  - record £7,000 (ie £2,000 + £5,000) on the debit side of the depreciation row
  - record £2,000 on the credit side of the provision for depreciation: premises row
  - record £5,000 on the credit side of the provision for depreciation: shop fittings row
- on the debit side of the profit and loss column record the depreciation for the year of £7,000
- on the credit side of the balance sheet column record the £2,000 and £5,000 provision for depreciation on the two classes of assets

Remember that:

- depreciation is the annual charge for depreciation
- provision for depreciation is the accumulated total of depreciation for each class of fixed asset

As this is the first year that Tara Smith has recorded depreciation, both depreciation and provision for depreciation amounts are the same. The figures for depreciation are shaded for ease of reference (note that the extended trial balance already incorporates adjustments for accruals and prepayments of expenses). As a result of depreciation, net profit is reduced by £7,000 (ie £2,000 + £5,000) to £4,975.

DEPRECIATION: A NON-CASH EXPENSE

It is very important to realise that depreciation is a non-cash expense: unlike the other expenses in profit and loss account, no cheque is written out, or cash paid, for depreciation. In cash terms, depreciation causes no outflow of money. Nevertheless, it is correct, in the final accounts of a business, to show an allowance for depreciation in the profit and loss account, and to reduce the value of the fixed asset in the balance sheet. This is because the business has had the use of the asset, and needs to record the fall in value as an expense to present a true picture of its financial state. Thus we are led back to the definition of depreciation as "the estimate of the amount of the loss in value of fixed assets over an estimated time period", ie it is an accounting adjustment.

As depreciation is a non-cash expense, it should be noted that depreciation is not a method of providing a fund of cash which can be used to replace the asset at the end of its life. In order to do this, it is necessary to create a separate fund into which cash is transferred at regular intervals. This technique is often known as a sinking fund, and it needs to be represented by a separate bank account, eg a deposit account, which can be drawn against when the new fixed asset is to be purchased.

SALE OF FIXED ASSETS

When a fixed asset is sold or disposed, it is necessary to bring together:

- the original cost of the asset
- provision for depreciation over the life of the asset
- sale proceeds

These figures are transferred from the appropriate accounts in the double-entry book-keeping system to an asset disposal account (also known as a sale of assets account). The disposals account will enable us to calculate the 'profit' or 'loss' on sale of the asset (more correctly the terms are 'over-provision' and 'under-provision' of depreciation, respectively).

The book-keeping transactions are:

- original cost of the asset
  - *debit* disposals account
  - *credit* fixed asset account
- depreciation provided to date
  - *debit* provision for depreciation account
  - *credit* disposals account

Note:
The amount of depreciation for the current accounting period may need to be calculated, eg if disposal takes place part of the way through a financial year and the firm's policy is to charge for part-years.

- sale proceeds
  - *debit* bank/cash account
  - *credit* disposals account
- loss on sale
  - *debit* profit and loss account
  - *credit* disposals account
- profit on sale
  - *debit* disposals account
  - *credit* profit and loss account

Small adjustments for under-provision or over-provision of depreciation will usually be needed because it is impossible, at the start of an asset's life, to predict exactly what it will sell for in a number of years' time.

CASE STUDY

SALE OF FIXED ASSETS

To illustrate the transactions to record the sale of fixed assets, we will use the machine purchased for £2,000 (net of VAT) on 1 January 1998, which is depreciated at twenty per cent each year, using the straight-line depreciation method. On 31 December 2000, the machine is sold for £600 (net of VAT); the company's accounting policy is to depreciate assets in the year of sale. The calculations are:

	£
cost price of machine (net of VAT)	2,000
less provision for depreciation to date	1,200
net book value at date of sale	800
selling price (net of VAT)	600
loss on sale	200

The book-keeping entries (excluding bank account and VAT account) are:

Machinery Account

Dr						Cr
1998		£	2000		£
1 Jan	Bank	2,000	31 Dec	Disposals account	2,000

Provision for Depreciation Account – Machinery

Dr					Cr
1998		£	1998		£
31 Dec	Balance c/d	400	31 Dec	Depreciation account	400
1999			1999		
31 Dec	Balance c/d	800	1 Jan	Balance b/d	400
			31 Dec	Depreciation account	400
		800			800
2000			2000		
31 Dec	Disposals account	1,200	1 Jan	Balance b/d	800
			31 Dec	Depreciation account	400
		1,200			1,200

Disposals Account

Dr					Cr
2000		£	2000		£
31 Dec	Machinery account	2,000	31 Dec	Prov for dep'n account	1,200
			31 Dec	Bank	600
			31 Dec	Profit and loss account (loss on sale)	200
		2,000			2,000

Profit and loss account (extract) .... for the year ended 31 December 2000		
	£	£
Gross profit		x
Less overheads:		
Depreciation: machinery	400	
Loss on sale of machinery	200	

Notes:

- In the machinery account, which is always kept 'at cost', the original price of the asset is transferred at the date of sale to disposals account. In this example, a nil balance remains on machinery account; however it is quite likely that the machinery account includes several machines, only one of which is being sold – in this case, there would be a balance on machinery account comprising the cost prices of the remaining machines.
- In provision for depreciation account, the amount of depreciation relating to the machine sold is transferred to disposals account. In this example, as only one machine is owned, the whole balance is transferred. However, if there were machines remaining, only part of the balance would be transferred – the amount remaining on the account relates to the remaining machines.
- Disposals account would balance without the need for a profit and loss account transfer if the depreciation rate used reflected exactly the fall in value of the machine. In practice, this is unlikely to happen, so a transfer to profit and loss account must be made. In this example, it is an under-provision of depreciation (loss on sale), and the profit and loss account lists an extra overhead. If there had been an over-provision of depreciation (profit on sale), an item of additional income would be shown in profit and loss account.

PART-EXCHANGE OF AN ASSET

Instead of selling an old fixed asset for cash, it is quite common to part-exchange it for a new asset. This is exactly the same as if a person trades in their old car for a new (or newer) one.

Once the part-exchange allowance has been agreed, the book-keeping entries for disposal are as detailed earlier except that, instead of sale proceeds, there will be:

- *debit* fixed asset account with the amount of the part-exchange allowance
- *credit* disposals account with the amount of the part-exchange allowance

The remainder of the purchase cost of the new fixed asset paid by cheque is debited to fixed asset account and credited to bank account in the usual way.

6.8 The following trial balance has been extracted by the book-keeper of Hazel Harris at 31 December 1998:

	Dr	*Cr*
	£	£
Bank loan		75,000
Capital		125,000
Purchases and sales	465,000	614,000
Building repairs	8,480	
Motor vehicle at cost	12,000	
Provision for depreciation on motor vehicles		2,400
Motor expenses	2,680	
Land and buildings at cost	100,000	
Bank overdraft		2,000
Furniture and fittings at cost	25,000	
Provision for depreciation on furniture and fittings		2,500
Wages and salaries	86,060	
Discounts	10,610	8,140
Drawings	24,000	
Rates and insurance	6,070	
Debtors and creditors	52,130	36,600
Value Added Tax		5,250
General expenses	15,860	
Stock at 1 January 1998	63,000	
	870,890	870,890

Notes at 31 December 1998:

- stock was valued at £88,000
- wages and salaries outstanding: £3,180
- rates and insurance paid in advance: £450
- depreciate the motor vehicle at 20 per cent using the straight-line method
- depreciate furniture and fittings at 10 per cent using the straight-line method
- buildings are not to be depreciated

You are to prepare the figures for the final accounts of Hazel Harris for the year ended 31 December 1998 using the extended trial balance method.

Optional activities: *the figures from the extended trial balance columns produced in these Activities can, in addition, be extracted to set out statements of income and expenditure (to determine net profit) and totalled lists of assets, liabilities and capital. You may also wish to set out the final accounts in full as preparation for NVQ Level 4 work .*

7 BAD DEBTS AND PROVISION FOR BAD DEBTS

this chapter covers . . .

Most businesses selling their goods and services to other businesses do not receive payment immediately. Instead, they often have to allow a period of credit and, until the payment is received, they have a current asset of debtors. Unfortunately, it is likely that not all debtors will eventually settle the amounts they owe, ie the amounts are bad debts which have to be written off. At the same time a business needs to make a provision for bad debts (or doubtful debts), which allows for debtors who may not pay.

In this chapter we will:

- *distinguish between bad debts and provision for bad debts*
- *prepare the accounting entries for bad debts, and consider the effect on the final accounts*
- *prepare the accounting entries to make a provision for bad debts, and consider the effect on the final accounts*

NVQ PERFORMANCE CRITERIA COVERED

unit 4: MAINTAINING FINANCIAL RECORDS AND PREPARING ACCOUNTS

element 2

record income and expenditure

- ❏ *the organisation's policies, regulations, procedures and timescales in relation to recording income and expenditure are observed*

element 4

prepare the extended trial balance

- ❏ *the organisation's policies, regulations, procedures and timescales in relation to preparing extended trial balances are observed*
- ❏ *the extended trial balance is accurately extended and totalled*

BAD DEBTS AND PROVISION FOR BAD DEBTS

A bad debt is a debt owing to a business which it considers will never be paid.

Let us consider a business with debtors of £10,000. This total will, most probably, be made up of a number of debtors' accounts. At any one time, a few of these accounts will be bad, and therefore the amount is uncollectable: these are bad debts, and they need to be written off, ie the business will give up trying to collect the debt and will accept the loss.

Provision for bad debts is the estimate by a business of the likely percentage of its debtors which may go bad during any one accounting period.

There are likely to be some debtors' accounts which, although they are not yet bad, may be giving some concern as to their ability to pay: a provision for bad debts (or doubtful debts) needs to be made in respect of these. The one thing the business with debtors of £10,000 cannot do is to show this debtors' amount as a current asset in the balance sheet: to do so would be to imply to the reader of the balance sheet that the full £10,000 is collectable. Instead, this gross debtors' figure might be reduced in two stages, for example:

- debtors' accounts with balances totalling £200 are to be written off as bad
- a general provision for bad debts is to be made amounting, in this case, to two per cent of remaining debtors

Thus the debtors figure becomes:

	£
Gross debtors	10,000
Less: bad debts written off	200
	9,800
Less: provision for bad debts at two* per cent	196
Net debtors (recorded in balance sheet)	9,604

* Note: The amount of the provision for bad debts will vary from business to business, depending on the past experience of receiving payment, the nature of the business and the current economic climate.

Bad debts and provision for bad debts is an application of the accounting concept of prudence (see Chapter 8). By reducing the debtors' figure, through the profit and loss account and balance sheet, a more realistic amount is shown of the amount that the business can expect to receive.

TREATMENT OF BAD DEBTS

Bad debts are written off when they become uncollectable. This means that all reasonable efforts to recover the amount owing have been exhausted, ie statements and letters have been sent to the debtor requesting payment and legal action, where appropriate, or the threat of legal action has failed to obtain payment.

In writing off a debtor's account as bad, the business is bearing the cost of the amount due. The debtor's account is closed and the amount (or amounts, where a number of accounts are dealt with in this way) is debited to *bad debts written off* account. This account stores up the amounts of account balances written off during the year (in much the same way as an expense account). At the end of the financial year, the balance of the account is transferred to profit and loss account, where it is described as *bad debts written off.*

In terms of book-keeping, the transactions are:

- *debit* bad debts written off account
- *credit* debtor's account

At the end of the financial year, bad debts written off account is transferred to profit and loss account:

- *debit* profit and loss account
- *credit* bad debts written off account

For example, the following debtor's account is in the sales ledger:

Dr		**T Hughes**			Cr
1998		£	1998		£
5 Jan	Sales	55	8 May	Bank	25
			6 Jul	Cash	5

It is now 15 December 1998 and you are reviewing the debtors' accounts before the end of the financial year on 31 December. Your business has sent statements and 'chaser' letters to T Hughes – the last letter was dated 30 September, and was returned marked 'gone away, not known at this address'. Nothing further has been heard from T Hughes. You take the decision to write off this account as a bad debt; the account will be closed off as shown on the next page:

book-keeping entries

creating the provision (year 1998):
£10,000 x 5% = £500

– *debit* profit and loss account
– *credit* provision for bad debts: adjustment account
– *debit* provision for bad debts: adjustment account
– *credit* provision for bad debts account

increasing the provision (year 1999):
£5,000 (increase in debtors) x 5% = £250

– *debit* profit and loss account
– *credit* provision for bad debts: adjustment account
– *debit* provision for bad debts: adjustment account
– *credit* provision for bad debts account

decreasing the provision (year 2000):
£3,000 (decrease in debtors) x 5% = £150

– *debit* provision for bad debts: adjustment account
– *credit* profit and loss account
– *debit* provision for bad debts account
– *credit* provision for bad debts: adjustment account

The book-keeping entries for

- provision for bad debts: adjustment account
- provision for bad debts account

are as follows:

Dr **Provision for Bad Debts: Adjustment Account** Cr

1998		£	1998		£
31 Dec	Provision for bad debts	500	31 Dec	Profit and loss account	500
1999			1999		
31 Dec	Provision for bad debts	250	31 Dec	Profit and loss account	250
2000			2000		
31 Dec	Profit and loss account	150	31 Dec	Provision for bad debts	150

Provision for Bad Debts Account

Dr		£			Cr £
1998			1998		
31 Dec	Balance c/d	500	31 Dec	Prov for bad debts: adjustment	500
1999			1999		
31 Dec	Balance c/d	750	1 Jan	Balance b/d	500
			31 Dec	Prov for bad debts: adjustment* *(increase in provision)	250
		750			750
2000			2000		
31 Dec	Prov for bad debts: adjustment* *(decrease in provision)	150	1 Jan	Balance b/d	750
31 Dec	Balance c/d	600			
		750			750
2001			2001		
			1 Jan	Balance b/d	600

the final accounts

The effect of the above transactions on the final accounts is shown as follows:

Year	Profit and loss account		Balance sheet		
	Expense	*Income*	*Debtors*	*Less provision for bad debts*	*Net debtors*
	£	£	£	£	£
1998	500	–	10,000	500	9,500
1999	250	–	15,000	750	14,250
2000	–	150	12,000	600	11,400

The profit and loss account and balance sheet extracts for each year are as follows:

1998

Profit and loss account (extract) for the year ended 31 December 1998

	£	£
Gross profit		x
Less overheads:		
Provision for bad debts: adjustment	500	

Balance sheet (extract) as at 31 December 1998

	£	£	£
Current assets			
Stock		x	
Debtors	10,000		
Less provision for bad debts	500		
		9,500	

1999

Profit and loss account (extract) for the year ended 31 December 1999

	£	£
Gross profit		x
Less overheads:		
Provision for bad debts: adjustment	250	

Balance sheet (extract) as at 31 December 1999

	£	£	£
Current assets			
Stock		x	
Debtors	15,000		
Less provision for bad debts	750		
		14,250	

2000

Profit and loss account (extract) for the year ended 31 December 2000

	£	£
Gross profit		x
Add income:		
Provision for bad debts: adjustment		150
		x

Balance sheet (extract) as at 31 December 2000

	£	£	£
Current assets			
Stock		x	
Debtors	12,000		
Less provision for bad debts	600		
		11,400	

Note:

When preparing final accounts in a Student Activity or in an Assessment, there will be a note to the trial balance telling you to make an adjustment to the provision for bad debts. Sometimes you will be told a percentage figure, eg 'provision for bad debts is to be maintained at five per cent of debtors'; alternatively, you may be told the new provision figure (be careful of the wording – distinguish between 'increase the provision to £750' and 'increase the provision by £750').

BAD DEBTS AND PROVISION FOR BAD DEBTS IN THE EXTENDED TRIAL BALANCE

bad debts

If bad debts already appear in the trial balance, simply show the amount in the profit and loss column: this will have the effect of reducing net profit. Do not alter the figure for debtors, as it will have been reduced already by the amount written off.

If a note to the trial balance tells you to write off, say, £100 of bad debts, then you will need to include a row on the extended trial balance for bad debts. In the adjustments column, show £100 as a debit to this row, and credit the debtors row. This will give an expense of £100 for profit and loss account, and will reduce debtors for the balance sheet by £100 (show net debtors in the balance sheet column).

provision for bad debts

In the extended trial balance layout you will see that, towards the bottom, a row is preprinted for provision for bad debts: adjustment. Use this as the 'holding' account to create, or increase, or decrease the provision.

For example, to increase an existing provision of £500 (which will be shown in the trial balance) by, say, £250, record the following in the extended trial balance:

- in the adjustments column
  - *debit* provision for bad debts: adjustment account
  - *credit* provision for bad debts account
- in the profit and loss column record the £250 amount of the provision for bad debts: adjustment as an expense in the debit column
- in the balance sheet column record the provision for bad debts as £750, ie the trial balance figure of £500 and the amount of £250 shown in the adjustments column

Where a new provision is to be created the above principles are followed; to reduce an existing provision, then the reverse of the above will be followed.

Remember that, in the extended trial balance:

- provision for bad debts: adjustment is shown in the profit and loss account and records the amount to create, increase or decrease the provision each year
- provision for bad debts is shown in the credit column of the balance sheet and is the accumulated total of the provision

CASE STUDY

CASE STUDY EXAMPLE: TARA SMITH

The extended trial balance of Tara Smith is shown on the next page, having been altered for:

- bad debts of £100 written off
- provision for bad debts of £250 created (note that there is no existing provision)

The columns which are affected are adjustments, profit and loss, and balance sheet – the altered figures are shaded for illustrative purposes.

EXTENDED TRIAL BALANCE	TARA SMITH TRADING AS "THE FASHION SHOP"				31 DECEMBER 1998			
Description	**Ledger balances**		**Adjustments**		**Profit and loss**		**Balance sheet**	
	Dr £	*Cr* £	*Dr* £	*Cr* £	*Dr* £	*Cr* £	*Dr* £	*Cr* £
Stocks at 1 Jan 1998	12,500				12,500			
Purchases	105,000				105,000			
Sales		155,000				155,000		
Administration expenses	6,200				6,200			
Wages	23,500				23,500			
Rent paid	750			75	675			
Telephone	500		100		600			
Interest paid	4,500				4,500			
Travel expenses	550				550			
Premises	100,000						100,000	
Provision for depreciation: premises				2,000				2,000
Shop fittings	20,000						20,000	
Provision for depreciation: shop fittings				5,000				5,000
Debtors	10,500			100			10,400	
Bank	5,450						5,450	
Cash	50						50	
Capital		75,000						75,000
Drawings	7,000						7,000	
Loan from bank		50,000						50,000
Creditors		14,500						14,500
Value Added Tax		2,000						2,000
Provision for bad debts				250				250
Closing stock: Profit & loss				10,500		10,500		
Closing stock: Balance sheet			10,500				10,500	
Accruals				100				100
Prepayments			75				75	
Depreciation			7,000		7,000			
Bad debts			100		100			
Provision for bad debts:adjustment			250		250			
Net profit/loss					4,625			4,625
	296,500	296,500	18,025	18,025	165,500	165,500	153,475	153,475

CHAPTER SUMMARY

- Not all debtors of a business will eventually settle the amounts they owe: such amounts are *bad debts* which have to be written off.
- A *provision for bad debts* (or *doubtful debts*) is made for debtors who may not pay.
- This sequence should be followed:
  - write off bad debts (if any)
  - create (or adjust) provision for bad debts
- To write off a bad debt:
  - *debit* bad debts written off account
  - *credit* debtor's account

  At the end of the financial year the bad debts written off account is transferred as an expense, to profit and loss account.
- A provision for bad debts is often based on a fixed percentage of debtors at the year-end.
- For book-keeping purposes, two accounts are used to create, increase or decrease a provision for bad debts:
  - provision for bad debts: adjustment account, to record the annual change
  - provision for bad debts account, to record the accumulated total
- In the balance sheet, provision for bad debts is deducted from debtors.
- Having created a provision for bad debts, it will usually be adjusted either upwards or downwards in subsequent years in line with the change in the level of debtors.

KEY TERMS

bad debt	a debt owing to a business which it considers will never be paid
bad debts written off account	the account to which the amounts of account balances written off as bad are transferred
provision for bad debts	an estimate by a business of the likely percentage of its debtors which may go bad during any one accounting period
provision for bad debts: adjustment account	used to record the annual change in the provision for bad debts
provision for bad debts account	used to record the accumulated total of the provision for bad debts
bad debts recovered	where a former debtor, whose account has been written off as bad, makes payment

The answers to these Student Activities are printed in the back of this book. Further questions and more fully extended Student Activities and Assessments are to be found in the accompanying Osborne Books' text *Financial Accounting Workbook*.

7.1 Ken Shah, a debtor of the business where you work, is unable to pay the amount owing and the accounts supervisor has decided to write off his account as a bad debt. This is recorded in the double-entry accounts by:

	Debit	Credit
(a)	bad debts written off	K Shah's account
(b)	K Shah's account	bad debts written off
(c)	cash account	K Shah's account
(d)	sales account	K Shah's account

Answer (a) or (b) or (c) or (d)

(Ignore VAT relief on bad debt write-off)

7.2 A trial balance shows debtors of £48,000 and a provision for bad debts of £2,200. It is decided to make the provision for bad debts equal to five per cent of debtors. What book-keeping entry will be made on the provision for bad debts account?

(a) debit £200

(b) debit £2,400

(c) credit £200

(d) credit £2,200

Answer (a) or (b) or (c) or (d)

7.3 You are the book-keeper at Waterston Plant Hire. At 31 December 1998, the end of the financial year, the business has gross debtors of £20,210. The owner decides to:

(a) write off, as bad debts, the accounts of:

P Ross	£55
J Ball	£105
L Jones	£50

(b) make a provision for bad debts of 2.5% of debtors (after writing off the above bad debts)

You are to explain how these transactions will be recorded in the final accounts at the end of the financial year.

7.4 Ross Engineering has an existing provision for bad debts of £300, based on 5 per cent of debtors. After writing off bad debts, the amounts of debtors at the end of the next two financial years are found to be:

30 June 1999	£8,000
30 June 2000	£7,000

The business continues to keep the provision for bad debts equal to 5 per cent of debtors.

As an accounts assistant at Ross Engineering, you are to show how the provision for bad debts will be adjusted at the end of the financial years ended 30 June 1999 and 30 June 2000, and how it will be recorded in the appropriate final accounts.

7.5 The following trial balance has been extracted by the book-keeper of Paul Sanders, who runs an office supplies business, as at 31 December 1998:

	Dr	*Cr*
	£	£
Purchases and sales	51,225	81,762
Returns	186	254
Stock at 1 January 1998	6,031	
Discounts	324	438
Motor expenses	1,086	
Wages and salaries	20,379	
Electricity	876	
Telephone	1,241	
Rent and rates	4,565	
Sundry expenses	732	
Bad debts written off	219	
Debtors and creditors	1,040	7,671
Value Added Tax		1,301
Bank	3,501	
Cash	21	
Motor vehicles at cost	15,000	
Provision for depreciation on motor vehicles		3,000
Office equipment at cost	10,000	
Provision for depreciation on office equipment		5,000
Capital		25,000
Drawings	8,000	
	124,426	124,426

Notes at 31 December 1998:

- stock was valued at £8,210
- electricity owing £102
- rent prepaid £251
- depreciate motor vehicles at 20 per cent and office equipment at 10 per cent per annum, using the straight-line method
- create a provision for bad debts of 5 per cent of debtors

You are to prepare the figures for the final accounts of Paul Sanders for the year ended 31 December 1998, using the extended trial balance method.

7.6 The following trial balance has been extracted by the book-keeper of James Jenkins, who owns a patisserie and coffee lounge, as at 30 June 1999:

	Dr	*Cr*
	£	£
Capital		36,175
Drawings	19,050	
Purchases and sales	105,240	168,432
Stock at 1 July 1998	9,427	
Debtors and creditors	3,840	5,294
Value Added Tax		1,492
Returns	975	1,237
Discounts	127	643
Wages and salaries	30,841	
Motor vehicle expenses	1,021	
Rent and rates	8,796	
Heating and lighting	1,840	
Telephone	355	
General expenses	1,752	
Bad debts written off	85	
Motor vehicle at cost	8,000	
Provision for depreciation on motor vehicle		3,500
Shop fittings at cost	6,000	
Provision for depreciation on shop fittings		2,000
Provision for bad debts		150
Cash	155	
Bank	21,419	
	218,923	218,923

Notes at 30 June 1999:

- stock was valued at £11,517
- motor vehicle expenses owing £55
- rent prepaid £275
- depreciate the motor vehicle at 25 per cent per annum, using the reducing balance method
- depreciate shop fittings at 10 per cent per annum, using the straight-line method
- the provision for bad debts is to be equal to 2.5 per cent of debtors

You are to prepare the figures for the final accounts of James Jenkins for the year ended 30 June 1999, using the extended trial balance method.

Optional activities: *the figures from the extended trial balance columns produced in these Activities can, in addition, be extracted to set out statements of income and expenditure (to determine net profit) and totalled lists of assets, liabilities and capital. You may also wish to set out the final accounts in full as preparation for NVQ Level 4 work .*

8 THE REGULATORY FRAMEWORK OF ACCOUNTING

this chapter covers . . .

In this chapter we will explain how the regulatory framework of accounting provides the 'rules' to be followed when preparing final accounts. These rules take the form of

- *accounting concepts*
- *accounting standards*

If the same rules have been followed, then broad comparisons can be made between the final accounts of different businesses.

We will also see how the accounting 'rules' relating to the valuation of stock are applied.

Later in the chapter we focus on the importance of the distinction between capital expenditure and revenue expenditure.

NVQ PERFORMANCE CRITERIA COVERED

unit 4: MAINTAINING FINANCIAL RECORDS AND PREPARING ACCOUNTS

element 3

collect and collate information for the preparation of final accounts

❑ *the organisation's policies, regulations, procedures and timescales relating to preparing final accounts are observed*

element 4

prepare the extended trial balance

❑ *an agreed valuation of closing stock is correctly entered on the extended trial balance*

ACCOUNTING CONCEPTS

There are several accounting concepts that are followed when preparing accounts:

- business entity
- money measurement
- historical cost
- duality
- materiality
- going concern
- accruals
- consistency
- prudence

business entity concept

This refers to the fact that final accounts record and report on the activities of one particular business. They do not include the assets and liabilities of those who play a part in owning or running the business. Thus the owner's personal assets and liabilities are kept separate from those of the business: the main links between the business and the owner's personal funds are capital and drawings.

money measurement concept

This means that, in the final accounts, all items are expressed in the common denominator of money. Only by using money can items be added together to give, for example, net profit, or a balance sheet total. The disadvantage of money measurement is that it is unable to record items which cannot be expressed in money terms. For example, a business with an efficient management, and good labour relations, will appear to have the same value as one that is overstaffed and has poor labour relations: only in the longer term, with different levels of profit and balance sheet structure, will the differences between the two become apparent.

historical cost concept

This concept, which is an extension of money measurement, follows the principle that assets and liabilities are recorded in the accounts at historical cost, ie the actual amount of the transaction. Thus a stock of goods for resale which cost £5,000 is recorded at that historical cost; a bank loan for £10,000 is recorded at that amount; a vehicle costing £12,500 is recorded at that amount.

The main advantages of the historical cost concept are that it is:

- verifiable – there is a prime document (eg an invoice) that confirms the amount recorded in the accounts

- objective – there are no valuations to apply, which are subjective and may vary depending on the circumstances (eg the value of a car will be different when offered for sale to a garage for cash, when offered as part-exchange for a new car, or when advertised as a private sale in the local paper)

The main disadvantages of the historical cost concept are that it cannot record:

- the change in value – upwards or downwards – of assets over time
- the effects of inflation

Falls in the value of fixed assets are dealt with by using depreciation methods in the accounts; from time-to-time, fixed assets such as land may be revalued upwards to reflect increases in market values. Both of these are subjective techniques, but are well-recognised in accounting. Inflation is rather more difficult, as there is no definitive way for dealing with it in the accounts.

duality concept

This concept means that each financial transaction is recorded by means of two opposite accounting entries (debit and credit), but of equal values. Thus double-entry book-keeping is an example of the duality concept in practice.

materiality concept

Some items in accounts have such a low monetary value that it is not worthwhile recording them separately, ie they are not 'material'.

Examples:

- Small expense items, such as donations to charities, the purchase of plants for the office, window cleaning, etc, do not justify their own separate expense account; instead they are grouped together in a sundry expenses account.
- End-of-year stocks of office stationery, eg paper clips, staples, photocopying paper, etc, are often not valued for the purpose of final accounts, because the amount is not material and does not justify the time and effort involved. This does mean, however, that the cost of all stationery purchased during the year is charged as an expense to profit and loss account – technically wrong, but not material enough to affect the final accounts.
- Low-cost fixed assets are often charged as an expense in profit and loss account, instead of being classed as capital expenditure, eg a stapler, waste-paper basket, etc. Strictly, these should be treated as fixed assets and depreciated each year over their estimated life; in practice, because the amounts involved are not material, they are treated as profit and loss account expenses.

Materiality depends very much on the size of the business. A large company may consider that items of less than £1,000 are not material; a small company will usually use a much lower figure. What is material, and what is not becomes a matter of judgement.

going concern concept

This presumes that the business to which the final accounts relate will continue to trade in the foreseeable future. The trading and profit and loss account and balance sheet are prepared on the basis that there is no intention to reduce significantly the size of the business or to liquidate the business. If the business was not a going concern, assets would have very different values, and the balance sheet would be affected considerably. For example, a large, purpose-built factory has considerable value to a going concern business but, if the factory had to be sold, it is likely to have a limited use for other industries, and therefore will have a lower market value. The latter case is the opposite of the going concern concept and would be described as a *gone concern*. Also, in a gone concern situation, extra depreciation would need to be charged as an expense to profit and loss account to allow for the reduced value of fixed assets.

accruals (or matching) concept

This means that expenses and revenues must be matched so that they concern the same goods or services and the same time period. We have already put this concept into practice in Chapter 5, where expenses and revenues were adjusted to take note of prepayments and accruals. The profit and loss account should always show the amount of the expense that should have been incurred, ie the expenditure for the year, whether or not it has been paid. This is the principle of income and expenditure accounting, rather than using receipts and payments as and when they fall due.

Further examples of the accruals concept are:

- debtors
- creditors
- depreciation
- bad debts
- provision for bad debts
- opening and closing stock adjustments in profit and loss account

consistency concept

This requires that, when a business adopts particular accounting methods, it should continue to use such methods consistently. For example, a business that decides to make a provision for depreciation on machinery at ten per cent per annum, using the straight-line method, should continue to use that percentage and method for future final accounts for this asset. Of course, having once chosen a particular method, a business is entitled to make changes provided there are good reasons for so doing, and a note to the final accounts would explain what has happened. By applying the consistency concept, direct comparison between the final accounts of different years can be made. Further examples of the use of the consistency concept are:

- stock valuation (see later in this chapter)
- the application of the materiality concept

prudence concept

This concept, also known as conservatism in accounting, requires that final accounts should always, where there is any doubt, report a conservative figure for profit or the valuation of assets. To this end, profits are not to be anticipated and should only be recognised when it is reasonably certain that they will be realised; at the same time all known liabilities should be provided for. A good example of the prudence concept is where a provision is made for bad debts (see Chapter 7) – the debtors have not yet gone bad, but it is expected, from experience, that a certain percentage will eventually need to be written off as bad debts. The valuation of stock (see later in this chapter) also follows the prudence concept. 'Anticipate no profit, but anticipate all losses' is a summary of the concept which, in its application, prevents an over-optimistic presentation of a business through the final accounts.

Note: The concepts apply equally to the final accounts of sole traders, partnerships and limited companies. In the case of limited companies the concepts of going concern, accruals, consistency and prudence are given legal force in the Companies Act 1985, and a company which does not apply them will receive a qualified audit report from its auditors.

ACCOUNTING POLICIES

Accounting policies are the methods used by an individual business to show the effect of transactions, and to record assets and liabilities, in its accounts. For example, straight-line and reducing balance are two ways of recording depreciation in the accounts – a business will select, as its accounting policy, a particular method for each class of fixed asset to be depreciated.

A business selects its accounting policies to fit in with the objectives of:

- relevance – the financial information is useful to users of accounts
- reliability – the financial information can be depended upon by users
- comparability – financial information can be compared with that from previous accounting periods

- understandability – users can understand the financial information provided

An accounting standard (see next section), Financial Reporting Standard No 18, entitled *Accounting policies*, sets out how businesses are to select and report their accounting policies.

ACCOUNTING STANDARDS

Over the last thirty years, accounting standards have been developed to provide the rules, or framework, of accounting. The intention has been to reduce the variety of alternative accounting treatments. This framework for accounting is represented by *Statements of Standard Accounting Practice* and *Financial Reporting Standards*.

Statements of Standard Accounting Practice (SSAPs) are no longer issued, but those still current come under the control of the Accounting Standards Board. This Board requires accountants to observe the applicable accounting standards, and to disclose and explain significant departures from the standards. A number of SSAPs have been replaced with *Financial Reporting Standards (FRSs)* as part of an attempt to reduce the number of permissible accounting treatments.

The main accounting standards relevant to level 3 of NVQ Accounting are set out below:

SSAP 5 Accounting for Value Added Tax

- VAT is a tax on the supply of goods and services, which is borne by the final consumer but is collected at each stage of the production and distribution chain.
- Most businesses with a turnover (sales) above a certain figure must be registered for VAT.
- At regular intervals, businesses pay the VAT Authorities (HM Customs and Excise Department):
  - the amount of output tax collected on sales made
  - less the amount of input tax on goods and services purchased

  If the amount of input tax is greater than output tax, the business claims a refund of the difference from HM Customs and Excise.
- A VAT-registered business does not normally include VAT in the income and expenditure of the business – whether for capital or revenue items. For example, the purchase of goods for £100 plus VAT is recorded in purchases account as £100 (the VAT is debited to VAT account). By contrast, a business not registered for VAT records the cost as £117.50 (current VAT rate of 17.5%).

- Some goods and services (such as postal services, loans of money, sales or lettings of land) are exempt from VAT – the effect of this is that the supplier cannot charge output tax, and can claim back only a proportion of input tax as agreed with the VAT authorities.
- Irrecoverable VAT is where a business registered for VAT cannot reclaim input tax (for example on cars, other than for resale); thus the total cost, including VAT, is entered into the accounts as the expenditure.
- A VAT-registered business does not normally include VAT in the fnancial statements – whether for capital or revenue items. A business not registered for VAT will include input VAT as a cost in the financial statements.

SSAP 9 Stocks and long-term contracts

- This sets out the broad rule that stock should be valued at cost or, where lower, selling price – see following section.

SSAP 13 Accounting for research and development

- Requires that all expenditure on research (ie undertaken to gain new technical knowledge, but which may not have a practical application) should be shown as an expense in the profit and loss account in the year in which it is incurred. (See Chapter 16)
- Development expenditure (ie development of a new product) is to be:

  either shown as an expense in the profit and loss account in the year in which it is incurred

  or can be shown (capitalised) on the balance sheet as an intangible fixed asset, provided that the product's commercial viability is assured; the intangible fixed asset will then be amortised (depreciated down to zero) in proportion to sales of the product as they materialise

FRS 15 Tangible fixed assets

- This requires that all fixed assets having a known useful economic life are to be depreciated (note that land is not depreciated – unless it is a mine or a quarry). See Chapters 6 and 16.
- Any acceptable depreciation method can be used to spread the cost of the fixed asset over its estimated useful economic life.
- Depreciation amounts are normally based on the cost of the fixed assets (where assets are revalued, depreciation is based on the revalued amount).

FRS 18 Accounting policies

The objective of this standard is to ensure that for all material items:

- a business selects the accounting policies most appropriate to its particular circumstances for the purpose of giving a true and fair view

- the accounting policies are reviewed regularly to ensure that they remain appropriate, and are changed when necessary
- sufficient information is disclosed in the financial statements to enable users to understand the accounting policies adopted and how they have been implemented

See also previous section.

VALUATION OF STOCK

The control and valuation of stock is an important aspect in the efficient management of a business. Manual or computer records are used to show the amount of stock held and its value at any time during the year. However, at the end of the financial year it is essential for a business to make a physical *stock-take* for use in the final accounts. This involves stock control personnel going into the stores, the shop, or the warehouse and counting each item. The counted stock for each type of stock held is then valued as follows:

number of items held x stock valuation per item = stock value

The auditors of a business may make random checks to ensure that the stock value is correct.

The value of stock at the beginning and end of the financial year is used to calculate the figure for cost of sales. Therefore, the stock value has an effect on profit for the year.

Stock is valued at:

- either what it cost the business to buy the stock (including additional costs to bring the product or service to its present location and condition, such as delivery charges)
- or the net realisable value – the actual or estimated selling price (less any further costs, such as selling and distribution)

This stock valuation is often described as being *at the lower of cost and net realisable value*. This valuation is taken from SSAP 9 and applies the *prudence concept*. It is illustrated as follows:

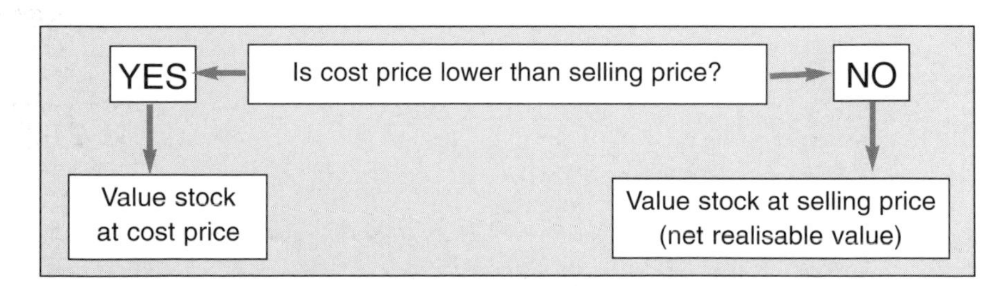

Thus two different stock values are compared:

- cost, including additional costs such as delivery charges
- net realisable value (the amount the stock will sell for), less any further costs such as selling and distribution

The lower of these two values is taken, and *different items or groups of stock are compared separately*. These principles are illustrated in the two Case Studies which follow.

CASE STUDY

'THE CLOTHING STORE'

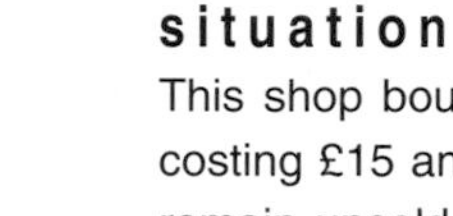

situation

This shop bought in a range of 'designer' beachwear in the Spring, with each item costing £15 and retailing for £30. Most of the stock is sold but, by Autumn, ten items remain unsold. These are put on the 'bargain rail' at £18 each. On 31 December, at the end of the shop's financial year, five items remain unsold. At what price will they be included in the year-end stock valuation?

Twelve months later, three items still remain unsold and have been reduced further to £10 each. At what price will they now be valued in the year-end stock valuation?

solution

- At 31 December, the five items will be valued at a cost of £15 each, ie 5 x £15 = £75.
- Twelve months later, the three items remaining unsold will be valued at a net realisable value of £10 each, ie 3 x £10 = £30.

Important note: Stock is *never* valued at selling price when selling price is above cost price. The reason for this is that selling price includes profit, and to value stock in this way would bring the profit into the accounts before it has been earned.

CASE STUDY

'PAINT AND WALLPAPER SUPPLIES'

situation

The year-end stocks for the two main groups of stock held by the business 'Paint and Wallpaper Supplies' are found to be:

	Cost	Net Realisable Value
	£	£
Paints	2,500	2,300
Wallpapers	5,000	7,500
	7,500	9,800

Which of the following stock valuations do you think is correct?

(a) £7,500

(b) £9,800

(c) £7,300

(d) £10,000

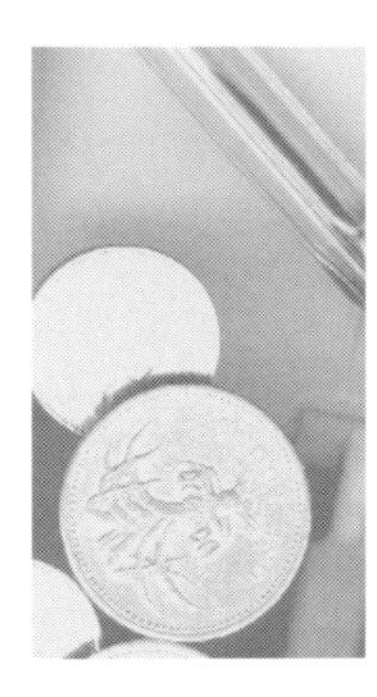

solution

Stock valuation (c) is correct, because it has taken the 'lower of cost and net realisable value' for each *group* of stock, ie

Paints (at net realisable value)	£2,300
Wallpapers (at cost)	£5,000
	£7,300

You will also note that this valuation is the lowest of the four possible choices, indicating that stock valuation follows the *prudence concept.*

commonly used stock valuation methods

Businesses use different methods to calculate the cost price of stock. Three commonly used methods are:

- FIFO (first in, first out) This method assumes that the first stocks acquired are the first to be disposed of, so that the valuation of stock on hand at any time consists of the most recently acquired stock.
- LIFO (last in, first out) Here it is assumed that the last stocks acquired are the first to be used, so that the stock on hand is made up of earlier purchases.
- AVCO (average cost) Here the average cost of items held at the beginning of the period is calculated; as new stocks are acquired a new average cost is calculated (usually based on a weighted average, using the number of units bought as the weighting).

The use of a particular method does not necessarily correspond with the method of physical distribution adopted in a firm's stores. For example, in a car factory one car battery of type X is the same as another, and no-one will be concerned if the storekeeper issues one from the latest batch received, even if the FIFO system has been adopted. However, perishable goods are always physically handled on the basis of first in, first out, even if the accounting stock records use another method.

Having chosen a suitable stock valuation method, a business would continue to use that method unless there were good reasons for making the change. This is in line with the consistency concept of accounting.

CASE STUDY

'THE CORNER STORES'

situation

One of the lines stocked by 'The Corner Stores' is tins of baked beans. The following are the purchases and sales of tins of beans for two weeks (note that there was no stock at the beginning of week 1):

Week 1:	100 tins of beans bought at a cost of 25p per tin
	50 tins sold at 40p per tin
Week 2:	100 tins of beans bought at a cost of 30p per tin
	75 tins sold at 40p per tin

What will be the stock valuation at the end of week 2, using

- FIFO (first in, first out)
- LIFO (last in, first out)
- AVCO (average cost)

and what gross profit has been made on beans over the two week period?

solution

At the end of week 2 there are 75 tins of beans in stock.

FIFO

Using FIFO, the week 2 closing stock consists of 75 tins at the latest price, ie 30p. Therefore the stock valuation is 75 x 30p = £22.50

LIFO

With LIFO the closing stock consists of:

50 tins from week 1 at 25p each	= £12.50
25 tins from week 2 at 30p each	= £ 7.50
75 tins	= £20.00

AVCO

We must calculate the average cost as follows:

50 tins in stock at end of week 1 at 25p	= £12.50
100 tins received in week 2 at 30p	= £30.00
150 tins at an average cost of 28.33p (£42.50 ÷ 150)	= £42.50
75 tins in stock at end of week at 28.33p each	= £21.25

The conclusion here is that, even with tins of baked beans, there is a difference in closing stock valuation depending on the method used:

FIFO	£22.50
LIFO	£20.00
AVCO	£21.25

From these results we can draw a general conclusion that, in times of rising prices, FIFO always gives the highest valuation, LIFO the lowest, and AVCO comes somewhere between the two (although not necessarily exactly half-way between the two).

You may wonder why it is necessary to spend so much time on looking at different stock valuation methods. The method adopted for stock valuation is important because of the effect it has on the profits of the business.
Let us now calculate how much profit this business made on its sales of baked beans. The profit and loss account is set out on the next page.

You will see that as a result of using different closing stock valuations, the gross profit is different. Here, with prices rising, FIFO gives the highest profit, LIFO the lowest, and

AVCO is between the two. Do not forget, also, that the closing stock for one accounting period becomes the opening stock for the next, and so the following accounting period will also be affected.

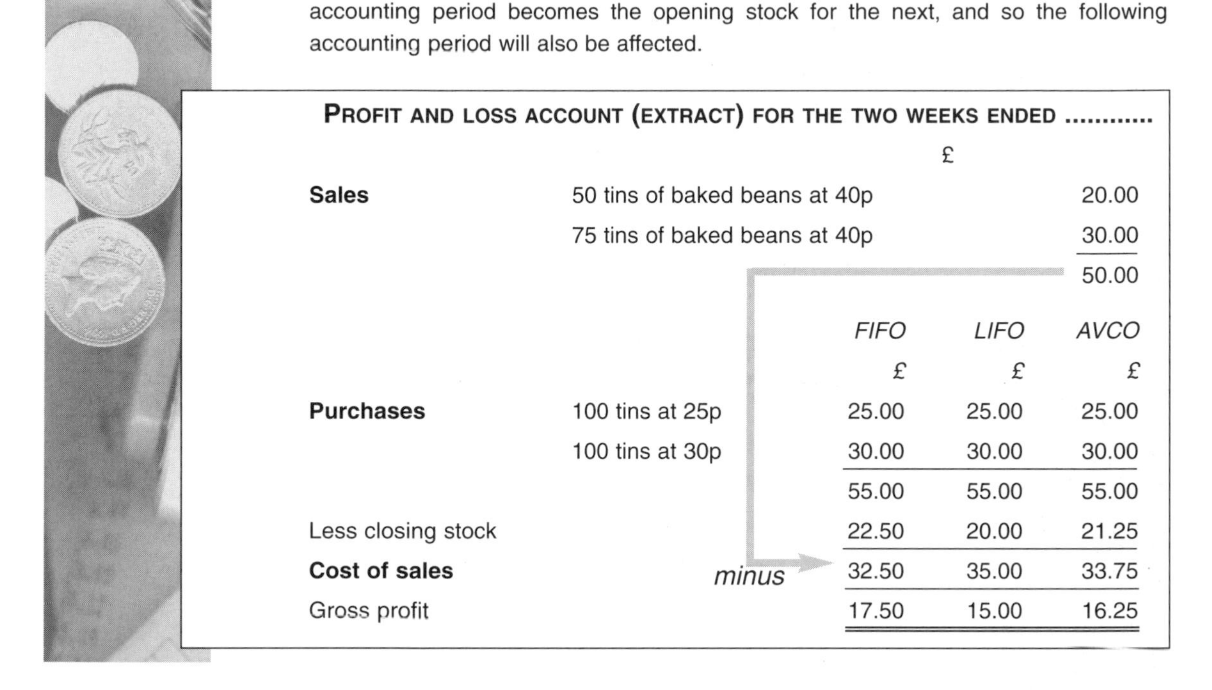

PROFIT AND LOSS ACCOUNT (EXTRACT) FOR THE TWO WEEKS ENDED ....

				£
Sales	50 tins of baked beans at 40p			20.00
	75 tins of baked beans at 40p			30.00
				50.00
		FIFO	*LIFO*	*AVCO*
		£	£	£
Purchases	100 tins at 25p	25.00	25.00	25.00
	100 tins at 30p	30.00	30.00	30.00
		55.00	55.00	55.00
Less closing stock		22.50	20.00	21.25
Cost of sales	*minus*	32.50	35.00	33.75
Gross profit		17.50	15.00	16.25

STOCK VALUATION IN A MANUFACTURING BUSINESS

A manufacturing business will often have stocks in three different forms:

- raw materials
- work-in-progress
- finished goods

The principle of 'lower of cost and net realisable value' is followed in the valuation of year-end stocks. However, for work-in-progress and finished goods, manufacturing costs which bring the product to its present location or condition are included in the cost price. This topic is covered in Chapter 15.

CAPITAL EXPENDITURE AND REVENUE EXPENDITURE

When preparing final accounts it is important to distinguish between *capital expenditure* and *revenue expenditure.*

Capital expenditure can be defined as *expenditure incurred on the purchase, alteration or improvement of fixed assets.* For example, the purchase of a car for use in the business is capital expenditure. Included in capital expenditure are such costs as:

- delivery of fixed assets
- installation of fixed assets
- improvement (but not repair) of fixed assets
- legal costs of buying property

Revenue expenditure is *expenditure incurred on running expenses*. For example, the cost of petrol or diesel for the car (above) is revenue expenditure. Included in revenue expenditure are the costs of:

- maintenance and repair of fixed assets
- administration of the business
- selling and distributing the goods or products in which the business trades

Capital expenditure is shown on the balance sheet, while revenue expenditure is charged as an expense to the profit and loss account. It is important to classify these types of expenditure correctly in the accounting system. For example, if the cost of the car was shown as an expense in profit and loss account, then net profit would be reduced considerably, or a net loss recorded; meanwhile, the balance sheet would not show the car as a fixed asset – clearly this is incorrect as the business owns the asset. Note, however, that there is a link between capital expenditure and the profit and loss account: as fixed assets are depreciated, the amount of depreciation is shown as an expense in the profit and loss account. This is an application of the accruals concept, ie the depreciation relates to the time period over which the fixed asset is used.

In some circumstances we must take care to distinguish between capital and revenue expenditure. For example:

- ***cost of building an extension to the factory £30,000, which includes £1,000 for repairs to the existing factory***
  - capital expenditure, £29,000
  - revenue expenditure, £1,000 (because it is for repairs to an existing fixed asset)
- ***a plot of land has been bought for £20,000, the legal costs are £750***
  - capital expenditure £20,750 (the legal costs are included in the capital expenditure, because they are the cost of acquiring the fixed asset, ie the legal costs are capitalised)
- ***the business' own employees are used to install a new air conditioning system: wages £1,000, materials £1,500***
  - capital expenditure £2,500 (an addition to the property). Note that, in cases such as this, revenue expenditure, ie wages and materials purchases, will need to be reduced to allow for the transfer to capital expenditure

- ***own employees used to repair and redecorate the premises: wages £500, materials £750***
  - revenue expenditure £1,250 (repairs and redecoration are running expenses)
- ***purchase of a new machine £10,000, payment for installation and setting up £250***
  - capital expenditure £10,250 (costs of installation of a fixed asset are capitalised)

Only by allocating capital expenditure and revenue expenditure correctly between the balance sheet and the profit and loss account can the final accounts reflect accurately the financial state of the business. The chart below shows the main items of capital expenditure and revenue expenditure associated with three major fixed assets – buildings, vehicles and computers.

	capital expenditure	*revenue expenditure*
BUILDINGS	• cost of building • cost of extension • carriage on raw materials used • legal fees • labour cost of own employees used on building • installation of utilities, eg gas, water, electricity	• general maintenance • repairs • redecoration
VEHICLES	• net cost, including any optional extras • delivery costs • number plates • changes to the vehicle	• fuel • road fund licence • extended warranty • painting company logo • insurance • servicing and repairs
COMPUTERS	• net cost • installation and testing • modifications, including memory upgrades, to meet specific needs of business • installation of special wiring • cost of air conditioning to computer room • staff training (where directly related to new equipment) • computer programs (but can be classified as revenue expenditure if cost is low and will have little impact on final accounts)	• floppy discs • printer paper and other consumables • insurance • computer programs (or can be classified as capital expenditure if cost is high and will have a large impact on final accounts)

CHAPTER SUMMARY

- The accounting concepts followed when preparing accounts are: business entity, money measurement, historical cost, duality, materiality, going concern, accruals (matching), consistency and prudence.
- Accounting standards comprise SSAPs and FRSs.
- The usual valuation for stock is at the lower of cost and net realisable value (SSAP 9).
- Commonly used stock valuation methods include:
  - FIFO (first in, first out)
  - LIFO (last in, first out)
  - AVCO (average cost, based on a weighted average)
- Having chosen one stock valuation method, a business should apply it consistently.
- It is important to allocate capital expenditure and revenue expenditure correctly between the balance sheet and the profit and loss account so that the final accounts reflect accurately the financial state of the business.

KEY TERMS

accounting concepts part of the 'rules' of accounting

business entity concept final accounts record and report on the activities of one particular business

money measurement concept in final accounts all items are expressed in terms of money

historical cost concept assets and liabilities are recorded in the accounts at the actual amount of the transaction

duality each financial transaction is recorded by two opposite accounting entries of equal value

materiality concept items with a low monetary value are not worthwhile recording in the accounts separately

going concern concept the presumption that the business to which the final accounts relate will continue to trade in the foreseeable future

accruals concept expenses and revenues are matched so that they concern the same goods or services and the same time period

consistency concept when a business adopts particular accounting methods, it should continue to use such methods consistently

prudence concept final accounts should always, where there is any doubt, report a conservative figure for profit or the valuation of assets

SSAP Statement of Standard Accounting Practice; part of the rules of accounting

FRS	Financial Reporting Standard; part of the rules of accounting
capital expenditure	expenditure incurred on the purchase, alteration or improvement of fixed assets
revenue expenditure	expenditure incurred on running expenses

STUDENT ACTIVITIES

The answers to these Student Activities are printed in the back of this book. Further questions and more fully extended Student Activities and Assessments are to be found in the accompanying Osborne Books' text *Financial Accounting Workbook*.

8.1 A business should not change its basis of valuing stock without good reason. This follows the concept of:

(a) money measurement

(b) going concern

(c) prudence

(d) consistency

Answer (a) or (b) or (c) or (d)

8.2 Explain the appropriate accounting concept in each of the following circumstances.

(a) A business has a customer who owes £1,000. Despite sending numerous statements of account to the debtor, payment has not been received. It has been decided to make a provision for bad debts in respect of this customer.

(b) From time-to-time a business buys a pack of blank video tapes in order to record business meetings. The tapes are re-used over a number of years and are sometimes kept as a permanent record of meetings. Accounting policy is to charge the cost of the tapes – £10 for a pack of five tapes – as an expense in profit and loss account.

(c) As an accounting trainee you are instructed to prepare two sets of a business' final accounts for a particular year, one of which uses straight-line depreciation while the other uses reducing balance depreciation. The owner of the business says that he will use the set which shows the lower profit.

(d) A business has a financial year end of 31 December 1997. In early February 1998, an electricity bill is received covering the period November 1997 – January 1998. It is decided to apportion two-thirds of the bill to the profit and loss account for 1997 and one-third to the profit and loss account for 1998.

8.3 A discussion is taking place between Jane Smith, a sole trader, who owns a furniture shop, and her husband, John, who solely owns an engineering business. The following points are made:

(a) John says that, having depreciated his firm's machinery last year on the reducing balance method, for this year he intends to use the straight-line method. By doing this he says that he will deduct less depreciation from profit and loss account, so his net profit will be higher and his bank manager will be impressed. He says he might revert back to reducing balance method next year.

(b) At the end of her financial year, Jane comments that the stock of her shop had cost £10,000. She says that, as she normally adds 50 per cent to cost price to give the selling price, she intends to put a value of £15,000 for closing stock in the final accounts.

(c) John's car is owned by his business but he keeps referring to it as my car. Jane reminds him that it does not belong to him, but to the firm. He replies that of course it belongs to him and, furthermore, if the firm went bankrupt, he would be able to keep the car.

(d) John's business has debtors of £30,000. He knows that, included in this figure is a bad debt of £2,500. He wants to show £30,000 as debtors in the year-end balance sheet in order to have a high figure for current assets.

(e) On the last day of her financial year, Jane sold a large order of furniture, totalling £3,000, to a local hotel. The furniture was invoiced and delivered from stock that day, before year-end stocktaking commenced. The payment was received early in the new financial year and Jane now asks John if she will be able to put this sale through the accounts for the new year, instead of the old, but without altering the figures for purchases and closing stock for the old year.

(f) John says that his accountant talks of preparing his accounts on a going concern basis. John asks Jane if she knows of any other basis that can be used, and which it is usual to follow.

You are to take each of the points and state the correct accounting treatment, referring to appropriate accounting concepts.

8.4 Stock is valued at:

(a) cost price

(b) net realisable value

(c) lower of cost and net realisable value

(d) selling price

Answer (a) or (b) or (c) or (d)

8.5 A stationery supplies business has 500 large ring binders in stock at the end of its financial year on 30 June 1999. The details are

- cost price £2.20 per ring binder
- selling price £4.00 each

As the ring binders have not sold well, the owner of the business has decided to overprint them with pictures in order to make them attractive to students starting courses at the local college in September. The cost of the overprinting will be £1 per binder and the 'special offer' price to students will then be £3 per binder.

What is the stock valuation for the 500 binders in stock on 30 June 1999?

(a) £2,000

(b) £1,500

(c) £1,100

(d) £1,000

Answer (a) or (b) or (c) or (d)

8.6 A furniture shop sells coffee tables amongst the lines that it sells. The stock movements for coffee tables in February 1998 were:

1 February	Stock of 10 tables brought forward at a cost of £30 each
4 February	Sold 2 tables
7 February	Sold 5 tables
10 February	Bought 12 tables at £32 each
12 February	Sold 6 tables
17 February	Sold 4 tables
20 February	Bought 8 tables at £31 each
24 February	Sold 4 tables
27 February	Sold 3 tables

Each table sells at £50.

Stock is valued on the FIFO (first in, first out) basis.

You are to calculate the value of:

(a) sales for February

(b) closing stock at 28 February

(c) cost of sales for February

8.7 A garden supplies shop has the following valuations for each group of stock at the end of its financial year:

	cost	*selling price*
	£	£
seeds	1,550	1,450
fertilisers and insecticides	2,270	3,560
tools	4,390	6,920

What valuation for closing stock will be used in its final accounts?

8.8 A business has, in error, overcalculated the value of its closing stock by £1,000. Before the error is corrected, what is the effect

(a) on this year's profit?

(b) on next year's profit?

8.9 A business has bought an accounting program for its computer system. The cost of the software is £99. Will this be treated as capital expenditure or revenue expenditure? Give reasons for your answer in the form of a memorandum to the owner of the business.

8.10 "Capital expenditure is money spent on fixed assets. As these are recorded on the balance sheet, then it is true to say that capital expenditure has no effect on the profit and loss account."

Discuss this statement, saying whether or not you agree with it and giving reasons for your answer.

9 CONTROL ACCOUNTS

this chapter covers . . .

Control accounts are 'master' accounts which record by means of totals the transactions passing through the accounts that they control. In this chapter we will look at:

- *the ledger system of accounts and the division of the ledger*
- *the concept of control accounts*
- *the layout of sales ledger and purchases ledger control accounts*
- *the use of control accounts as an aid to the management of a business*
- *control accounts and book-keeping*

NVQ PERFORMANCE CRITERIA COVERED

unit 4: MAINTAINING FINANCIAL RECORDS AND PREPARING ACCOUNTS

element 3

collect and collate information for the preparation of final accounts

- ❑ *relevant accounts and reconciliations are correctly prepared to allow the preparation of final accounts*
- ❑ *investigations into business transactions are conducted with tact and courtesy*
- ❑ *discrepancies and unusual features are identified and either resolved or referred to the appropriate person*

TYPES OF ACCOUNTS

Within a book-keeping system there are different types of accounts: a distinction is made between *personal* and *impersonal* accounts. Personal accounts are in the names of people or businesses, eg the accounts for debtors and creditors. Impersonal accounts are the other accounts; these are usually divided between *real accounts*, which represent things such as computers, motor vehicles, machinery, stock of goods, etc, and *nominal accounts*, which record income and expenses such as sales, purchases, wages, etc.

The diagram below distinguishes between the different types of accounts.

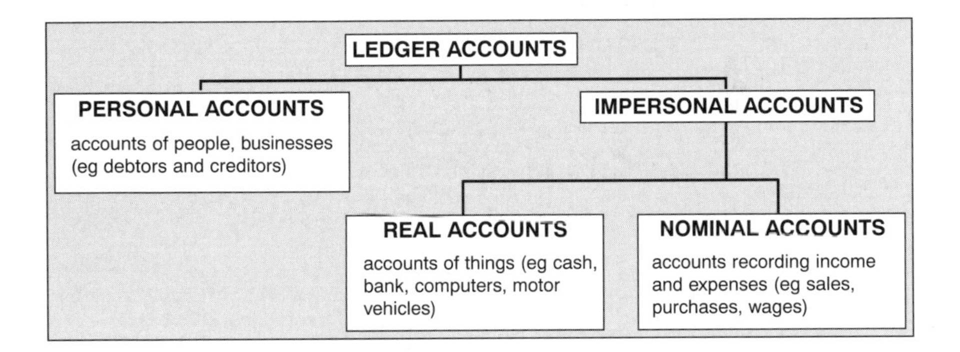

DIVISION OF THE LEDGER

The duality concept of double-entry book-keeping involves, as we have seen, making two entries in the ledger accounts for each business transaction. The traditional meaning of a ledger is a weighty leather-bound volume into which each account was entered on a separate page. With such a hand-written book-keeping system, as more and more accounts were opened, the point was reached where another ledger book was needed. Finally, in order to sort the accounts into a logical order, the accounting system was divided into four main sections, and this practice continues today:

- *sales ledger*, containing the accounts of debtors
- *purchases ledger*, containing the accounts of creditors
- *cash books*, containing the main cash book (which combines both cash account and bank account), and the petty cash book
- *general (or nominal) ledger*, containing the nominal accounts (income and expenses) and the real accounts (accounts of things)

These four divisions comprise 'the ledger', and are illustrated on the next page.

DIVISION OF THE LEDGER

sales ledger

Sales ledger contains the accounts of debtors, and records:

- sales made on credit to customers of the business
- sales returns by customers
- payments received from debtors
- cash discount allowed for prompt settlement

Sales ledger does not record cash sales.

Sales ledger contains an account for each debtor and records the transactions with that debtor. Usually a sales ledger control account is used to summarise the transactions on the accounts of debtors.

purchases ledger

Purchases ledger contains the accounts of creditors, and records:

- purchases made on credit from suppliers of the business
- purchases returns made by the business
- payments made to creditors
- cash discount received for prompt settlement

Purchases ledger does not record cash purchases.

Purchases ledger contains an account for each creditor and records the transactions with that creditor. Usually a purchases ledger control account is used to summarise the transactions on the accounts of creditors.

cash books

Cash Book

- records all transactions for bank account and cash account
- cash book is also often used for listing the amounts of cash discount received and allowed, and Value Added Tax, before transfer of the totals to the relevant accounts

Petty Cash Book

- records low-value cash payments – usually for expenses – that are too small to be entered in the main cash book

general (nominal) ledger

The general (nominal) ledger contains the other accounts of the business:

Nominal Accounts

- sales account (cash and credit sales), sales returns
- purchases account (cash and credit purchases), purchases returns
- expenses and income, loans, capital, drawings
- Value Added Tax (where the business is VAT registered)
- profit and loss

Real Accounts

- fixed assets, eg computers, motor vehicles, machinery
- stock

THE CONCEPT OF CONTROL ACCOUNTS

Control accounts are 'master' accounts which control a number of subsidiary ledger accounts. Control accounts work in the following way:

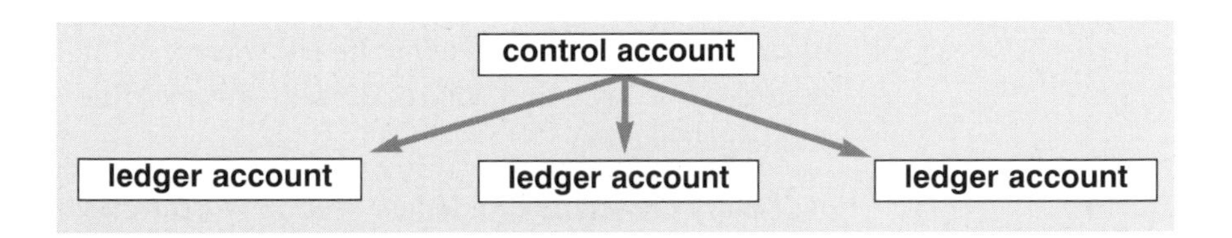

The control account (also known as a *totals account*) is used to record the totals of transactions passing through the subsidiary accounts. In this way, the balance of the control account will always be equal to the total balances of the subsidiary accounts, unless an error has occurred. Two commonly-used control accounts are:

- sales ledger control account – the total of the debtors
- purchases ledger control account – the total of the creditors

In the illustration above we have seen how a control account acts as a master account for a number of subsidiary accounts. The principle is that, if the total of the opening balances for subsidiary accounts is known, together with the total of amounts increasing these balances, and the total of amounts decreasing these balances, then the total of the closing balances for the subsidiary accounts can be calculated.

For example:

	£
Total of opening balances	50,000
Add increases	10,000
	60,000
Less decreases	12,000
Total of closing balances	48,000

The total of the closing balances can now be checked against a separate listing of the balances of the subsidiary accounts to ensure that the two figures agree. If so, it proves that the ledgers within the section are correct (subject to any errors such as misposts and compensating errors). Let us now apply this concept to one of the divisions of the ledger – sales ledger.

The diagram on page 139 shows the personal accounts which form the entire sales ledger of a particular business (in practice there would, of course, be more than four accounts involved). The sales ledger control account acts as a totals account, which records totals of the transactions passing through the individual accounts that it controls. Notice how transactions appear in the control account *on the same side* as they appear in the individual accounts. The sales ledger control account can be reconciled with the balances of the individual accounts which it controls (see below). Thus, control accounts act as an aid to locating errors: if the control account and subsidiary accounts agree, then the error is likely to lie elsewhere. In this way the control account acts as a checking and control device – proving the arithmetical accuracy of the ledger section.

Normally the whole of a ledger section is controlled by one control account, eg sales ledger control account or purchases ledger control account. However, it is also possible to have a number of separate control accounts for subdivisions of the sales ledger and purchases ledger, eg sales ledger control account A-K, purchases ledger control account S-Z, etc. It is for a business – the user of the accounting system – to decide what is most suitable, taking into account the number of accounts in the sales and purchases ledger, together with the type of book-keeping system – manual or computerised.

In the diagram on the next page the sales ledger control account and subsidiary accounts are agreed at the beginning and end of the month, as follows:

Reconciliation of sales ledger control account with debtor balances

	1 January 1998	*31 January 1998*
	£	£
A Ackroyd	100	150
B Barnes	200	200
C Cox	50	180
D Douglas	150	150
Sales ledger control account	500	680

Note: The business will decide how often to reconcile the control account with the subsidiary accounts – weekly, monthly, quarterly or annually.

SALES LEDGER CONTROL ACCOUNT

The layout of a sales ledger control account (or debtors' control account) is shown on page 140. Study the layout carefully and then read the text which explains the additional items.

Dr	SALES LEDGER CONTROL ACCOUNT				Cr
1998		£	1998		£
1 Jan	Balances b/d	500	31 Jan	Bank	443
31 Jan	Sales	700	31 Jan	Discount allowed	7
			31 Jan	Sales returns	70
			31 Jan	Balances c/d	680
		1,200			1,200
1 Feb	Balances b/d	680			

Dr	A Ackroyd				Cr
1998		£	1998		£
1 Jan	Balance b/d	100	10 Jan	Bank	98
6 Jan	Sales	150	10 Jan	Discount allowed	2
			31 Jan	Balance c/d	150
		250			250
1 Feb	Balance b/d	150			

Dr	B Barnes				Cr
1998		£	1998		£
1 Jan	Balance b/d	200	13 Jan	Bank	195
6 Jan	Sales	250	13 Jan	Discount allowed	5
			27 Jan	Sales returns	50
			31 Jan	Balance c/d	200
		450			450
1 Feb	Balance b/d	200			

Dr	C Cox				Cr
1998		£	1998		£
1 Jan	Balance b/d	50	20 Jan	Bank	50
15 Jan	Sales	200	29 Jan	Sales returns	20
			31 Jan	Balance c/d	180
		250			250
1 Feb	Balance b/d	180			

Dr	D Douglas				Cr
1998		£	1998		£
1 Jan	Balance b/d	150	30 Jan	Bank	100
20 Jan	Sales	100	31 Jan	Balance c/d	150
		250			250
1 Feb	Balance b/d	150			

relationship of the sales ledger control account to the individual sales ledger accounts

Dr	Sales Ledger Control Account		Cr
	£		£
Balances b/d (large amount)		Balances b/d (small amount)	
Credit sales		Cash/cheques received from debtors	
Returned cheques		Cash discount allowed	
Interest charged to debtors		Sales returns	
Balances c/d (small amount)		Bad debts written off	
		Set-off/contra entries	
		Balances c/d (large amount)	
Balances b/d (large amount)		Balances b/d (small amount)	

balances b/d

In the layout above there is a figure for balances b/d on both the debit side and the credit side of the control account. The usual balance on a debtor's account is debit and so this will form the large balance on the debit side. However, from time-to-time, it is possible for some debtors to have a credit balance on their accounts. This may come about, for example, because they have paid for goods, and then returned them, or because they have overpaid in error: the business owes them the amount due, ie they have a credit balance for the time being. Such credit balances are always going to be in the minority and so they will be for the smaller amount. Clearly, if there are small credit balances at the beginning of the month, there are likely to be credit balances at the month-end, and these need to be recorded separately as balances carried down – do not 'net off' the two types of balances. In a balance sheet, the small credit balances should be included with creditors.

credit sales

Only credit sales – and not cash sales – are entered in the control account because only credit sales are recorded in the debtors' accounts. The total sales of the business will comprise both credit and cash sales.

returned cheques

If a debtor's cheque is returned unpaid by the bank, ie the cheque has 'bounced', then entries have to be made in the book-keeping system to record this. These entries are:

– *debit* debtor's account

– *credit* cash book (bank columns)

As a transaction has been made in a debtor's account, then the amount must also be recorded in the sales ledger control account – on the debit side.

interest charged to debtors

Sometimes a business will charge a debtor for slow payment of an account. The accounting entries are:

– *debit* debtor's account

– *credit* interest received account

As a debit transaction has been made in the debtor's account, so a debit entry must be recorded in the control account.

bad debts written off

The book-keeping entries for writing off a bad debt (see Chapter 7) are:

– *debit* bad debts written off account

– *credit* debtor's account

A credit transaction is entered in a debtor's account. This is because the control account 'masters' the sales ledger and so the transaction must also be recorded as a credit transaction in the control account.

set-off/contra entries

See page 144.

PURCHASES LEDGER CONTROL ACCOUNT

The specimen layout for the purchases ledger control account (or creditors' control account) is shown below.

The layout is explained on the next page.

Dr	Purchases Ledger Control Account		Cr
	£		£
Balances b/d small amount)		Balances b/d (large amount)	
Cash/cheques paid to creditors		Credit purchases	
Cash discount received		Interest charged by creditors	
Purchases returns		Balances c/d (small amount)	
Set-off/contra entries			
Balances c/d (large amount)			
Balances b/d (small amount)		Balances b/d (large amount)	

balances b/d

As with sales ledger control account, it is possible to have balances on both sides of the account. For purchases ledger, containing the accounts of creditors, the large balance b/d is always on the credit side. However, if a creditor has been overpaid, the result may be a small debit balance b/d. It may also be that there are closing balances on both sides of the account at the end of the period. In the balance sheet, any small debit balances should be included with debtors.

credit purchases

Only credit purchases – and not cash purchases – are entered in the control account. However, the total purchases of the business will comprise both credit and cash purchases.

interest charged by creditors

If creditors charge interest because of slow payment, this must be recorded on both the creditor's account and the control account.

set-off/contra entries

See page 144.

reconciliation of purchases ledger control account

The diagram on page 143 shows how a purchases ledger control account acts as a totals account for the creditors of a business. Reconciliation of the balances on the purchases ledger control account and subsidiary accounts is made as follows:

Reconciliation of purchases ledger control account with creditor balances

	1 January 1998	*31 January 1998*
	£	£
F Francis	100	200
G Gold	200	350
H Harris	300	500
I Ingram	400	900
Purchases ledger control account	1,000	1,950

Dr	PURCHASES LEDGER CONTROL ACCOUNT				Cr
1998		£	1998		£
31 Jan	Purchases returns	150	1 Jan	Balances b/d	1,000
31 Jan	Bank	594	31 Jan	Purchases	1,700
31 Jan	Discount received	6			
31 Jan	Balances c/d	1,950			
		2,700			2,700
			1 Feb	Balances b/d	1,950

Dr	F Francis				Cr
1998		£	1998		£
17 Jan	Bank	98	1Jan	Balance b/d	100
17 Jan	Discount received	2	3 Jan	Purchases	200
31 Jan	Balance c/d	200			
		300			300
			1 Feb	Balance b/d	200

Dr	G Gold				Cr
1998		£	1998		£
15 Jan	Purchases returns	50	1 Jan	Balance b/d	200
28 Jan	Bank	100	9 Jan	Purchases	300
31 Jan	Balance c/d	350			
		500			500
			1 Feb	Balance b/d	350

Dr	H Harris				Cr
1998		£	1998		£
28 Jan	Purchases returns	100	1 Jan	Balance b/d	300
30 Jan	Bank	200	17 Jan	Purchases	500
31 Jan	Balance c/d	500			
		800			800
			1 Feb	Balance b/d	500

Dr	I Ingram				Cr
1998		£	1998		£
22 Jan	Bank	196	1 Jan	Balance b/d	400
22 Jan	Discount received	4	27 Jan	Purchases	700
31 Jan	Balance c/d	900			
		1,100			1,100
			1 Feb	Balance b/d	900

relationship of the purchases ledger control account to the individual purchase ledger accounts

SET-OFF/CONTRA ENTRIES

These entries occur when the same person or business has an account in both sales ledger and purchases ledger, ie they are both buying from, and selling to, the business whose accounts we are preparing. For example, M Patel Limited has the following accounts in the sales and purchases ledgers:

SALES LEDGER

Dr	**A Smith**		Cr
	£		£
Balance b/d	200		

PURCHASES LEDGER

Dr	**A Smith**		Cr
	£		£
		Balance b/d	300

From these accounts we can see that:

- A Smith owes M Patel Limited £200 (sales ledger)
- M Patel Limited owes A Smith £300 (purchases ledger)

To save each having to write out a cheque to send to the other, it is possible (with A Smith's agreement) to set-off one account against the other, so that they can settle their net indebtedness with one cheque. The book-keeping entries in M Patel's books will be:

– *debit* A Smith (purchases ledger) £200

– *credit* A Smith (sales ledger) £200

The accounts will now appear as:

SALES LEDGER

Dr	**A Smith**		Cr
	£		£
Balance b/d	200	Set-off: purchases ledger	200

PURCHASES LEDGER

Dr	A Smith		Cr
	£		£
Set-off: sales ledger	200	Balance b/d	300

The net result is that M Patel Limited owes A Smith £100. The important point to note is that, because transactions have been recorded in the personal accounts, an entry needs to be made in the two control accounts:

– *debit* purchases ledger control account

– *credit* sales ledger control account

SOURCES OF INFORMATION FOR CONTROL ACCOUNTS

Control accounts use totals (remember that their other name is 'totals accounts') for the week, month, quarter or year – depending on what time period is decided upon by the business. The totals come from a number of sources in the accounting system:

sales ledger control account

- total credit sales (including VAT) – from the 'gross' column of the sales day book
- total sales returns (including VAT) – from the 'gross' column of the sales returns day book
- total cash/cheques received from debtors – from the cash book
- total discount allowed – from the discount allowed column of the cash book, or from discount allowed account
- bad debts – from the journal, or bad debts written off account

purchases ledger control account

- total credit purchases (including VAT) – from the 'gross' column of the purchases day book
- total purchases returns (including VAT) – from the 'gross' column of the purchases returns day book
- total cash/cheques paid to creditors – from the cash book
- total discount received – from the discount received column of the cash book, or from discount received account

CONTROL ACCOUNTS AS AN AID TO MANAGEMENT

When the manager of a business needs to know the figure for debtors or creditors – important information for the manager – the balance of the appropriate control account will give the information immediately: there is no need to add up the balances of all the individual debtors' or creditors' accounts. With a computer accounting system, control accounts can be printed at any time.

The use of control accounts makes fraud more difficult – particularly in a manual accounting system. If a fraudulent transaction is to be recorded on a personal account, the transaction must also be entered in the control account. As the control account will be either maintained by a supervisor, or checked regularly by the manager, the control accounts add another level of security within the accounting system.

We have already seen in this chapter how control accounts can help in locating errors. Remember, though, that a control account only proves the arithmetical accuracy of the accounts which it controls – there could still be errors, such as misposts and compensating errors, within the ledger section.

A further use of control accounts is to help with the construction of final accounts when a business has not kept double-entry accounts and a trial balance cannot be extracted – see Chapter 12, which deals with *incomplete records*.

CONTROL ACCOUNTS AND BOOK-KEEPING

A business must decide how to use control accounts in its book-keeping system. The commonest way of doing this is to incorporate the control accounts into double-entry book-keeping.

The control accounts therefore form part of the double-entry system: the balances of the sales ledger control account and the purchases ledger control account are recorded in the trial balance as the figures for debtors and creditors respectively. This means that the personal accounts of debtors and creditors are not part of double-entry, but are separate *memorandum accounts* which record how much each debtor owes, and how much is owed to each creditor. From time-to-time, the balances of the memorandum accounts are agreed with the balance of the appropriate control account.

The diagrams on the next two pages show how the sales ledger control account and the purchases ledger control account are incorporated into the double-entry book-keeping system (general ledger), with the individual debtors' and creditors' accounts kept in the form of memorandum accounts.

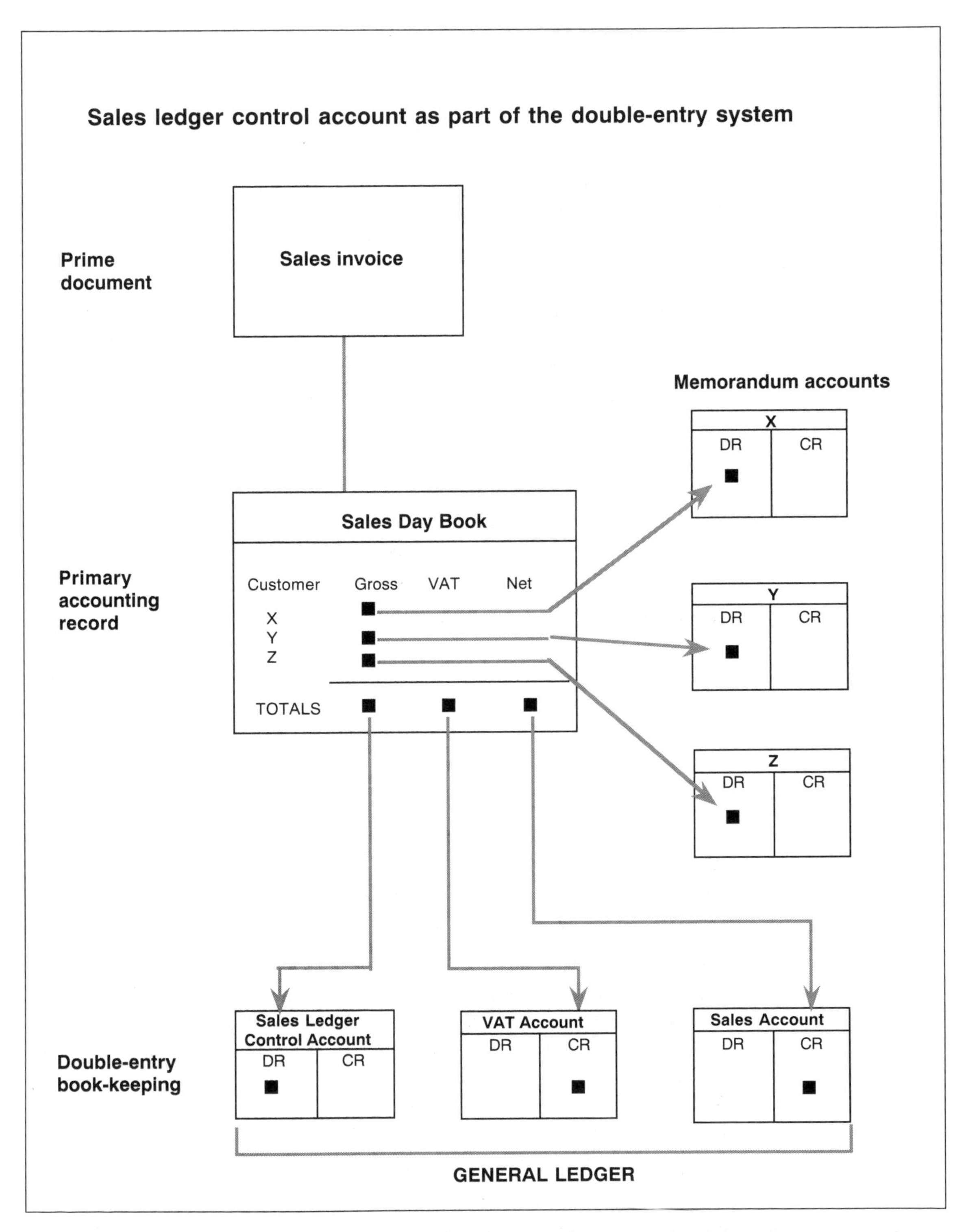

Sales ledger control account incorporated into the double-entry book-keeping system; the debtors' accounts are memorandum accounts

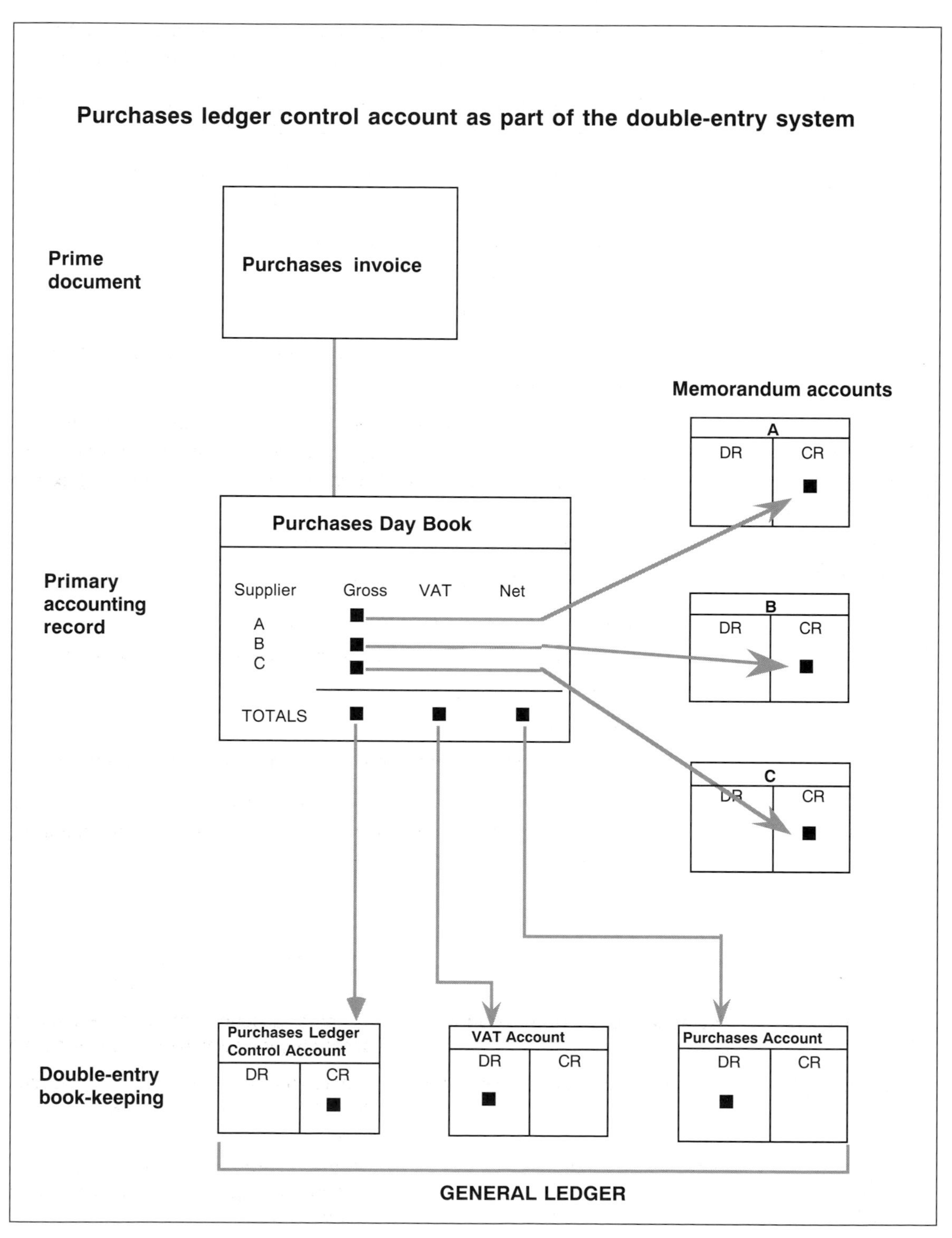

Purchases ledger control account incorporated into the double-entry book-keeping system; the creditors' accounts are memorandum accounts.

CHAPTER SUMMARY

- Accounts are either personal (eg accounts of debtors and creditors) or impersonal ('real' items such as assets or 'nominal' items such as income).
- The ledger is divided for convenience into four sections: sales ledger, purchases ledger, cash book and general (or nominal) ledger
- Control accounts (or totals accounts) are 'master' accounts, which control a number of subsidiary accounts within the ledger.
- Two commonly used control accounts are:
  - sales ledger control account
  - purchases ledger control account
- Transactions are recorded on the same side of the control account as on the subsidiary accounts.
- Set-off/contra entries occur when one person has an account in both sales and purchases ledger, and it is agreed to set-off one balance against the other to leave a net balance. This usually results in the following control account entries:
  - debit purchases ledger control account
  - credit sales ledger control account
- Control accounts are an aid to management:
  - they give up-to-date information on the total of debtors or creditors
  - by making fraud more difficult
  - in helping to locate errors
  - in assisting with the preparation of accounts from incomplete records
- Control accounts are normally incorporated into the double-entry book-keeping system. The subsidiary accounts are set up as separate memorandum accounts.

KEY TERMS

control account	a 'master' account which controls a number of subsidiary accounts
sales ledger control account	a 'master' account which controls debtors' accounts (or a section of the sales ledger)
purchases ledger control account	'master' account which controls creditors' accounts (or a section of the purchases ledger)
set-off/contra entries	where balances in sales ledger and purchases ledger are to be set-off against one another
memorandum account	an account which is not part of the double-entry system

STUDENT ACTIVITIES

The answers to these Student Activities are printed in the back of this book. Further questions and more fully extended Student Activities and Assessments are to be found in the accompanying Osborne Books' text *Financial Accounting Workbook*.

9.1 You have the following information:

• opening creditor balances at start of month	£18,600
• cash/cheques paid to creditors during month	£9,400
• purchases for month	£9,100
• purchases returns for month	£800

What is the figure for closing creditor balances at the end of the month?

(a) £18,100

(b) £19,100

(c) £36,300

(d) £17,500

Answer (a) or (b) or (c) or (d)

9.2 Which one of the following does not appear in sales ledger control account?

(a) bad debts written off

(b) discount received

(c) sales returns

(d) cash/cheques received from debtors

Answer (a) or (b) or (c) or (d)

9.3 Prepare a sales ledger control account for the month of June 1998 from the following information:

1998		£
1 Jun	Sales ledger balances	17,491
30 Jun	Credit sales for month	42,591
	Sales returns	1,045
	Payments received from debtors	39,024
	Cash discount allowed	593
	Bad debts written off	296

The debtors figure at 30 June is to be entered as the balancing figure.

9.4 Prepare a purchases ledger control account for the month of April 1998 from the following information:

1998		£
1 Apr	Purchases ledger balances	14,275
30 Apr	Credit purchases for month	36,592
	Purchases returns	653
	Payments made to creditors	31,074
	Cash discount received	1,048
	Transfer of credit balances to sales ledger	597

The creditors figure at 30 April is to be entered as the balancing figure.

9.5 The sales ledger of Rowcester Traders contains the following accounts on 1 February 1998:

Arrow Valley Retailers, balance £826.40 debit

B Brick (Builders) Limited, balance £59.28 debit

Mereford Manufacturing Company, balance £293.49 debit

Redgrove Restorations, balance £724.86 debit

Wyvern Warehouse Limited, balance £108.40 debit

The following transactions took place during February:

3 Feb	Sold goods on credit to Arrow Valley Retailers £338.59, and to Mereford Manufacturing Company £127.48
7 Feb	Redgrove Restorations returned goods £165.38
15 Feb	Received a cheque from Wyvern Warehouse Limited for the balance of the account after deduction of 2.5% cash discount
17 Feb	Sold goods on credit to Redgrove Restorations £394.78, and to Wyvern Warehouse Limited £427.91
20 Feb	Arrow Valley Retailers settled an invoice for £826.40 by cheque after deducting 2.5% cash discount
24 Feb	Mereford Manufacturing Company returned goods £56.29
28 Feb	Transferred the balance of Mereford Manufacturing Company's account to the company's account in the purchases ledger
28 Feb	Wrote off the account of B Brick (Builders) Limited as a bad debt

You are to:

(a) write up the personal accounts in the sales ledger of Rowcester Traders for February 1998, balancing them at the end of the month

(b) prepare a sales ledger control account for February 1998, balancing it at the end of the month

(c) reconcile the control account balance with the debtors' accounts at 1 February and 28 February 1998.

Note: VAT is to be ignored on all transactions and day books are not required.

10 THE JOURNAL – CORRECTION OF ERRORS

this chapter covers . . .

The journal is the primary accounting record for non-regular transactions, eg purchase and sale of fixed assets on credit, correction of errors, end-of-year transfers (such as depreciation and provision for bad debts), and other transfers.

As a primary accounting record, the journal is not part of double-entry book-keeping; instead the journal is used to list transactions before they are entered into the accounts. In this way, the journal completes the accounting system by providing the primary accounting record for non-regular transactions.

NVQ PERFORMANCE CRITERIA COVERED

unit 4: MAINTAINING FINANCIAL RECORDS AND PREPARING ACCOUNTS

element 3

collect and collate information for the preparation of final accounts

❑ *all relevant information is correctly identified and recorded*

❑ *the trial balance is accurately prepared and, where necessary, a suspense account is opened and reconciled*

element 4

prepare the extended trial balance

❑ *material errors disclosed by the trial balance are identified, traced and referred to the appropriate authority*

❑ *discrepancies, unusual features or queries are identified and either resolved or referred to the appropriate person*

USES OF THE JOURNAL

The journal completes the accounting system by providing the primary accounting record for non-regular transactions, which are not recorded in any other primary accounting record. The categories of such non-regular transactions include:

- opening entries
- purchase and sale of fixed assets on credit
- correction of errors
- other transfers

The reasons for using a journal are:

- to provide a primary accounting record for non-regular transactions
- to eliminate the need for remembering why non-regular transactions were put through the accounts – the journal acts as a notebook
- to reduce the risk of fraud, by making it difficult for unauthorised transactions to be entered in the accounting system
- to reduce the risk of errors, by listing the transactions that are to be put into the double-entry accounts
- to ensure that entries can be traced back to a prime document, thus providing an audit trail for non-regular transactions

THE JOURNAL – A PRIMARY ACCOUNTING RECORD

The journal is a primary accounting record; it is not, therefore, part of the double-entry book-keeping system. The journal is used to list the transactions that are then to be put through the accounts. The accounting system for non-regular transactions is as follows:

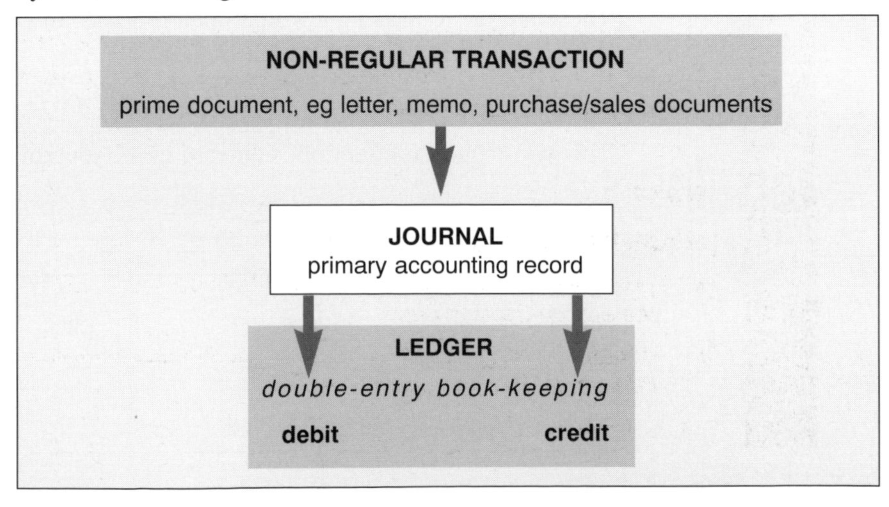

Look at the way the journal is set out, and then read the notes that follow.

Date	Details	Folio	Dr	Cr
			£	£

- the names of the accounts to be debited and credited in the book-keeping system are written in the details column; it is customary to show the debit transaction first
- the money amount of each debit and credit is stated in the appropriate columns
- the folio column cross-references to the division of the ledger where each account will be found (it can also include an account number)
- a journal entry always balances, ie debit and credit entries are for the same amount or total
- it is usual to include a brief narrative explaining why the transaction is being carried out, and making reference to the prime document whenever possible (in Assessments you should always include a narrative unless specifically told otherwise)
- each journal entry is complete in itself and is ruled off to separate it from the next entry

These principles are applied in the examples which follow. Note that, for sales ledger and purchases ledger, we will assume that control accounts are incorporated into the double-entry book-keeping system and that the accounts for each debtor and creditor are kept in memorandum form.

OPENING ENTRIES

These are the transactions which open the accounts of a new business. For example, a first business transaction is:

1 Jan 1998 Started in business with £10,000 in the bank

This non-regular transaction is entered in the journal as follows:

Date	Details	Folio	Dr	Cr
1998			£	£
1 Jan	Bank	CB	10,000	
	Capital	GL		10,000
	Opening capital introduced			

After the journal entry has been made, the transaction can be recorded in the double-entry accounts.

Here is another opening entries transaction to be recorded in the journal:

2 Feb 1998 *Started in business with cash £100, bank £5,000, stock £1,000, machinery £2,500, creditors £850*

The journal entry is:

Date	Details	Folio	Dr	Cr
1998			£	£
2 Feb	Cash	CB	100	
	Bank	CB	5,000	
	Stock account	GL	1,000	
	Machinery	GL	2,500	
	Purchase ledger control	GL		850
	Capital	GL		7,750
			8,600	8,600
	Assets and liabilities at the start of business			

Notes:

- Capital is the balancing figure, ie assets minus liabilities.
- The journal is the primary accounting record for all opening entries, including cash and bank; however the normal primary accounting record for other cash/bank transactions is the cash book.
- The amounts from the journal entry will now need to be recorded in the double-entry accounts.

PURCHASE AND SALE OF FIXED ASSETS ON CREDIT

The purchase and sale of fixed assets are non-regular business transactions which are recorded in the journal as the primary accounting record. Only *credit* transactions are entered in the journal (because cash/bank transactions are recorded in the cash book as the primary accounting record). However, a business (or an Assessment) may choose to journalise cash entries: strictly, though, this is incorrect as two primary accounting records are being used.

15 Apr 1998 *Bought a machine for £1,000 plus VAT (at 17.5%) on credit from Machinery Supplies Limited, purchase order no 2341.*

Date	Details	Folio	Dr	Cr
1998			£	£
15 Apr	Machinery	GL	1,000	
	VAT	GL	175	
	Purchases ledger control*	GL		1,175
			1,175	1,175
	Purchase of machine from creditor, Machinery Supplies Limited: purchase order 2341			

20 May 1998 *Car sold for £2,500 on credit to Wyvern Motors Limited (no VAT chargeable).*

Date	Details	Folio	Dr	Cr
1998			£	£
20 May	Sales ledger control*	GL	2,500	
	Disposals	GL		2,500
	Sale of car, registration no Q201 HAB to debtor, Wyvern Motors Limited			

* Instead of entering these transactions in the purchases ledger and sales ledger, an alternative treatment would be to open general ledger accounts for the creditor (Machinery Supplies Limited) and the debtor (Wyvern Motors Limited). This would avoid confusion with trade creditors (in the purchases ledger) and trade debtors (in the sales ledger).

CORRECTION OF ERRORS

In any book-keeping system there is always the possibility of an error. Ways to avoid errors, or ways to reveal them sooner, include:

- division of the accounting function between a number of people, so that no one person is responsible for both the debit and credit entries of a business transaction
- regular circulation of statements to debtors, who will check the transactions on their accounts and advise any discrepancies
- checking of statements received from creditors
- extraction of a trial balance at regular intervals
- the preparation of bank reconciliation statements
- checking cash and petty cash balances against cash held
- the use of control accounts
- the use of a computer accounting program

Despite all of these, errors will still occur from time-to-time and, in this section, we will look at:

- correction of errors not shown by a trial balance
- correction of errors shown by a trial balance, using a suspense account

errors not shown by a trial balance

In Chapter 3 we have already seen that some types of errors in a book-keeping system are not revealed by a trial balance. These are:

- error of omission
- reversal of entries
- mispost/error of commission
- error of principle
- error of original entry (or transcription)
- compensating error

Although these errors are not shown by a trial balance, they are likely to come to light if the procedures suggested on the previous page are followed. For example, a debtor will soon let you know if her account has been debited with goods she did not buy. When an error is found, it needs to be corrected by means of a journal entry which shows the book-keeping entries that have been made.

We will now look at an example of each of the errors not shown by a trial balance, and will see how it is corrected by means of a journal entry. (A practical hint which may help in correcting errors is to write out the 'T' accounts as they appear with the error. Then write in the correcting entries and see if the result has achieved what was intended.)

ERROR OF OMISSION

Credit sale of goods, £200 plus VAT (at 17.5%) on invoice 4967 to H Jarvis completely omitted from the accounting system; the error is corrected on 12 May 1998

Date	Details	Folio	Dr	Cr
1998			£	£
12 May	Sales ledger control	GL	235	
	Sales	GL		200
	VAT	GL		35
	Invoice 4967 omitted from accounts:			
	in the memorandum sales ledger –			
	debit H Jarvis £235			

This type of error can happen in a very small business – often where the book-keeping is done by one person. For example, an invoice, when typed out, is 'lost' down the back of a filing cabinet. In a large business, particularly one using a computer accounting system, it should be impossible for this error to occur. Also, if documents are numbered serially, then none should be mislaid.

REVERSAL OF ENTRIES

A payment, on 5 May 1998 by cheque of £50 to a creditor, S Wright (receipt no 93459) has been debited in the cash book and credited to purchases ledger control and Wright's account; the error is corrected on 14 May 1998

Date	Details	Folio	Dr	Cr
1998			£	£
14 May	Purchases ledger control	GL	50	
	Bank	CB		50
	Purchases ledger control	GL	50	
	Bank	CB		50
			100	100
	Correction of £50 reversal of entries: receipt 93459: in the memorandum purchases ledger – debit S Wright £50 – debit S Wright £50			

To correct this type of error it is best to reverse the entries that have been made incorrectly (the first two journal entries), and then to put through the correct entries. Although it will correct the error, it is wrong to debit £100 to purchases ledger control account and to credit £100 to bank account. This is because there was never a transaction for this amount – the original transaction was for £50.

As noted earlier, it is often an idea to write out the 'T' accounts, complete with the error, and then to write in the correcting entries. As an example, the two accounts involved in this last error are shown with the error made on 5 May, and the corrections made on 14 May indicated by the shading:

Dr	**Purchases Ledger Control Account**		Cr
1998	£	1998	£
14 May Bank	50	5 May Bank	50
14 May Bank	50		

Dr			Bank Account		Cr
1998		£	1998		£
5 May	Purchases ledger control	50	14 May	Purchases ledger control	50
			14 May	Purchases ledger control	50

The accounts now show a net debit transaction of £50 on the purchases ledger control account, and a net credit transaction of £50 on bank account, which is how this payment to a creditor should have been recorded in the first place.

MISPOST/ERROR OF COMMISSION

Credit sales of £47, including VAT (at 17.5%), on invoice no 321 have been debited to the account of J Adams, instead of the account of J Adams Limited; the error is corrected on 15 May 1998

Date	Details	Folio	Dr	Cr
1998			£	£
15 May	Sales ledger control	GL	47	
	Sales ledger control	GL		47
	Correction of mispost (invoice 321):			
	in the memorandum sales ledger			
	– debit J Adams Limited £47			
	– credit J Adams £47			

This type of error can be avoided, to some extent, by the use of account numbers, and by persuading the customer to quote the account number or reference on each transaction.

ERROR OF PRINCIPLE

The cost of petrol, £30 (excluding VAT) on receipt no 34535 has been debited to vehicles account; the error is corrected on 20 May 1998

Date	Details	Folio	Dr	Cr
1998			£	£
20 May	Vehicle running expenses	GL	30	
	Vehicles	GL		30
	Correction of error: receipt 34535			

This type of error is similar to a mispost except that, instead of the wrong person's account being used, it is the wrong class of account. In this example, the vehicle running costs must be kept separate from the cost of the asset (the vehicle), otherwise the expense and asset accounts will be incorrect, leading to profit for the year being overstated and the fixed asset being shown in the balance sheet at too high a figure.

ERROR OF ORIGINAL ENTRY

Postages of £45 paid by cheque entered in the accounts as £54; the error is corrected on 27 May 1998

Date	Details	Folio	Dr	Cr
1998			£	£
27 May	Bank	CB	54	
	Postages	GL		54
	Postages	GL	45	
	Bank	CB		45
			99	99
	Correction of error: postages of £45 entered into the accounts as £54			

This error could have been corrected by debiting bank and crediting postages with £9, being the difference between the two amounts. However, there was no original transaction for this amount, and it is better to reverse the wrong transaction and put through the correct one. A reversal of figures either has a difference of nine (as above), or an amount divisible by nine. An error of original entry can also be a 'bad' figure on a cheque or an invoice, which is entered wrongly into both accounts.

COMPENSATING ERROR

Rates account is added up by £100 more than it should be (ie it is overadded, or overcast); sales account is also overcast by the same amount; the error is corrected on 29 May 1998

Date	Details	Folio	Dr	Cr
1998			£	£
29 May	Sales	GL	100	
	Rates	GL		100
	Correction of overcast on rates account and sales account			

Here, an account with a debit balance – rates – has been overcast; this is compensated by an overcast on an account with a credit balance – sales. There are several permutations on this theme, eg two debit balances, one overcast, one undercast (ie underadded); a debit balance undercast, a credit balance undercast. Note the following important points:

- The journal is the primary accounting record for non-regular transactions. The journal entries must then be recorded in the book-keeping system.
- For all the journal entries shown above which involve sales ledger or purchases ledger, we have assumed that control accounts are used, which are incorporated into the double-entry book-keeping system; remember that the transactions must also be recorded in the memorandum accounts for debtors or creditors.

TRIAL BALANCE ERRORS: USE OF SUSPENSE ACCOUNT

There are many types of errors revealed by a trial balance. Included amongst these are:

- omission of one part of the double-entry transaction
- recording two debits or two credits for a transaction
- recording a different amount for a transaction on the debit side from the credit side
- errors in the calculation of balances (not compensated by other errors)
- error in transferring the balance of an account to the trial balance
- error of addition in the trial balance

When errors are shown, the trial balance is 'balanced' by recording the difference in a suspense account, as shown in the Case Study below.

CASE STUDY

TEMESIDE TRADERS: SUSPENSE ACCOUNT

The book-keeper of Temeside Traders is unable to balance the trial balance on 30 June 1998. As the error or errors cannot be found quickly the trial balance is balanced by recording the difference in a suspense account, as follows:

	Dr	*Cr*
	£	£
Trial balance totals	100,000	99,850
Suspense account		150
	100,000	100,000

A suspense account is opened in the general ledger with, in this case, a credit balance of £150 – see next page.

Dr		Suspense Account			Cr
1998		£	1998		£
			30 Jun	Trial balance difference	150

A detailed examination of the book-keeping system is now made in order to find the errors. As errors are found, they are corrected by means of a journal entry. The journal entries will balance, with one part of the entry being either a debit or credit to suspense account. In this way, the balance on suspense account is eliminated by book-keeping transactions. Using the above suspense account, the following errors are found and corrected on 15 July 1998:

- sales account is undercast by £100
- a payment to a creditor, A Wilson, for £65, has been recorded in the bank as £56
- telephone expenses of £55 have not been entered in the expenses account
- stationery expenses £48 have been debited to both the stationery account and the bank account

These errors are corrected by the journal entries shown below. Note that the journal narrative includes details of cheque numbers and dates taken from the records of the business.

Date	Details	Folio	Dr	Cr
1998			£	£
15 Jul	Suspense	GL	100	
	Sales	GL		100
	Undercast on 27/5/98 now corrected			
15 Jul	Bank	CB	56	
	Suspense	GL		56
	Suspense	GL	65	
	Bank	CB		65
	Payment to A Wilson for £65 (cheque no. 783726) on 30/5/98 entered in bank as £56 in error		121	121
15 Jul	Telephone expenses	GL	55	
	Suspense	GL		55
	Omission of entry in expenses account paid by cheque no. 783734			
15 Jul	Suspense	GL	48	
	Bank	CB		48
	Suspense	GL	48	
	Bank	CB		48
	Correction of error: payment by cheque 783736 debited in error to bank account		96	96

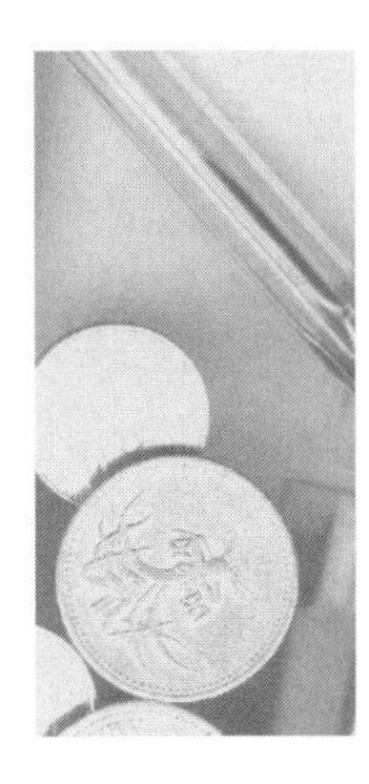

After these journal entries have been posted in the accounts, suspense account appears:

Dr		Suspense Account			Cr
1998		£	1998		£
15 Jul	Sales	100	30 Jun	Trial balance difference	150
15 Jul	Bank	65	15 Jul	Bank	56
15 Jul	Bank	48	15 Jul	Telephone expenses	55
15 Jul	Bank	48			
		261			261

Thus all the errors have now been found, and suspense account has a nil balance.

EFFECT ON PROFIT AND BALANCE SHEET

The correction of errors, whether shown by a trial balance or not, often has an effect on the profit figure calculated before the errors were found. For example, an undercast of sales account, when corrected, will increase profit and, of course, the profit figure shown in the balance sheet. Some errors, however, only affect the balance sheet, eg an error involving a creditor's account. The diagram below shows the effect of errors when corrected on the profit figure and the balance sheet.

	correction of error	profit	balance sheet
profit and loss account	sales undercast/understated	increase	profit increase
	sales overcast/overstated	decrease	profit decrease
	purchases undercast/understated	decrease	profit decrease
	purchases overcast/overstated	increase	profit increase
	opening stock undervalued	decrease	profit decrease
	opening stock overvalued	increase	profit increase
	closing stock undervalued	increase	profit increase /stock increase
	closing stock overvalued	decrease	profit decrease/stock decrease
	expense undercast/understated	decrease	decrease in profit
	expense overcast/overstated	increase	increase in profit
	income undercast/understated	increase	increase in profit
	income overcast/overstated	decrease	decrease in profit
balance sheet	asset undercast/understated	–	increase asset
	asset overcast/overstated	–	decrease asset
	liability undercast/understated	–	increase liability
	liability overcast/overstated	–	decrease liability

OTHER TRANSFERS

All other non-regular transactions need to be recorded in the journal. Many of these take place at the end of a firm's financial year and are concerned with:

- transfers to profit and loss account
- accruals and prepayments
- expenses charged to the owner's drawings
- goods for the owner's use
- depreciation
- disposal of fixed assets
- bad debts written off
- provision for bad debts

transfers to profit and loss account

As we have seen earlier (Chapter 4), the profit and loss account forms part of double-entry book-keeping. Therefore, each amount recorded in profit and loss account must have an opposite entry in another account: such transfers are recorded in the journal as the primary accounting record.

31 Dec 1998 *Balance of wages account, £23,500, transferred to profit and loss account (debit profit and loss account; credit wages account)*

Date	Details	Folio	Dr	Cr
1998			£	£
31 Dec	Profit and loss	GL	23,500	
	Wages	GL		23,500
	Transfer to profit and loss of expenditure for the year			

31 Dec 1998 *Closing stock has been valued at £12,500 and is to be entered into the accounts*

Date	Details	Folio	Dr	Cr
1998			£	£
31 Dec	Stock	GL	12,500	
	Profit and loss	GL		12,500
	Stock valuation at 31 December 1998 transferred to profit and loss account			

Remember that the closing stock valuation for the year is recorded in stock account as an asset (*debit* stock account; *credit* profit and loss account).

accruals and prepayments

The amounts of accruals and prepayments (see Chapter 5) are recorded in the accounts: such transfers are recorded in the journal as the primary accounting record.

31 Dec 1998 *The balance of telephone account is £500. A telephone bill for £100 is received on 4 January 1999 and relates to costs incurred in 1998.*

Date	Details	Folio	Dr	Cr
1998			£	£
31 Dec	Profit and loss	GL	600	
	Telephone	GL		500
	Accruals	GL		100
			600	600
	Transfer to profit and loss account of expenditure for the year			

The above transaction leaves a credit balance on accruals account, being the amount due at 31 December 1998.

31 Dec 1998 *The balance of rent paid account is £750. Of this, £675 relates to 1998, while £75 is a prepayment for 1999*

Date	Details	Folio	Dr	Cr
1998			£	£
31 Dec	Profit and loss	GL	675	
	Prepayments	GL	75	
	Rent paid	GL		750
			750	750
	Transfer to profit and loss account of expenditure for the year			

The above transaction leaves a debit balance on prepayments account, being the amount prepaid at 31 December 1998.

expenses charged to owner's drawings

Sometimes the owner of a business uses business facilities for private use, eg telephone, or car. The owner will agree that part of the expense shall be charged to him or her as drawings, while the other part represents a business expense. The book-keeping entry to record the adjustment is:

- *debit* drawings account
- *credit* expense account, eg telephone

31 Dec 1998 *The balance of telephone account is £600; of this, one-quarter is the estimated cost of the owner's private usage*

The journal entry is:

Date	Details	Folio	Dr	Cr
1998			£	£
31 Dec	Drawings	GL	150	
	Telephone	GL		150
	Transfer of private use to drawings account			

goods for the owner's use

When the owner of a business takes some of the goods in which the business trades for his or her own use, the double-entry book-keeping is:

- *debit* drawings account
- *credit* purchases account

15 Oct 1998 *Owner of the business takes goods for own use, £105 (no VAT)*

The journal entry is:

Date	Details	Folio	Dr	Cr
1998			£	£
15 Oct	Drawings	GL	105	
	Purchases	GL		105
	Goods taken for own use by the owner			

Notes:

- Where a business is VAT-registered, VAT must be accounted for on goods taken by the owner

- An alternative method of accounting for goods for own use is:
  - *debit* drawings account
  - *credit* sales account

This method is favoured by the Inland Revenue for taxation purposes; however, either is acceptable for the purpose of financial accounting – which method is used will depend on the custom and practice of the business.

depreciation

As we have seen in Chapter 6, the amount of depreciation on fixed assets is recorded in the profit and loss account:

- *debit* profit and loss account
- *credit* depreciation account

31 Dec 1998 Depreciation on a machine is calculated at £400 for the year

The journal entry is:

Date	Details	Folio	Dr	Cr
1998			£	£
31 Dec	Profit and loss	GL	400	
	Depreciation	GL		400
	Depreciation charge for year on machine			

As already seen in Chapter 6, the amount credited to depreciation account (the annual charge for depreciation) is then transferred to provision for depreciation account (which records the accumulated total of depreciation for each class of asset):

- *debit* depreciation account
- *credit* provision for depreciation account

The journal entry for depreciation on the machine is:

Date	Details	Folio	Dr	Cr
1998			£	£
31 Dec	Depreciation	GL	400	
	Provision for depreciation account – machinery	GL		400
	Transfer of depreciation charge for year to provision for depreciation account			

disposal of fixed assets

When a fixed asset is sold or disposed, the book-keeping entries (see page 92) bring together:

- the original cost of the asset
- depreciation provided over the life of the asset
- sale proceeds

31 Dec 2000 *A machine had been bought on 1 January 1998 (ie three years ago) for £2,000 (net of VAT). Provision for depreciation (including the current year) totals £1,200. On 31 December 2000 the machine is sold for £600 plus VAT (cheque received)*

The journal entry is:

Date	Details	Folio	Dr	Cr
2000			£	£
31 Dec	Disposals	GL	2,000	
	Machinery	GL		2,000
	Provision for depreciation account			
	– machinery	GL	1,200	
	Disposals	GL		1,200
	Bank	CB	705	
	Disposals	GL		600
	VAT	GL		105
	Profit and loss	GL	200	
	Disposals	GL		200
			4,105	4,105
	Sale of machine no. 123456; loss on sale £200 transferred to profit and loss account			

(If you wish to check the book-keeping entries for this transaction, they are set out in full on page 93.)

bad debts written off

We have already seen, in Chapter 7, the double-entry book-keeping entries to write off a debtor's account as bad:

– *debit* bad debts written off account

– *credit* debtor's account

15 Dec 1998 *Write off the account of T Hughes, which has a balance of £25, as a bad debt*

The journal entry is:

Date	Details	Folio	Dr	Cr
1998			£	£
15 Dec	Bad debts written off	GL	25	
	Sales ledger control	GL		25
	Account of T Hughes written off as a bad debt – see memo dated 14 December 1998			

provision for bad debts

In Chapter 7 we saw that the creation of a provision for bad debts is recorded in the profit and loss account:

- *debit* profit and loss account
- *credit* provision for bad debts: adjustment account

31 Dec 1998 A provision for bad debts of £500 is to be created

The journal entry is:

Date	Details	Folio	Dr	Cr
1998			£	£
31 Dec	Profit and loss	GL	500	
	Provision for bad debts: adjustment	GL		500
	Creation of a provision for bad debts			

As already seen in Chapter 7, the amount credited to provision for bad debts: adjustment account (the annual change in the provision) is then transferred to provision for bad debts account (which records the accumulated total of the provision):

- *debit* provision for bad debts: adjustment account
- *credit* provision for bad debts account

The journal entry to record this transfer is:

Date	Details	Folio	Dr	Cr
1998			£	£
31 Dec	Provision for bad debts: adjustment	GL	500	
	Provision for bad debts	GL		500
	Transfer of charge for year to provision for bad debts account			

An existing provision for bad debts will usually be increased or decreased as the level of debtors changes. The book-keeping entries (see Chapter 7) are:

increasing the provision

- *debit* profit and loss account
- *credit* provision for bad debts: adjustment account

decreasing the provision

- *debit* provision for bad debts: adjustment account
- *credit* profit and loss account

31 Dec 1999 *The existing provision for bad debts is to be increased by £250*

The journal entry is:

Date	Details	Folio	Dr	Cr
1999			£	£
31 Dec	Profit and loss	GL	250	
	Provision for bad debts: adjustment	GL		250
	Increase in provision for bad debts			

This is then transferred to provision for bad debts account as follows:

Date	Details	Folio	Dr	Cr
1999			£	£
31 Dec	Provision for bad debts: adjustment	GL	250	
	Provision for bad debts	GL		250
	Transfer of charge for year to provision for bad debts account			

CHAPTER SUMMARY

- The journal is used to list non-regular transactions.
- The journal is a primary accounting record – it is not a double-entry account.
- The journal is used for:
  - opening entries
  - purchase and sale of fixed assets on credit
  - correction of errors
  - other transfers (including year-end transfers)
- Correction of errors is always a difficult topic to put into practice: it tests knowledge of book-keeping procedures and it is all too easy to make the error worse than it was in the first place! The secret of dealing with this topic well is to write down – in account format – what has gone wrong. It should then be relatively easy to see what has to be done to put the error right.
- Errors not shown by a trial balance: error of omission, reversal of entries, mispost/error of commission, error of principle, error of original entry (or transcription), compensating error.
- Errors shown by a trial balance include: omission of one part of the book-keeping transaction, recording two debits/credits for a transaction, recording different amounts in the two accounts, calculating balances incorrectly, transferring wrong balances to the trial balance.
- All errors are non-regular transactions and need to be corrected by means of a journal entry: the book-keeper then records the correcting transactions in the accounts.
- When error(s) are shown by a trial balance, the amount of the error is placed in a suspense account. As the errors are found, journal entries are made which 'clear out' the suspense account.
- Correction of errors may have an effect on profit calculated before the errors were found, and on the balance sheet.

KEY TERMS

journal – the primary accounting record for non-regular transactions

opening entries – the transactions which open the accounts of a new business

suspense account – account in which to place an error in the trial balance, pending further investigation

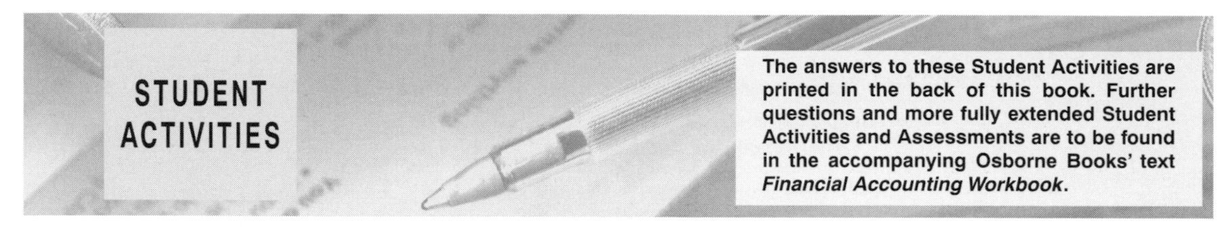

10.1 Which one of the following will *not* be recorded in the journal?

(a) credit purchase of a fixed asset

(b) cash sale of goods to a customer

(c) write-off of a bad debt

(d) correction of an error not shown by the trial balance

Answer (a) or (b) or (c) or (d)

10.2 A trial balance fails to agree by £75 and the difference is placed to a suspense account. Later it is found that a credit sale for this amount has not been entered in the sales account. Which one of the following journal entries is correct?

(a) debit suspense account £75; credit sales account £75

(b) debit suspense account £150; credit sales account £150

(c) debit sales account £75; credit suspense account £75

(d) credit sales account £75

Answer (a) or (b) or (c) or (d)

10.3 Lucy Wallis started in business on 1 May 1998 with the following assets and liabilities:

	£
Motor vehicle	6,500
Fixtures and fittings	2,800
Opening stock	4,100
Cash	150
Loan from husband	5,000

You are to prepare Lucy's opening journal entry, showing clearly her capital at 1 May 1998.

10.4 The trial balance of Thomas Wilson balanced. However, a number of errors have been found in the book-keeping system:

(a) Credit sale of £150 to J Rigby has not been entered in the accounts.

(b) A payment by cheque for £125 to H Price Limited, a creditor, has been recorded in the account of H Prince.

(c) The cost of a new delivery van, £10,000, has been entered to vehicle expenses account.

(d) Postages of £55, paid by cheque, have been entered on the wrong sides of both accounts.

(e) The totals of the purchases day book and the purchases returns day book have been undercast by £100.

(f) A payment for £89 from L Johnson, a debtor, has been entered in the accounts as £98.

You are to take each error in turn and:

- state the type of error
- show the correcting journal entry

Note: VAT is to be ignored

10.5 Jeremy Johnson extracts a trial balance from his book-keeping records on 30 September 1998. Unfortunately the trial balance fails to balance and the difference, £19 debit, is placed to a suspense account pending further investigation.

The following errors are later found:

(a) A cheque payment of £85 for office expenses has been entered in the cash book but no entry has been made in the office expenses account.

(b) A payment for photocopying of £87 by cheque has been correctly entered in the cash book, but is shown as £78 in the photocopying account.

(c) The sales returns day book has been overcast by £100.

(d) Commission received of £25 has been entered twice in the account.

You are to:

- make journal entries to correct the errors
- show the suspense account after the errors have been corrected

10.6 Show the journal entries for the following transfers which relate to Trish Hall's business for the year ended 31 December 1998:

(a) Closing stock is to be recorded in the accounts at a valuation of £22,600.

(b) Telephone expenses for the year, amounting to £890, are to be transferred to profit and loss account.

(c) Salaries account shows a balance of £22,950, but £980 is owing; the amount due for the year is to be transferred to profit and loss account.

(d) Photocopying expenses account shows a balance of £1,240, but this includes copier rental of £80 in respect of January and February 1999; the amount due for the year is to be transferred to profit and loss account.

(e) Motoring expenses account shows a balance of £800; one-quarter of this relates to Trish Hall's private motoring.

(f) Trish has taken goods for her own use of £175 (no VAT).

(g) Depreciation on fixtures and fittings for the year is calculated at £500.

(h) A machine had been bought on 1 January 1996 for £5,000 (net of VAT). Provision for depreciation (including the current year) totals £3,750. On 31 December 1998 the machine is sold for £2,000 plus VAT, a cheque being received.

(i) The following sales ledger accounts are to be written off as bad (bad debt relief is not available): Nick Marshall, £55; Crabbe & Company, £30; A Hunt, £40.

These are the only bad debts written off during the year; the total is to be transferred to profit and loss account.

(j) The provision for bad debts is £550; the amount is to be reduced to £450.

11 BANK RECONCILIATION STATEMENTS

this chapter covers . . .

Bank reconciliation statements form part of the check and control process of the accounting system. They provide a link between the balance at bank shown in the cash book of a firm's book-keeping system and the balance shown on the bank statement received from the bank.

The reasons why the cash book and bank statement may differ are because:

- *there are timing differences caused by*
  - *unpresented cheques, ie the time delay between writing out (drawing) a cheque and recording it in the cash book, and the cheque being entered on the bank statement*
  - *outstanding lodgements, ie amounts paid into the bank, but not yet recorded on the bank statement*
- *the cash book has not been updated with items which appear on the bank statement and which should also appear in the cash book, eg bank charges*

Assuming that there are no errors in each, both cash book and bank statement are correct, but need to be reconciled with each other, ie the closing balances need to be agreed.

NVQ PERFORMANCE CRITERIA COVERED

unit 4: MAINTAINING FINANCIAL RECORDS AND PREPARING ACCOUNTS

element 3

collect and collate information for the preparation of final accounts

- ❑ *relevant accounts and reconciliations are correctly prepared to allow the preparation of final accounts*
- ❑ *investigations into business transactions are conducted with tact and courtesy*

TIMING DIFFERENCES

The two main timing differences between the bank columns of the cash book and the bank statement are:

- *unpresented cheques*, ie cheques drawn, not yet recorded on the bank statement
- *outstanding lodgements*, ie amounts paid into the bank, not yet recorded on the bank statement

The first of these – unpresented cheques – is caused because, when a cheque is written out, it is immediately entered on the payments side of the cash book, even though it may be some days before the cheque passes through the bank clearing system and is recorded on the bank statement. Therefore, for a few days at least, the cash book shows a lower balance than the bank statement in respect of this cheque. When the cheque is recorded on the bank statement, the difference will disappear. We have looked at only one cheque here, but a business will often be issuing many cheques each day, and the difference between the cash book balance and the bank statement balance may be considerable.

With the second timing difference – outstanding lodgements – the firm's cashier will record a receipt in the cash book as he or she prepares the bank paying-in slip. However, the receipt may not be recorded by the bank on the bank statement for a day or so, particularly if it is paid in late in the day (when the bank will put it into the next day's work), or if it is paid in at a bank branch other than the one at which the account is maintained. Until the receipt is recorded by the bank the cash book will show a higher bank account balance than the bank statement. Once the receipt is entered on the bank statement, the difference will disappear.

These two timing differences are involved in the calculation known as the bank reconciliation statement. The business cash book must not be altered for these because, as we have seen, they will correct themselves on the bank statement as time goes by.

UPDATING THE CASH BOOK

Besides the timing differences described above, there may be other differences between the bank columns of the cash book and the bank statement, and these do need to be entered in the cash book to bring it up-to-date. For example, the bank might make an automatic standing order payment on behalf of a business – such an item is correctly debited by the bank, and it might be that the bank statement acts as a reminder to the business cashier of the payment: it should then be entered in the cash book.

Examples of items that show in the bank statement and need to be entered in the cash book include:

receipts

- standing order and BACS (Bankers' Automated Clearing Services) receipts credited by the bank, eg payments from debtors (customers)
- bank giro credit (credit transfer) amounts received by the bank, eg payments from debtors (customers)
- dividend amounts received by the bank
- interest credited by the bank

payments

- standing order and direct debit payments
- bank charges and interest
- unpaid cheques debited by the bank (ie cheques from debtors paid in by the business which have 'bounced' and are returned by the bank marked 'refer to drawer')

For each of these items, the firm's cashier needs to check to see if they have been entered in the cash book; if not, they need to be recorded (provided that the bank has not made an error). If the bank has made an error, it must be notified as soon as possible and the incorrect transactions reversed by the bank in its own accounting records.

THE BANK RECONCILIATION STATEMENT

This forms the link between the balances shown in the bank statement and the cash book.

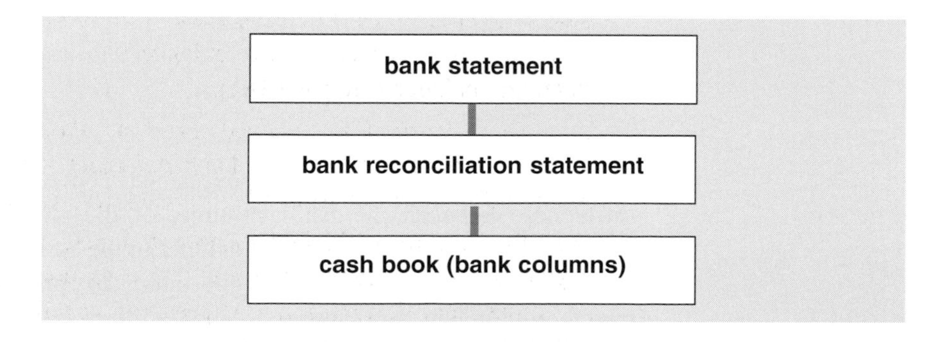

Upon receipt of a bank statement, reconciliation of the two balances is carried out in the following way:

- tick off the items that appear in both cash book and bank statement
- the unticked items on the bank statement are entered into the bank columns of the cash book to bring it up-to-date (provided none are errors made by the bank)
- the bank columns of the cash book are now balanced to find the revised figure
- the remaining unticked items from the cash book will be the timing differences
- the timing differences are used to prepare the bank reconciliation statement, which takes the following format (with example figures):

XYZ TRADING LIMITED
Bank Reconciliation Statement as at 31 October 1998

		£	£
Balance at bank as per bank statement			245
Less: unpresented cheques			
J Lewis	cheque no. 0012378	60	
ABC Limited	cheque no. 0012392	100	
Eastern Oil Company	cheque no. 0012407	80	
			240
			5
Add: outstanding lodgements		220	
		300	
			520
Balance at bank as per cash book			525

Notes:

- The layout shown above starts from the bank statement balance, and works towards the cash book balance. A common variation of this layout is to start with the cash book balance and to work towards the bank statement balance (see page 181).
- If a bank overdraft is involved, brackets should be used around the numbers to indicate this for the bank statement or cash book balance. The timing differences are still added or deducted, as appropriate.
- Once the bank reconciliation statement agrees, it should be filed because it proves that the bank statement and cash book were reconciled at a particular date. If, next time it is prepared, it fails to agree, the previous statement is proof that reconciliation was reached at that time.

CASE STUDY

BANK RECONCILIATION STATEMENT

situation

The cashier of Severn Trading Company has written up the firm's cash book (bank columns) for the month of February 1999, as follows (the cheque number is shown against payments):

Dr		Cash Book			Cr
Date	Details	Bank	Date	Details	Bank
1999		£	1999		£
1 Feb	Balance b/d	1,340.50	3 Feb	Appleton Ltd 123456	675.25
7 Feb	A Abbott	208.50	12 Feb	Rent 123457	125.00
14 Feb	Cash	500.00	17 Feb	D Smith & Co 123458	421.80
21 Feb	D Richards Ltd	162.30	25 Feb	G Christie 123459	797.55
27 Feb	Cash	500.00	28 Feb	Balance c/d	954.00
28 Feb	P Paul Ltd	262.30			
		2,973.60			2,973.60
1 Mar	Balance b/d	954.00			

The bank statement for February 1999 has just been received:

National Bank plc

Branch Bartown

TITLE OF ACCOUNT Severn Trading Company

ACCOUNT NUMBER 67812318

STATEMENT NUMBER 45

DATE	PARTICULARS	PAYMENTS	RECEIPTS	BALANCE
1999		£	£	£
1 Feb	Balance brought forward			1340.50 CR
8 Feb	Credit		208.50	1549.00 CR
10 Feb	Cheque no. 123456	675.25		873.75 CR
17 Feb	Credit		500.00	1373.75 CR
17 Feb	Cheque no. 123457	125.00		1248.75 CR
24 Reb	Credit		162.30	1411.05 CR
24 Feb	BACS credit: J Jarvis Ltd		100.00	1511.05 CR
26 Feb	Cheque no. 123458	421.80		1089.25 CR
26 Feb	Direct debit: A-Z Finance	150.00		939.25 CR
28 Feb	Credit		500.00	1439.25 CR
28 Feb	Bank charges	10.00		1429.25 CR

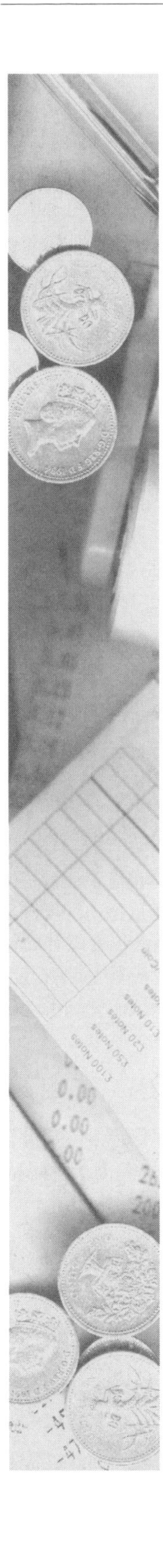

solution

As the month-end balance at bank shown by the cash book, £954.00, is not the same as that shown by the bank statement, £1,429.25, it is necessary to prepare a bank reconciliation statement. The steps are:

1. Tick off the items that appear in both cash book and bank statement.
2. The unticked items on the bank statement are entered into the bank columns of the cash book to bring it up-to-date. These are:
   - receipt 24 Feb BACS credit, J Jarvis Limited £100.00
   - payments 26 Feb Direct debit, A-Z Finance £150.00
     28 Feb Bank Charges, £10.00

   In double-entry book-keeping, the other part of the transaction will need to be recorded in the accounts, eg in J Jarvis Ltd's account in the sales ledger, etc.

3. The cash book is now balanced to find the revised balance:

Dr	Cash Book (bank columns)				Cr
1999		£	1999		£
	Balance b/d	954.00	26 Feb	A-Z Finance	150.00
24 Feb	J Jarvis Ltd	100.00	28 Feb	Bank Charges	10.00
			28 Feb	Balance c/d	894.00
		1,054.00			1,054.00
1 Mar	Balance b/d	894.00			

4. The remaining unticked items from the cash book are used in the bank reconciliation statement:
   - receipt 28 Feb – P Paul Limited £262.30
   - payment 25 Feb – G Christie (cheque no 123459) £797.55

   These items are timing differences, which should appear on next month's bank statement.

5. The bank reconciliation statement is now prepared, starting with the bank statement balance of £1,429.25 .

SEVERN TRADING COMPANY

Bank Reconciliation Statement as at 28 February 1999

	£
Balance at bank as per bank statement	1,429.25
Less: unpresented cheque, no. 123459	797.55
	631.70
Add: outstanding lodgement, P Paul Limited	262.30
Balance at bank as per cash book	894.00

This statement has been produced which starts with the bank statement balance, and finishes with the amended balance from the cash book, ie the two figures are reconciled.

notes on the case study

- The *unpresented cheque* is deducted from the bank statement balance because, until it is recorded by the bank, the bank statement shows a higher balance than the cash book.
- The *outstanding lodgement* is added to the bank statement balance because, until it is recorded by the bank, the bank statement shows a lower balance than the cash book.

PREPARING A BANK RECONCILIATION STATEMENT

In order to help you with the Student Activities at the end of the chapter, here is a step-by-step summary of the procedure. Reconciliation of the bank statement balance with that shown in the cash book should be carried out in the following way:

1. From the bank columns of the cash book tick off, in both cash book and bank statement, the receipts that appear in both.
2. From the bank columns of the cash book tick off, in both cash book and bank statement, the payments that appear in both.
3. Identify the items that are unticked on the bank statement and enter them in the cash book on the debit or credit side, as appropriate. (If, however, the bank has made a mistake and debited or credited an amount in error, this should not be entered in the cash book, but should be notified to the bank for them to make the correction. The amount will need to be entered on the bank reconciliation statement.)
4. The bank columns of the cash book are now balanced to find the up-to-date balance.
5. Start the bank reconciliation statement with the final balance figure shown on the bank statement.
6. In the bank reconciliation statement *deduct* the unticked payments shown in the cash book – these will be unpresented cheques.
7. In the bank reconciliation statement, *add* the unticked receipts shown in the cash book – these are outstanding lodgements.
8. The resultant money amount on the bank reconciliation statement is the balance at bank as per the cash book.

The layout which is often used for the bank reconciliation statement is that shown on page 177. The layout starts with the bank statement balance and finishes with the cash book balance. However, there is no reason why it should not commence with the cash book balance and finish with the bank statement balance: with this layout it is necessary to:

- *add* unpresented cheques
- *deduct* outstanding lodgements

The bank reconciliation statement of Severn Trading Company (see page 179) would then appear as:

SEVERN TRADING COMPANY
Bank Reconciliation Statement as at 28 February 1999

	£
Balance at bank as per cash book	894.00
Add: unpresented cheque, no 123459	797.55
	1,691.55
Less: outstanding lodgement, P Paul Limited	262.30
Balance at bank as per bank statement	1,429.25

RECONCILIATION OF OPENING BALANCES

If you look back to the Case Study on page 178, you will see that both the cash book (bank columns) and the bank statement balance both started the month with the same balance: 1 February 1999 £1,340.50. In reality, it is unlikely that the opening cash book and bank statement balances will be the same.

It will be necessary, in these circumstances, to prepare an *opening* bank reconciliation statement in order to prove that there are no errors between cash book and bank statement at the start of the month. This is set out in the same format as the end-of-month bank reconciliation statement, and is best prepared immediately after ticking off the items that appear in both cash book and bank statement. The earliest unpresented cheques drawn and outstanding lodgements will comprise the opening bank reconciliation statement.

Of course, where last month's bank reconciliation statement is available, such as in business, there is no need to prepare an opening reconciliation.

The layout for the opening balance reconciliation, with sample figures, is shown on the next page.

Opening Bank Reconciliation Statement as at 1 June 1999

		£	£
Opening balance at bank as per bank statement			245
Less: unpresented cheques			
J Chumleigh	cheque no. 0012323	60	
R Warner	cheque no. 0012325	100	
S Lobb	cheque no. 0012435	80	
			240
			5
Add: outstanding lodgements		220	
		300	
			520
Opening balance at bank as per cash book			525

An alternative way of presenting the layout is to start with the opening cash book balance and finish with the opening bank statement balance. In this case you would add unpresented cheques and deduct outstanding lodgements.

IMPORTANCE OF BANK RECONCILIATION STATEMENTS

1. A bank reconciliation statement forms an important part of the check and control process of the accounting system. When you prepare it the transactions in the bank columns of the cash book are compared with those recorded on the bank statement. In this way, any errors in the cash book or bank statement will be found and can be corrected (or advised to the bank, if the bank statement is wrong).
2. The bank statement is an independent accounting record, therefore it will assist in deterring fraud by providing a means of verifying the cash book balance.
3. By writing the cash book up-to-date, the business has an amended figure for the bank balance to be shown in the trial balance.
4. It is good business practice to prepare a bank reconciliation statement each time a bank statement is received. The reconciliation statement should be prepared as quickly as possible so that any queries – either with the bank statement or in the firm's cash book – can be resolved. Many firms will specify to their accounting staff the timescales for preparing bank reconciliation statements – as a guideline, if the bank statement is received weekly, then the reconciliation statement should be prepared within five working days.

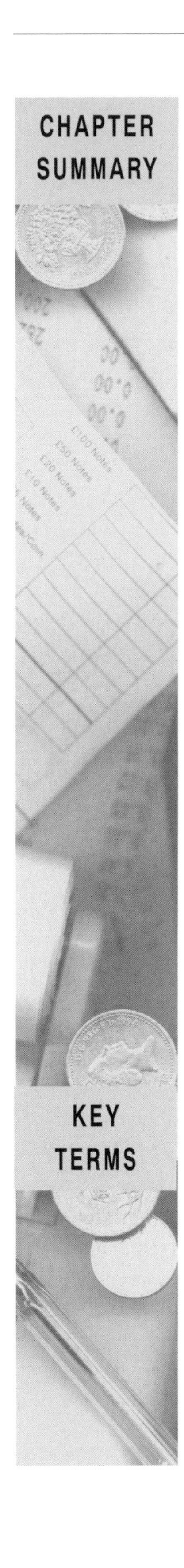

CHAPTER SUMMARY

- A bank reconciliation statement is used as part of the check and control process of the accounting system to agree the balance shown by the bank statement with that shown by the bank columns of the cash book.

- Certain differences between the two are timing differences. The main timing differences are:
  - unpresented cheques
  - outstanding lodgements

  These differences will be corrected by time and, most probably, will be recorded on the next bank statement.

- Certain differences appearing on the bank statement need to be entered in the cash book to bring it up-to-date. These include:

  Receipts
  - standing order and BACS receipts credited by the bank
  - bank giro credit amounts received by the bank
  - dividend amounts received by the bank
  - interest credited by the bank

  Payments
  - standing order and direct debit payments
  - bank charges and interest
  - unpaid cheques debited by the bank

- The bank reconciliation statement makes use of the timing differences.

- Once prepared, a bank reconciliation statement is proof that the bank statement and the cash book (bank columns) were agreed at a particular date.

KEY TERMS

bank reconciliation statement — forms the link between the balances shown in the bank statement and the cash book

timing differences — any discrepancies between the bank statement and the cash book that will be corrected over time, such as unpresented cheques and outstanding lodgements

unpresented cheques — cheques drawn, but not yet recorded on the bank statement

outstanding lodgements — amounts paid into the bank, but not yet recorded on the bank statement

STUDENT ACTIVITIES

The answers to these Student Activities are printed in the back of this book. Further questions and more fully extended Student Activities and Assessments are to be found in the accompanying Osborne Books' text *Financial Accounting Workbook*.

11.1 When preparing a bank reconciliation statement, which one of the following is a timing difference?

(a) unpresented cheques

(b) direct debit payments

(c) bank charges and interest

(d) BACS receipts

Answer (a) or (b) or (c) or (d)

11.2 A firm's bank statement shows a balance of £400. Unpresented cheques total £350; outstanding lodgements total £200. What is the balance at bank shown by the cash book?

(a) £100

(b) £200

(c) £250

(d) £400

Answer (a) or (b) or (c) or (d)

11.3 The bank columns of Tom Reid's cash book for December 1999 are as follows:

1999	*Receipts*	£	1999	*Payments*		£
1 Dec	Balance b/d	280	9 Dec	W Smith	345123	40
13 Dec	P Jones	30	13 Dec	Rent	345124	50
17 Dec	H Homer	72	16 Dec	Wages	345125	85
29 Dec	J Hill	13	20 Dec	B Kay	345126	20
			31 Dec	Balance c/d		200
		395				395

He then received his bank statement which showed the following transactions for December 1999:

BANK STATEMENT		Payments	Receipts	Balance
1999		£	£	£
1 Dec	Balance brought forward			280 CR
13 Dec	Credit		30	310 CR
15 Dec	Cheque no. 345123	40		270 CR
17 Dec	Cheque no. 345124	50		220 CR
22 Dec	Credit		72	292 CR
23 Dec	Cheque no. 345125	85		207 CR

You are to prepare a bank reconciliation statement which agrees the bank statement balance with the cash book total.

11.4 The bank columns of Jane Doyle's cash book for May 1999 are as follows:

1999	*Receipts*	£	1999	*Payments*		£
1 May	Balance b/d	300	3 May	P Stone	867714	28
7 May	Cash	162	14 May	Alpha Ltd	867715	50
17 May	C Brewster	89	28 May	E Deakin	867716	110
27 May	Cash	60				
28 May	Cash	40				

She received her bank statement which showed the following transactions for May 1999:

BANK STATEMENT		Payments	Receipts	Balance
1999		£	£	£
1 May	Balance brought forward			326 CR
3 May	Credit		54	380 CR
5 May	Cheque no. 867714	28		352 CR
6 May	Cheque no. 867713	80		272 CR
7 May	Credit		162	434 CR
17 May	Standing order: A-Z Insurance	25		409 CR
19 May	Credit		89	498 CR
20 May	Cheque no. 867715	50		448 CR
26 May	Credit		60	508 CR
31 May	Bank Charges	10		498 CR

You are to:

(a) write the cash book up-to-date at 31 May 1999

(b) prepare an opening bank reconciliation statement at 1 May 1999

(c) prepare a bank reconciliation statement at 31 May 1999

12 INCOMPLETE RECORDS

this chapter covers . . .

So far our studies of financial accounting have concentrated on the double-entry system and, from this, we have extracted a trial balance and prepared for the production of final accounts. However, many smaller businesses do not use the double-entry system, and no trial balance is available. Such businesses keep some records – incomplete records – and, at the end of the year, it is the task of the accountant to construct the final accounts from these.

This chapter looks at

- *the information available when constructing final accounts from incomplete records*
- *how information that is required can be calculated*
- *the use of gross profit mark-up and margin in incomplete records accounting*

NVQ PERFORMANCE CRITERIA COVERED

unit 4: MAINTAINING FINANCIAL RECORDS AND PREPARING ACCOUNTS

element 2

record income and expenditure

❑ *the organisation's policies, regulations, procedures and timescales in relation to recording income and expenditure are observed*

❑ *incomplete data is identified and either resolved or referred to the appropriate person*

element 3

collect and collate information for the preparation of final accounts

❑ *investigations into business transactions are conducted with tact and courtesy*

WHAT ARE INCOMPLETE RECORDS?

Incomplete records is the term used where the book-keeping system does not use double-entry principles and no trial balance is available. Some records are kept and the accountant will construct final accounts by

- using the information available (see below)
- seeing what information may not be available, and how 'missing' figures can be calculated

information available to the accountant

The basic financial record kept by most businesses is a cash book, often operated as a *single-entry* system. In practice, even if a cash book has not been kept, it is usually possible to reconstruct it from banking records, although this task can prove to be time-consuming. Other financial information will be available so that, in all, the accountant has the following to work from:

- cash book – the basic record for any single entry system
- banking details – statements, paying-in books, cheque counterfoils
- invoices – both received (for purchases) and sent (for sales) during the year
- expenses – during the year
- assets and liabilities – fixed and current assets, long-term and current liabilities, both at the beginning and end of the year
- fixed assets – bought or sold during the year

Information which may not be available, and will need to be calculated includes:

- capital at the beginning of the financial year
- purchases and sales for the year
- cash book summary
- profit for the year

the tools of accounting

In the two Case Studies which follow (pages 188 and 194) we shall see how to take the financial information that is available and, using the *tools of accounting*, to construct the accounts that are required. The tools of accounting that may be needed are:

- the use of an opening trial balance, or statement of assets and liabilities
- the construction of a cash account and/or bank account

- the use of control accounts – sales ledger control account and purchases ledger control account

In addition, the following may be of use:

- the accounting equation (assets – liabilities = capital)
- gross profit mark-up and margin (see page 199)
- the format of the profit and loss account and balance sheet

The two Case Studies make use of these tools of accounting, although it should be emphasised that no two incomplete records situations are the same; however practice will help to develop your skills in this aspect of financial accounting.

CASE STUDY

JAYNE PERRY – STATIONERY SUPPLIES

The following information has been taken from the incomplete records of Jayne Perry, who runs a small stationery supplies business.

LIST OF ASSETS AND LIABILITIES

	1 Jan 1998	31 Dec 1998
	£	£
Shop fittings	8,000	8,000
Stock	25,600	29,800
Debtors	29,200	20,400
Bank balance	5,000	not known
Creditors	20,800	16,000
Expenses owing	200	300

BANK SUMMARY FOR 1998

	£
Receipts from debtors	127,800
Payments to creditors	82,600
Drawings	12,500
Business expenses	30,600

In the text which follows we shall see how Jayne Perry's accountant will construct the final accounts for 1998 from incomplete records. The information to be calculated is:

- opening capital, at the beginning of the financial year
- cash book summary for the year
- purchases and sales for the year
- profit for the year, and a year-end statement of assets, liabilities and capital

Note: VAT is to be ignored on all transactions

OPENING CAPITAL

Opening capital is needed in Jayne Perry's case because a year-end statement of assets, liabilities and capital is to be prepared. In other situations with incomplete records, opening capital may be stated, being the difference between assets and liabilities. To calculate the capital at the beginning of the financial year, we use the formula *assets – liabilities = capital.*

This is presented as a *statement of assets and liabilities* as follows:

JAYNE PERRY
STATEMENT OF ASSETS AND LIABILITIES
as at 1 January 1998

	£	£
Assets		
Shop fittings		8,000
Stock		25,600
Debtors		29,200
Bank balance		5,000
		67,800
Less Liabilities		
Creditors	20,800	
Expenses owing	200	
		21,000
Capital at 1 January 1998		46,800

Notes:

- Here, the bank balance is an asset, ie money in the bank; if it was marked as an overdraft, it would be included amongst the liabilities.
- Look out for the opening bank balance or overdraft being stated elsewhere in the information; for example, a bank summary may be given which starts with the bank figure at the beginning of the year – this figure must be included in the statement of assets and liabilities, which is used to calculate opening capital.

CASH BOOK SUMMARY

A cash book summary enables us to find out the cash and bank balances at the year-end. (Sometimes this is not necessary, as a cash book may have been prepared already by the owner of the business.) In practice, the entries on the firm's bank statement can be used to produce a summary of receipts and payments for the year. In the case of Jayne Perry's business, the cash book (bank columns) are:

Dr		Cash Book (bank columns)			Cr
1998		£	1998		£
1 Jan	Balance b/d	5,000		Payments to creditors	82,600
	Receipts from debtors	127,800		Drawings	12,500
				Expenses	30,600
			31 Dec	Balance c/d	7,100
		132,800		MISSING FIGURE	132,800
1999			1999		
1 Jan	Balance b/d	7,100			

The bank balance of £7,100 on 31 December 1998 is calculated by filling in the missing figure.

Notes:

- When preparing a cash book summary, look out for an opening bank balance that is *overdrawn*; this is entered on the credit side.
- At the end of the cash book summary, a credit balance brought down is an overdraft.

PURCHASES AND SALES

In calculating purchases and sales, we need to take note of the creditors and debtors at both the beginning and the end of the year. The important point to note is that payments to creditors are *not* the same as purchases for the year (because of the change in the level of creditors). Likewise, receipts from debtors are not the same as sales (because of the change in debtors). Only in a business which trades solely on cash terms and has no debtors/creditors would the receipts and payments be the figures for sales and purchases.

calculating purchases and sales

The method of calculating the purchases and sales figures is:

- **purchases for year** = payments to creditors in year, *less* creditors at the beginning of the year, *plus* creditors at the end of the year
- **sales for year** = receipts from debtors in year, *less* debtors at the beginning of the year, *plus* debtors at the end of the year

When calculating purchases and sales, also take note of any cash discounts received and allowed, and – for sales – bad debts written off.

The figures from Jayne Perry's business are:

purchases	= £82,600 - £20,800 + £16,000	= £77,800
sales	= £127,800 - £29,200 + £20,400	= £119,000

use of control accounts

The use of control accounts (or totals accounts) is recommended for calculating purchases and sales in incomplete records questions. We can use the information for purchases given in the Case Study as follows:

Dr — Purchases Ledger Control Account — Cr

1998		£	1998		£
-	Payments to creditors	82,600	1 Jan	Balances b/d	20,800
31 Dec	Balances c/d	16,000	-	Purchases *(missing figure)*	?
		98,600			98,600
1999			1999		
			1 Jan	Balances b/d	16,000

The missing figure of purchases for the year is calculated as:

£98,600 – £20,800 = £77,800.

In a similar way, the sales figure can be calculated:

Dr — Sales Ledger Control Account — Cr

1998		£	1998		£
1 Jan	Balances b/d	29,200	-	Receipts from debtors	127,800
-	Sales (missing figure)	?	31 Dec	Balances c/d	20,400
		148,200			148,200
1999			1999		
1 Jan	Balances b/d	20,400			

The missing figure of sales for the year is £148,200 – £29,200 = £119,000.

The control account method, although its use is not essential in incomplete records questions, does bring a discipline to calculating the two important figures of purchases and sales. Do not forget that the control accounts give the figures for *credit* purchases and sales: cash purchases and sales need to be added, where applicable, to obtain total purchases and sales for the year.

purchases and sales – summary

Whichever method of calculating purchases or sales is used – calculation, or a control account – four pieces of information are usually required:

- opening balance
- closing balance
- payments or receipts for the year
- purchases or sales for the year

Provided that any three are known, the fourth can be calculated – the figure for purchases and sales was the missing figure in the examples above. However if, for example, we know the opening and closing debtors totals, together with sales for the year, then it is a simple matter to calculate the missing figure for receipts from debtors.

Remember that, if they are applicable, cash discounts allowed and received, and – for sales – bad debts written off, should also be incorporated into the control accounts.

PREPARATION OF FIGURES FOR THE FINAL ACCOUNTS

profit and loss account

Having calculated the figures for purchases and sales, we can now prepare the profit and loss account. The section as far as gross profit is:

JAYNE PERRY

PROFIT AND LOSS ACCOUNT

for the year ended 31 December 1998

	£	£
Sales		119,000
Opening stock	25,600	
Purchases	77,800	
	103,400	
Less Closing stock	29,800	
Cost of sales		73,600
Gross profit		45,400

The overheads section of the profit and loss account follows but, before we are able to complete this, we need to know the figure for expenses for the year. The relevant information from the Case Study is:

- bank payments for expenses during year, £30,600
- expenses owing at 1 January 1998, £200
- expenses owing at 31 December 1998, £300

Like the calculation of purchases and sales, we cannot simply use the bank payments figure for expenses; we must take note of cash payments, together with accruals (and prepayments). The calculation is:

> **expenses for year** = bank and cash payments less accruals at the beginning of the year (or plus prepayments), plus accruals at the end of the year (or less prepayments)

Thus the figure for Jayne Perry's business expenses is:

£30,600 – £200 + £300 = £30,700.

Alternatively, expenses can be calculated by means of a control account:

Dr — Expenses Control Account — Cr

1998		£	1998		£
-	Cash/bank	30,600	1 Jan	Balance b/d	200
31 Dec	Balance c/d	300	31 Dec	Profit and loss account *(missing figure)*	?
		30,900			30,900
1999			1999		
			1 Jan	Balance b/d	300

The missing figure is £30,900 - £200 = £30,700.

Jayne Perry's profit and loss account concludes as follows:

	£
Gross profit	45,400
Less overheads:	
Expenses	30,700
Net profit	14,700

balance sheet

The figures for a statement of assets, liabilities and capital (the basis of the balance sheet) can now be prepared using the assets and liabilities from the Case Study. The formula is: assets *minus* liabilities *equals* capital.

JAYNE PERRY
STATEMENT OF ASSETS, LIABILITIES AND CAPITAL
as at 31 December 1998

	£	£
ASSETS		
Shop fittings		8,000
Stock		29,800
Debtors		20,400
Bank		7,100
TOTAL ASSETS		65,300
LIABILITIES		
Creditors	16,000	
Accruals	300	
TOTAL LIABILITIES		16,300
CAPITAL		*49,000

*The capital figure can also be calculated as follows: opening capital £46,800 *add* net profit for year £14,700 *less* drawings £12,500 *equals* £49,000.

optional student activity

Draw up Jayne Perry's balance sheet from the figures given here.

CASE STUDY

ELECTROPARTS

We will now look at a more comprehensive example of incomplete records accounting. This incorporates points on depreciation and the sale of a fixed asset and concludes with the production of final accounts. You may like to work through the Case Study before comparing your solution with the one shown.

situation

John Anstey owns a small business, Electroparts, which supplies spare parts for a wide range of electrical goods – cookers, fridges, freezers, kettles, dishwashers, etc. Most of his customers are self-employed repairers who buy parts for specific jobs from his trade counter – John allows them credit terms; some sales are made to members of the public carrying out 'do-it-yourself' repairs – these customers pay in cash at the time of sale. All purchases from suppliers are made on credit.

John does not keep a full set of accounting records; however, the following information has been produced for the year ended 31 December 1998:

assets and liabilities of Electroparts at 1 January 1998

		£	£
ASSETS	Buildings at cost	100,000	
	Less provision for depreciation	10,000	
			90,000
	Fixtures and fittings at cost	15,000	
	Less provision for depreciation	7,500	
			7,500
			97,500
	Stock	24,400	
	Debtors	21,650	
	Prepayment: general expenses	140	
	Cash	250	
			46,440
	TOTAL ASSETS		143,940
LIABILITIES	Creditors	15,950	
	Bank overdraft	12,850	
	TOTAL LIABILITIES		28,800
CAPITAL			115,140

summary of the bank account (year ended 31 December 1998)

	£		£
Cash sales	45,280	Balance b/d	12,850
Receipts from debtors	177,410	Payments to creditors	149,620
Sale proceeds of fixtures		General expenses	17,340
and fittings	1,950	Wages	18,280
		Drawings	25,390
		Balance c/d	1,160
	224,640		224,640

other information:

- On 31 December 1998, stock was valued at £28,400
- Depreciation is calculated at the rate of 2% on the cost of buildings and 10% on the cost of fixtures and fittings held at the end of the financial year. No depreciation is calculated in the year of sale/disposal
- Fixtures and fittings purchased on 1 January 1996 for £2,500 were sold on 30 September 1998, the purchaser paying by cheque
- The proceeds from cash sales are placed in the till and paid into the bank account at the end of the day, apart from a cash float which is retained in the till; the amount of the cash float was £250 until October, when it was increased to £500
- On 31 December 1998, creditors were £18,210, debtors were £23,840 and £210 was owing for general expenses
- During the year, bad debts of £870 have been written off

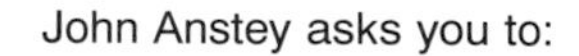

John Anstey asks you to:

1. Calculate the amount of credit sales during the year
2. Calculate the total sales during the year
3. Calculate the amount of purchases during the year
4. Calculate the profit or loss on the sale of fixtures and fittings
5. Calculate the figure for general expenses to be shown in the profit and loss account for the year ended 31 December 1998
6. Prepare the profit and loss account for the year ended 31 December 1998
7. Prepare the balance sheet at 31 December 1998

Note: VAT is to be ignored on all transactions

solution

1

Dr **Sales Ledger Control Account** Cr

1998		£	1998		£
1 Jan	Balances b/d	21,650	-	Receipts from debtors	177,410
	Credit sales		-	Bad debts written off	870
	(missing figure)	180,470	31 Dec	Balances c/d	23,840
		202,120			202,120

2

	£
Credit sales (see above)	180,470
Cash sales	45,280
Increase in cash float	250
Total sales for year	226,000

3

Dr **Purchases Ledger Control Account** Cr

1998		£	1998		£
-	Payments to creditors	149,620	1 Jan	Balances b/d	15,950
31 Dec	Balance c/d	18,210	-	Purchases *(missing figure)*	151,880
		167,830			167,830

4 **Profit or loss on disposal of fixtures and fittings**

Depreciation per year	£250	
Number of years' depreciation	2	(1996, 1997; no depreciation in year of sale)
Provision for depreciation	£500	

continued on next page

Net book value at date of sale	£2,000	(£2,500 – £500 depreciation)
Sale proceeds	£1,950	
Loss on sale	£50	

5

Dr **General Expenses Control Account** Cr

1998		£	1998		£
1 Jan	Balance b/d	140	31 Dec	Profit and loss account	
	Bank	17,340		*(missing figure)*	17,690
31 Dec	Balance c/d	210			
		17,690			17,690

6

JOHN ANSTEY, TRADING AS 'ELECTROPARTS'
PROFIT AND LOSS ACCOUNT
for the year ended 31 December 1998

	£	£
Sales		226,000
Opening stock	24,400	
Purchases	151,880	
	176,280	
Less Closing stock	28,400	
Cost of sales		147,880
Gross profit		78,120
Less overheads:		
General expenses	17,690	
Loss on sale of fixtures and fittings	50	
Depreciation: buildings	2,000	
fixtures and fittings	*1,250	
Bad debts written off	870	
Wages	18,280	
		40,140
Net profit		37,980

***Note**

Fixtures and fittings at cost on 1 January 1998	£15,000
Less cost price of fixtures and fittings sold 30 September 1998	£2,500
Fixtures and fittings at cost on 31 December 1998	£12,500
Depreciation at 10%	£1,250

optional student activity

Draw up a list of assets and liabilities from which the balance sheet can be prepared.

7

JOHN ANSTEY, TRADING AS 'ELECTROPARTS'
BALANCE SHEET
as at 31 December 1998

	£	£	£
Fixed assets	*Cost*	*Provision for depreciation*	*Net*
Buildings	100,000	12,000	88,000
Fixtures and fittings	12,500	*8,250	4,250
	112,500	20,250	92,250
Current assets			
Stock		28,400	
Debtors		23,840	
Bank		1,160	
Cash		500	
		53,900	
Less Current liabilities			
Creditors	18,210		
Accrual: general expenses	210		
		18,420	
Working capital			35,480
NET ASSETS			127,730
FINANCED BY			
Capital			
Opening capital (from assets and liabilities at 1 January 1998)			115,140
Add Net profit			37,980
			153,120
Less Drawings			25,390
Closing capital			127,730

***Note**

Provision for depreciation of fixtures and fittings at 1 January 1998	7,500
Less provision for depreciation on asset sold	500
	7,000
Depreciation for year (see profit and loss account)	1,250
Provision for depreciation of fixtures and fittings at 31 December 1998	8,250

THE USE OF GROSS PROFIT MARK-UP AND MARGIN

It is often necessary to use accounting ratios and percentages in the preparation of final accounts from incomplete records. The topic of ratios and percentages is covered more fully in Osborne Books' *Costing, Reports & Returns Tutorial.*

The two main percentages used for incomplete records accounting are:

- gross profit mark-up
- gross profit margin

It is quite common for a business to establish its selling price by reference to either a mark-up or a margin. The difference between the two is that:

- mark-up is a profit percentage added to *buying* or *cost* price
- margin is a percentage profit based on the *selling* price

For example, a product is bought by a retailer at a cost of £100; the retailer sells it for £125, ie

cost price + gross profit = selling price

£100 + £25 = £125

The ***mark-up*** is:

$$\frac{\text{gross profit}}{\text{cost price}} \times \frac{100}{1} = \frac{\text{£}25}{\text{£}100} \times \frac{100}{1} = \mathbf{25\%}$$

The ***margin*** is:

$$\frac{\text{gross profit}}{\text{selling price}} \times \frac{100}{1} = \frac{\text{£}25}{\text{£}125} \times \frac{100}{1} = \mathbf{20\%}$$

In incomplete records accounting, mark-up or the margin percentages can be used to calculate either cost of sales (which, if opening stock and closing stock are known, will enable the calculation of purchases) or sales. We will now look at two examples.

example 1

- Cost of sales is £150,000
- Mark-up is 40%
- What are sales?

$$\text{Gross profit} = \text{£}150{,}000 \times \frac{40}{100} = \text{£}60{,}000$$

Sales = cost of sales + gross profit, ie £150,000 + £60,000 = **£210,000**

example 2:

- Sales are £450,000
- Margin is 20%
- Opening stock is £40,000; closing stock is £50,000
- What are purchases?

Gross profit = £450,000 x $\frac{20}{100}$ = £90,000

Cost of sales = sales – gross profit, ie £450,000 – £90,000 = £360,000

The purchases calculation is:

Opening stock		£40,000
+	Purchases (missing figure)	?
–	Closing stock	£50,000
=	Cost of sales	£360,000
Purchases		= **£370,000**

STOCK LOSSES

A loss of stock may occur as a result of an event such as a fire, a flood or a theft. When such a loss occurs, an estimate of the value of the stock lost needs to be made in order for the business to make an insurance claim (always assuming that the stock was adequately insured). The value is calculated by preparing an accounting summary to the date of the event, and often making use of margins and mark-ups. The calculations are best carried out in three steps:

1.	Opening stock	
	+	Purchases
	=	Cost of stock available for sale
2.	Sales	
	–	Gross profit (using normal gross profit margin)
	=	Cost of sales
3.	Cost of stock available for sale (from 1, above)	
	–	Cost of sales (2, above)
	=	Estimated closing stock
	–	Value of stock remaining or salvaged
	=	Value of stock lost through fire, flood or theft

CASE STUDY

CLOTHING SUPPLIES – THEFT OF STOCK

situation

Peter Kamara runs Clothing Supplies, a small clothing wholesalers. Peter is convinced that various items of clothing have been stolen during the year and he asks you to calculate, from the accounting details, the value of stock stolen. The following information is available:

- sales for the year, £500,000
- opening stock at the beginning of the year, £15,000
- purchases for the year, £310,000
- closing stock at the end of the year, £22,000
- the gross profit margin achieved on all sales is 40 per cent

solution

CALCULATION OF STOCK LOSS FOR THE YEAR

	£	£
Opening stock		15,000
Purchases		310,000
Cost of stock available for sale		325,000
Sales	500,000	
Less Normal gross profit margin (40%)	200,000	
Cost of sales		300,000
Estimated closing stock		25,000
Less Actual closing stock		22,000
Value of stock loss		3,000

CHAPTER SUMMARY

- Incomplete records is the term used where the book-keeping system does not use double-entry principles.

- In order to prepare final accounts, the accountant may well have to calculate:
  - capital at the beginning of the financial year
  - purchases and sales for the year
  - cash book summary
  - profit for the year
- On the basis of these calculations, the accountant can then construct the final accounts without recourse to a trial balance.

- Two ratios and percentages used in incomplete records accounting are:
  - gross profit mark-up
  - gross profit margin

- The value of stock losses caused by fire, flood or theft is calculated using margins and mark-ups.

KEY TERMS

incomplete records	a book-keeping system in which double-entry principles are not used
gross profit mark-up	profit percentage added to the buying price
gross profit margin	profit percentage based on the selling price
stock loss	loss of stock caused by fire, flood or theft

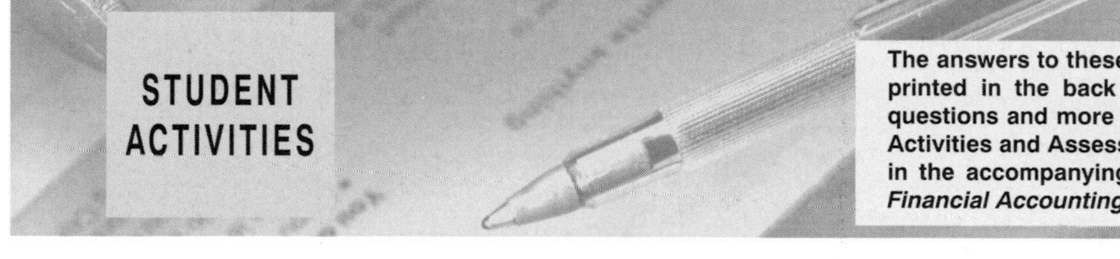

The answers to these Student Activities are printed in the back of this book. Further questions and more fully extended Student Activities and Assessments are to be found in the accompanying Osborne Books' text *Financial Accounting Workbook*.

12.1 • Cost of sales for the year is £200,000.
• Mark-up is 30%.
What are sales for the year?

12.2 • Sales for the year are £100,000.
• Gross profit margin is 25%.
• Opening stock is £10,000; closing stock is £12,000.
What are purchases for the year?

12.3 You are preparing accounts from incomplete records. Debtors at the start of the year were £2,500, and at the end were £3,250. Cheques received from debtors total £17,850; cash sales total £2,500. What is the sales figure for the year?

12.4 Jane Price owns a fashion shop called 'Trendsetters'. She has been in business for one year and, although she does not keep a full set of accounting records, the following information has been produced for the first year of trading, which ended on 31 December 1998:

Summary of the business bank account for the year ended 31 December 1998:

	£
Capital introduced	60,000
Receipts from sales	153,500
Payments to suppliers	95,000
Advertising	4,830
Wages	15,000
Rent and rates	8,750
General expenses	5,000
Shop fittings	50,000
Drawings	15,020

Summary of assets and liabilities as at 31 December 1998:

	£
Shop fittings at cost	50,000
Stock	73,900
Debtors	2,500
Creditors	65,000

Other information:

- Jane wishes to depreciate the shop fittings at 20% per year using the straight-line method
- At 31 December 1998, rent is prepaid by £250, and wages of £550 are owing

You are to:

(a) Calculate the amount of sales during the year.

(b) Calculate the amount of purchases during the year.

(c) Calculate the figures for

- rent and rates
- wages

to be shown in the profit and loss account for the year ended 31 December 1998

(d) Prepare Jane Price's profit and loss account for the year ended 31 December 1998.

(e) Prepare a list of assets, liabilities and capital as at 31 December 1998.

(f) *Optional task*: draw up Jane Price's balance sheet as at 31 December 1998.

Note: VAT is to be ignored on all transactions

12.5 James Harvey runs a stationery supplies shop. He is convinced that one of his employees is stealing stationery. He asks you to calculate from the accounting records the value of stock stolen. The following information is available:

- sales for the year, £180,000
- opening stock at the beginning of the year, £21,500
- purchases for the year, £132,000
- closing stock at the end of the year, £26,000
- the gross profit margin achieved on all sales is 30 per cent

You are to calculate the value of stock stolen (if any) during the year.

13 CLUB AND SOCIETY ACCOUNTS

this chapter covers . . .

Up until now, we have been dealing with the financial accounting records of businesses. We have seen how profit – the primary objective of a business – is calculated in the profit and loss account. We now turn to the accounts of non-profit making organisations – such as clubs and societies – where the primary objective is to provide facilities and services to members. In this chapter we will look at:

- *the differences in accounting terminology between business and non-profit making organisations*
- *the preparation of club/society year-end accounts*
- *the different accounting treatments for aspects of club/society accounts*

It is for the treasurer of the club/society to maintain proper accounting records, and these will be audited either by another member, or by an outside accountant. The important point is that the highest standards of financial recording should still be maintained, and often those who work in accounting find themselves elected to the job of treasurer of a club or society.

NVQ PERFORMANCE CRITERIA COVERED

unit 4: MAINTAINING FINANCIAL RECORDS AND PREPARING ACCOUNTS

element 3

collect and collate information for the preparation of final accounts

- ❑ *all relevant information is correctly identified and recorded*
- ❑ *investigations are conducted with tact and courtesy*
- ❑ *the organisation's policies, regulations, procedures and timescales relating to preparing final accounts are observed*

element 4

prepare the extended trial balance

- ❑ *the extended trial balance is accurately extended and totalled*

ACCOUNTING TERMINOLOGY

Businesses and non-profit making organisations – such as clubs and societies – differ in their aims and accounting terminology, as seen in the table below.

	Business	**Non-profit making organisation**
PRIMARY OBJECTIVE	To make a profit	To provide facilities and services to members
MAIN ACCOUNTING STATEMENTS	Profit and loss account	Income and expenditure account
	Balance sheet	Balance sheet
FINANCIAL PERFORMANCE	Profit	Surplus of income over expenditure
	Loss	Deficit of expenditure over income
FUNDING	Capital	Accumulated fund

ACCOUNTING RECORDS OF A CLUB/SOCIETY

Few clubs and societies keep accounting records in double-entry form. For most clubs, the treasurer keeps a cash book, which is a simple version of the cash book used by businesses. It records receipts paid into the bank and payments made from the bank, together with cash receipts and payments. The cash book is ruled off and balanced at the end of the financial year.

Often a summary of the cash book is presented to members in the form of a *receipts and payments account* (see the Case Study on page 208); for a very small club, this information forms the 'year-end accounts'. However, there are two accounting problems in using a receipts and payments account:

- accruals and prepayments cannot be made
- the distinction between capital and revenue expenditure cannot be made

Thus, whilst a receipt and payments account may be suitable for a small club which meets infrequently or deals in small amounts of money, a larger club needs to produce final accounts in the form of:

- income and expenditure account
- balance sheet

INCOME AND EXPENDITURE ACCOUNT

The income and expenditure account of a club or society lists the income and deducts the expenditure using a layout similar to a profit and loss account. The account will then show:

- *either* a surplus of income over expenditure
- *or* a deficit of expenditure over income

The income and expenditure account is prepared from the receipts and payments account, taking note of:

- accruals
- prepayments
- depreciation of fixed assets

Capital expenditure, eg the purchase of a new lawnmower for a cricket club, is not recorded in the income and expenditure account, although depreciation of the lawnmower will be shown.

A major source of income for a club is members' subscriptions. Some members will prepay subscriptions for the next financial year, while others will be late in paying, or may never pay at all, ceasing to be members. Unless the club has a different policy, the treasurer calculates the subscriptions that *should have been received*, ie

	subscriptions received in year
add	subscriptions prepaid at start of year
less	subscriptions owing at start of year
less	subscriptions paid in advance at end of the year
add	subscriptions due but unpaid at end of the year
equals	subscription income for year to be shown in income and expenditure account

This is best calculated by means of a control account in the following way:

Subscriptions Control Account

Dr	£		Cr £
Balance at start of year (subscriptions owing)		Balance at start of year (subscriptions prepaid)	
Income and expenditure account (subscription income for year)		Subscriptions received in year	
Balance at end of year (subscriptions prepaid)		Balance at end of year (subscriptions owing)	

In the balance sheet of the club, subscriptions in advance are recorded as a current liability, while subscriptions due but unpaid are a current asset – debtors for subscriptions. This method of handling subscriptions takes note of prepayments and accruals and is the way in which we would deal with such items in the accounts of a business. However, in practice, the treasurer of a club may decide not to record subscriptions due but unpaid as debtors because, unlike a business, the club will not sue for unpaid amounts. The most realistic approach is to ignore such subscriptions – if they are subsequently paid, they can be brought into that year's income.

Other sources of income for clubs/societies include:

- trading activities, eg a bar, catering facilities
- donations received
- room lettings to other organisations
- special activities, eg jumble sale, dinner dance

BALANCE SHEET

The balance sheet of a club/society is presented in a very similar way to that of a business. The major difference is that, instead of capital, a club has an *accumulated fund.* If the accumulated fund is not known at the start of the financial year, it is calculated as:

assets *less* liabilities *equals* accumulated fund

In the balance sheet a surplus from the income and expenditure account is added to the accumulated fund, while a deficit is deducted.

TRADING ACTIVITIES

Although the primary objective of clubs and societies and other non-profit making organisations is to provide facilities and services to members, many organisations carry out an activity on a regular basis with the intention of making a profit. Examples of such trading activities include:

- a bar for the use of members
- provision of catering facilities for members
- the purchase of goods to sell to members on favourable terms, eg seeds and fertilisers by a gardening society

In the year-end accounts, the treasurer should prepare a separate account for such activities so as to show the profit or loss. The layout of this account is exactly the same as that for a trading business, with opening stock, closing stock, purchases and sales. Any direct costs associated with the trading activity – such as the wages of bar staff – will be included. The profit or loss on trading activities is then taken to the income and expenditure account.

FUND-RAISING EVENTS

Most clubs and societies organise fund-raising events from time-to-time, eg jumble sales, raffles, coffee mornings, etc. It is usual to show the separate profit or loss on such events within the income and expenditure account. This is done by linking the income and the expenses together, for example:

	£	£
Income		
Christmas Fayre		
takings	550	
less expenses	210	
profit		340

CASE STUDY

SOUTH DEMPSEY TENNIS CLUB

situation

You have taken over as treasurer of South Dempsey Tennis Club. At the beginning of the financial year, on 1 January 1998, the assets and liabilities of the club were:

- bank balance, £431
- furniture and fittings, £1,000
- sports equipment, £1,250
- bar stock, £210

For the year ended 31 December 1998, you prepared the following receipts and payments account:

RECEIPTS AND PAYMENTS ACCOUNT
for the year ended 31 December 1998

RECEIPTS	£	PAYMENTS	£
Balance b/d	431	Rent	2,500
Subscriptions	1,875	Electricity	295
Bar takings	3,700	Bar purchases	1,210
Donation	100	Bar wages	790
Sale of raffle tickets	310	Raffle prizes	120
		Sports equipment	500
		Secretary's expenses	730
		Sundry expenses	220
		Balance c/d	51
	6,416		6,416

The shortcomings of the receipts and payments account are that:

- It ignores the fact that subscriptions of £1,875 include £175 paid by members in advance for next year.
- There is bar stock of £320 at the end of the year.
- Rent of £500 has been paid for the first quarter of next year (a prepayment)
- The acquisition of sports equipment of £500 is shown along with other payments; it needs to be identified and listed on the balance sheet as a fixed asset.
- At the end of the year, furniture is valued at £800, and sports equipment is valued at £1,500.

As the receipts and payments account does not show an entirely true picture of the club's affairs for the year, you decide to convert it into an extended trial balance in order to prepare the

- income and expenditure account
- balance sheet

solution

The steps to prepare the year-end accounts of the club are:

- an opening trial balance – to calculate the accumulated fund at the start of the year
- a closing trial balance – incorporating amounts from the receipts and payments account (or summary of the club's cash book)
- an extended trial balance – with adjustments for accruals, prepayments, depreciation, stock; income and expenditure account; balance sheet
- year-end accounts in conventional format

The opening trial balance is as follows:

SOUTH DEMPSEY TENNIS CLUB
Opening trial balance as at 1 January 1998

	Dr	*Cr*
	£	£
Bank balance	431	
Furniture and fittings	1,000	
Sports equipment	1,250	
Bar stock at 1 Jan 1998	210	
Accumulated fund		*2,891
	2,891	2,891

* calculated as the 'missing figure'

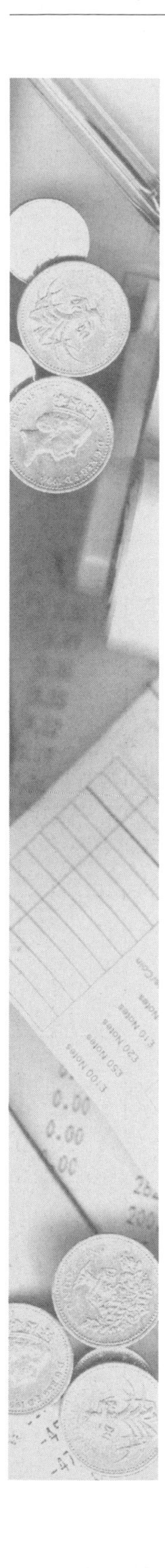

The year-end trial balance is shown in the ledger balances columns of the extended trial balance (see next page). The figures incorporate the opening trial balance and the amounts from the receipts and payments account. Note that sports equipment is shown as £1,750 (ie £1,250 from the opening trial balance, plus additions of £500 shown in the receipts and payments account).

The other columns of the extended trial balance are now completed in the same way as we have done previously. Note the adjustments columns include:

- Depreciation of fixed assets

  furniture, £1,000 – £800 = £200 depreciation

  sports equipment, £1,750 – £1,500 = £250 depreciation

- Subscriptions in advance of £175; thus the amount recorded in the income and expenditure columns is £1,875 – £175 = £1,700. Note that subscriptions which are due but unpaid are often, in practice, ignored for the year's accounts – they are often paid late, if indeed they are paid at all.

- Rent prepaid £500; thus the amount recorded in the income and expenditure column is £2,500 – £500 = £2,000.

- Bar closing stock of £320, which is dealt with in the same way as the closing stock of a business.

The income (credit) column of the income and expenditure account totals £6,130 while the expenditure (debit) column totals £6,025. Thus the club has £105 surplus of income over expenditure which is transferred to the credit side of the balance sheet. The adjustments for depreciation, subscriptions in advance (a liability of the club as it is a prepayment of income), rent prepaid and bar closing stocks are shown in the balance sheet columns.

The figures from the extended trial balance can then be presented in conventional format as shown on pages 212 and 213. Note the following points:

- The profit on the bar has been calculated separately in a 'bar trading account' and then brought into the income and expenditure account. It is usual for clubs and societies to show the figures relating to main trading activities in a separate account.

- The donation received has been shown as income; as it is a relatively small amount this would seem to be the correct treatment (see also page 214). Had it been a much larger amount, it would have been taken directly to the balance sheet.

- The profit on the raffle has been disclosed within the income and expenditure account; an alternative treatment would be to show the cost of raffle prizes as expenditure.

- A 'surplus of income over expenditure' (as here) is the equivalent of a business making a net profit, while a 'deficit of expenditure over income' is the equivalent of a net loss. The surplus is added to the accumulated fund – the equivalent of a business' capital – in the balance sheet (a deficit of expenditure over income would be deducted).

EXTENDED TRIAL BALANCE SOUTH DEMPSEY TENNIS CLUB 31 DECEMBER 1998

Description	Ledger balances		Adjustments		Income & expenditure		Balance sheet	
	Dr £	Cr £	Dr £	Cr £	Dr £	Cr £	Dr £	Cr £
Bank	51						51	
Furniture and fittings	1,000						1,000	
Provision for depreciation: furniture & fittings				200				200
Sports equipment (£1,250 + £500)	1,750						1,750	
Provision for depreciation: sports equipment				250				250
Bar stock at 1 Jan 1998	210				210			
Accumulated fund		2,891						2,891
Subscriptions		1,875	175			1,700		
Bar takings		3,700				3,700		
Donation		100				100		
Sale of raffle tickets		310				310		
Rent paid	2,500			500	2,000			
Electricity	295				295			
Bar purchases	1,210				1,210			
Bar wages	790				790			
Raffle prizes	120				120			
Secretary's expenses	730				730			
Sundry expenses	220				220			
Closing stock: Income & Expenditure				320		320		
Closing stock: Balance sheet			320				320	
Accruals				175				175
Prepayments			500				500	
Depreciation			450		450			
Surplus/deficit					105			105
	8,876	8,876	1,445	1,445	6,130	6,130	3,621	3,621

SOUTH DEMPSEY TENNIS CLUB
BAR TRADING ACCOUNT
for the year ended 31 December 1998

	£	£
Bar takings		3,700
Opening stock	210	
Purchases	1,210	
	1,420	
Less Closing stock	320	
	1,100	
Bar wages	790	
		1,890
Profit on bar		1,810

SOUTH DEMPSEY TENNIS CLUB
INCOME AND EXPENDITURE ACCOUNT
for the year ended 31 December 1998

	£	£
Income		
Profit on bar		1,810
Subscriptions		1,700
Donation		100
Sale of raffle tickets	310	
Less raffle prizes	120	
Profit on raffle		190
		3,800
Less Expenditure		
Rent	2,000	
Electricity	295	
Secretary's expenses	730	
Sundry expenses	220	
Depreciation:		
furniture	200	
sports equipment	250	
		3,695
Surplus of income over expenditure		105

SOUTH DEMPSEY TENNIS CLUB
BALANCE SHEET
as at 31 December 1998

	£	£
Fixed assets		
Furniture and fittings (at valuation)		800
Sports equipment (at valuation)		1,500
		2,300
Current assets		
Bar stock	320	
Prepayment (rent)	500	
Bank	51	
	871	
Less Current liabilities		
Subscriptions in advance	175	
Working capital		696
NET ASSETS		2,996
REPRESENTED BY		
Accumulated fund		2,891
Surplus of income over expenditure		105
		2,996

CLUB ACCOUNTS: PROBLEM AREAS

There are a number of possible areas that need to be clarified by a newly appointed treasurer of a club or society. These are the club's policy on:

- overdue subscriptions
- life membership
- entrance/joining fees
- donations received
- depreciation

The club's rules should state how these are to be handled in the accounts; if not, a new treasurer will have to see how they were dealt with in previous years, or ask the committee for a decision.

overdue subscriptions

We have seen earlier that the practical policy adopted by most treasurers is to ignore overdue subscriptions (but an adjustment *is* made for prepaid subscriptions). However, in Assessments and unless instructed otherwise, overdue subscriptions should be treated as accruals, and subscriptions in advance as prepayments.

life membership

Some clubs and societies offer life membership in exchange for a one-off payment. The problem for the treasurer is whether to record this payment as income for the year in which it is received, or to credit it to a reserve account (eg Life Subscriptions Account), the balance of which is then transferred bit-by-bit over a number of years to the income and expenditure account. The time period for this will depend on the nature of the club: for example, the 'Over-eighties Gentleman's Dining Club' is likely to transfer its life subscriptions account to income rather more quickly than will a stamp collecting club.

A club of which I am a member has the following accounting policy:

"Three per cent of the life subscriptions account is released to income each year."

The policy for accounting for life membership will always be stated clearly in an Assessment.

entrance or joining fees

Often a one-off charge is made in the year of joining a club as an entrance fee. It is possible to justify making such a charge by arguing that it covers the cost of processing new members' applications; on the other hand it gives extra income to the club and, once a person is a member, it acts as an incentive for them to remain a member (because, if their membership lapsed, the joining fee would be payable again upon rejoining).

The treasurer needs to know how to account for the joining fee:

- *either,* it is treated as income for the year of joining (but this could distort income if a membership 'drive' was held in one particular year)
- *or,* it is credited to an entrance fees account which is transferred to income over a number of years

donations received

There are two alternative accounting treatments which can be used for donations received:

- record the amount as income in the income and expenditure account, *or*
- record the amount as an addition to the accumulated fund in the balance sheet

The first method treats the donation as income for the year, while the second capitalises the amount (ie records it on the balance sheet). As to which is to be used depends very much on the amount of the donation in relation to the size of the club's activities – the accounting concept of materiality applies. For example, a £10 donation would normally be recorded as income; however, a legacy of several thousands of pounds from a deceased club member ought to be capitalised and added to the accumulated fund. If the club rules do not state how donations received are to be dealt with in the accounts, the treasurer must use his or her own judgement and will probably apply the materiality concept.

Remember that, in practice, donations will not always be cash amounts, other assets could be donated, eg a plot of land, a work of art. Here the asset will need to be valued and recorded in the accounts. In the case of assets other than cash, it is likely that they will need to be capitalised and recorded on the balance sheet.

depreciation

As in the final accounts of a business, fixed assets should be depreciated in club accounts; the same principles will apply (see Chapter 6). Depreciation for the year is charged as an expense in the income and expenditure account, while the asset is shown in the balance sheet at cost less provision for depreciation, to give the net book value.

Often clubs simply value fixed assets at the end of each financial year. The fall in value, subject to any acquisitions or sales, is the depreciation for the year which is charged as an expense in the income and expenditure account. The fixed asset will then be shown at the reduced value in the year end balance sheet.

PRACTICAL POINTS FOR TREASURERS

As noted in the introduction to this chapter, the treasurer of a club/society is responsible for maintaining proper accounting records. The same high standards of financial recording as would be applied to the accounts of a business should be used by the club treasurer. Two areas are of particular importance:

authority to spend

Before making payments, the treasurer must ensure that he or she has the authority to spend the club's money. For 'one-off' transactions, eg the purchase of a new lawnmower by a cricket club, the minutes of the relevant committee meeting will show that the purchase was agreed. For regular activities eg small expenses such as printing, electricity, the club's rules will authorise the treasurer to make payment against invoices received.

documentary evidence

The treasurer should ensure that there is documentary evidence for every transaction passing through the accounts of the club. For example, payments should only be made against invoices received in the name of the club, while a receipt should be given for all money received. In this way, an audit trail is created. All documents should be retained for the use of the club's auditor, who will check the accounting records after the end of each financial year. The documents should then be stored for at least six years in case there are subsequent queries.

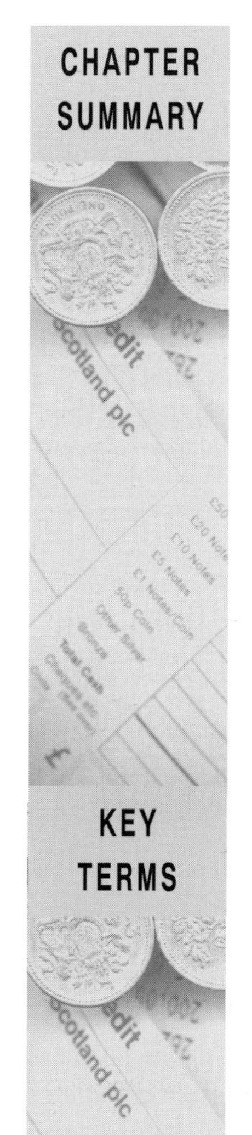

CHAPTER SUMMARY

- Unlike a business, a non-profit making organisation – such as a club or society – does not base its activities on profit, but operates for the benefit of its members.
- Many clubs and societies have large sums of money passing through their hands and, like businesses, need tight accounting controls.
- The year-end accounts of a club consist of
  - income and expenditure account
  - balance sheet
- Where a club carries out a trading activity with the intention of making a profit, a separate account is often prepared for the activity.
- Accounting policies on which the treasurer needs guidance from the club's committee are:
  - overdue subscriptions
  - life membership
  - entrance/joining fees
  - donations received
  - depreciation

KEY TERMS

receipts and payments account	summary of the cash book showing the main sources and uses of money
income and expenditure account	the equivalent of a business' profit and loss account
surplus of income over expenditure	the equivalent of a business' profit
deficit of expenditure over income	the equivalent of a business' loss
accumulated fund	assets less liabilities; the equivalent of the capital of a business

The answers to these Student Activities are printed in the back of this book. Further questions and more fully extended Student Activities and Assessments are to be found in the accompanying Osborne Books' text *Financial Accounting Workbook*.

13.1 A club's receipts and payments account is:

(a) similar to a balance sheet

(b) a summarised cash and bank account

(c) similar to a profit and loss account

(d) a deposit account at the bank

Answer (a) or (b) or (c) or (d)

13.2 The loss made by a club is recorded in its year-end accounts as:

(a) drawings

(b) deficit

(c) surplus

(d) depreciation

Answer (a) or (b) or (c) or (d)

13.3 In a club balance sheet, subscriptions paid in advance are recorded as:

(a) a current asset

(b) a current liability

(c) an addition to the accumulated fund

(d) a fixed asset

Answer (a) or (b) or (c) or (d)

13.4 The following information is available to the treasurer of Wyemeadow Golf Club for the year ended 31 December 1999:

1 January	Subscriptions prepaid	£1,250
	Subscriptions owing	£2,750
31 December	Subscriptions received during the year	£25,500
	Subscriptions prepaid for 2000	£1,750
	Subscriptions owing for 1999	£3,250

Note: all subscriptions due at 1 January 1999 have now been paid and are included in the receipts for the year.

You are to calculate the amount of subscription income to be shown in the income and expenditure account for the year ended 31 December 1999.

13.5 Westside Sports Club was set up on 1 July 1998. You are the treasurer and, at the end of the first year, you prepare a receipts and payments account as follows:

RECEIPTS AND PAYMENTS ACCOUNT

for the year ended 30 June 1999

RECEIPTS	£	PAYMENTS	£
Subscriptions	1,540	Equipment	1,500
Competition entry fees	498	Postage and stationery	197
Sale of snacks	1,108	Rent	550
		Competition expenses	320
		Purchase of snacks	520
		Balance c/d	59
	3,146		3,146

Additional information at 30 June 1999:

- subscriptions paid in advance for next year, £80
- rent owing, £100
- stock of snacks is valued at £70
- equipment is to be depreciated at 20%

You are to prepare the figures for the income and expenditure account and balance sheet of Westside Sports Club for the year ended 30 June 1999 using the extended trial balance method.

13.6 You have recently taken over as the treasurer of the Hallow Choir. The accounts of the previous year (to 31 December 1998) have been prepared, but only as a receipts and payments account as follows:

RECEIPTS AND PAYMENTS ACCOUNT

for the year to 31 December 1998

RECEIPTS	£	PAYMENTS	£
Balance b/d	112	Concert costs	1,250
Subscriptions	750	Conductor's fee	300
Music festival prize	500	Music purchase	450
Concert ticket sales	825	Printing of programmes	60
Fund raising activities (raffles)	427	Balance c/d	554
	2,614		2,614

Additionally, you note that:

- £65 of subscriptions, included in the £750, are paid in advance for 1999
- the club owes £40 for programme printing
- stocks of music, which are treated as fixed assets, are lent to club members free of charge; in last year's balance sheet they were valued at £875; for the current year's balance sheet they are to be valued at £1,125

You are to prepare the figures for the income and expenditure account and balance sheet of Hallow Choir for the year ended 31 December 1998, using the extended trial balance method.

13.7 The assets and liabilities of the Southwick Social Club as at 1 July 1998 were:

- bank balance, £580
- bar stock, £540
- furniture and equipment, £2,500
- rent owing, £120

For the year ended 30 June 1999, the treasurer prepared the following receipts and payments account:

RECEIPTS AND PAYMENTS ACCOUNT

for the year ended 30 June 1999

RECEIPTS	£	PAYMENTS	£
Balance b/d	580	Bar purchases	3,975
Subscriptions	2,790	Dinner dance expenses	1,280
Bar takings	6,380	Secretary's expenses	890
Dinner dance ticket sales	790	Bar wages	1,530
		Rent	940
		Furniture and equipment	1,710
		Balance c/d	215
	10,540		10,540

Additional information at 30 June 1999:

- bar stocks are valued at £630
- furniture and equipment is valued at £3,500
- subscriptions prepaid for next year, £210
- rent owing, £190

You are to prepare the figures for the income and expenditure account and balance sheet of Southwick Social Club for the year ended 30 June 1999, using the extended trial balance method.

14 PARTNERSHIP ACCOUNTS

this chapter covers . . .

So far, when discussing financial accounts, we have considered the accounts of a sole trader, ie one person in business. However, a partnership is a common form of business unit, and can be found in the form of:

- *sole traders who have joined together with others in order to raise finance and expand the business*
- *family businesses, such as builders, car repairers, gardeners*
- *professional firms such as solicitors, accountants, doctors, dentists*

In this chapter we look at

- *the definition of a partnership*
- *the accounting requirements of the Partnership Act 1890*
- *the accounting requirements which may be incorporated into a partnership agreement*
- *the use of capital accounts and current accounts*

NVQ PERFORMANCE CRITERIA COVERED

unit 4: MAINTAINING FINANCIAL RECORDS AND PREPARING ACCOUNTS

element 3

collect and collate information for thepreparation of final accounts

- ❑ *all relevant information is correctly identified and recorded*
- ❑ *the organisation's policies, regulations, procedures and timescales relating to preparing final accounts are observed*

element 4

prepare the extended trial balance

- ❑ *the extended trial balance is accurately extended and totalled*

DEFINITION OF A PARTNERSHIP

The Partnership Act of 1890 defines a partnership as

the relation which subsists between persons carrying on a business in common with a view of profit.

Normally, partnerships consist of between two and twenty partners (exceptions being large professional firms, eg solicitors and accountants). Partnerships are cheap and easy to set up, but the main disadvantages are the frequency of internal disputes and the liability in law of each partner for the dealings and business debts of the *whole* firm.

accounting requirements of a partnership

The accounting requirements of a partnership are

- either to follow the rules set out in the Partnership Act 1890
- or – and more likely – for the partners to agree amongst themselves, by means of a *partnership agreement* (see page 222), to follow different accounting rules

Unless the partners agree otherwise, the Partnership Act 1890 states the following accounting rules:

- profits and losses are to be shared equally between the partners
- no partner is entitled to a salary
- partners are not entitled to receive interest on their capital
- interest is not to be charged on partners' drawings
- when a partner contributes more capital than agreed, he or she is entitled to receive interest at five per cent per annum on the excess

As noted above, the partners may well decide to follow different accounting rules – these will be set out in a partnership agreement (see page 222).

YEAR-END ACCOUNTS OF A PARTNERSHIP

A partnership prepares the same type of year-end accounts as a sole trader business:

- profit and loss account
- balance sheet

The main difference is that, immediately after the profit and loss account, follows an *appropriation section* (often described as an appropriation account). This shows how the net profit from profit and loss account is shared amongst the partners.

example of the sharing of profit

Exe, Wye and Zed are partners sharing profits and losses equally; their profit and loss account for the current year shows a net profit of £30,000. The appropriation of profits appears as:

EXE, WYE AND ZED
PROFIT AND LOSS APPROPRIATION ACCOUNT
for the year ended ....

	£
Net profit	30,000
Share of profits:	
Exe	10,000
Wye	10,000
Zed	10,000
	30,000

The above is a simple appropriation of profits. More complex appropriation accounts – which form part of the year end financial statements of partnerships – are covered at level 4 of NVQ Accounting.

PARTNERSHIP AGREEMENT

The accounting rules from the Partnership Act are often varied with the agreement of all partners, by means of a partnership agreement. In particular, a *partnership agreement* will usually cover the following:

- **division of profits and losses between partners** – the Partnership Act states that unless it is otherwise laid down in the partnership agreement, profits and losses are to be shared *equally*
- **partners' salaries/commission** – these may be agreed between partners; for example a partner who has not contributed capital may be paid a salary instead of receiving a share of profits
- **interest allowed on capital** – a rate of interest may be paid to partners on the capital invested to compensate them for tying up capital in the business (money which could have earned interest elsewhere)
- **interest charged on partners' drawings** – a rate of interest may be charged to partners to penalise the taking of drawings early in the financial year, a practice which can deplete the resources of the business

The money amounts involved for each of these points – where allowed by the partnership agreement – are shown in the partnership appropriation account (covered in detail at level 4 of NVQ Accounting).

CAPITAL ACCOUNTS AND CURRENT ACCOUNTS

The important accounting difference between a sole trader and a partnership is that each partner usually has a capital account *and* a current account. The capital account is normally *fixed*, and only alters if a permanent increase or decrease in capital contributed by the partner takes place. The current account is *fluctuating* and it is to this account that:

- share of profits is credited
- share of losses is debited
- salary (if any) is credited
- interest allowed on partners' capital is credited
- drawings are debited
- interest charged on partners' drawings is debited

Thus, the current account is treated as a *working* account, while capital account remains fixed, except for capital introduced or withdrawn.

A partner's current account will have the following layout:

Dr	**Partner A: Current Account**		Cr
	£		£
Drawings		Balance b/d	
Interest charged on drawings*		Share of net profit	
		Salary (or commissions)*	
Balance c/d		Interest allowed on capital*	

* if these items are allowed by the partnership agreement

Note that whilst the normal balance on a partner's current account is credit, when the partner has drawn out more than his or her share of the profits, then the balance will be debit.

CASE STUDY

ABLE AND BAKER, IN PARTNERSHIP

This Case Study demonstrates the use of partners' capital and current accounts, incorporating:

- *a change in capital*
- *interest allowed on partners' capital*
- *a partnership salary*
- *interest charged on partners' drawings*

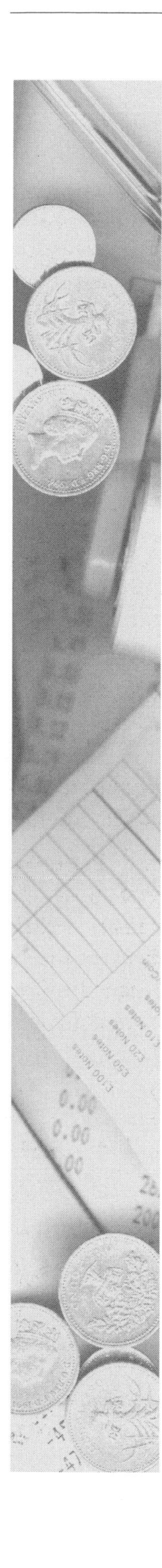

situation

Able and Baker are in partnership; their partnership agreement includes the following:

- interest is allowed on partners' capital at the rate of five per cent per year
- Baker is entitled to a salary of £8,000 per year
- interest is charged on partners' drawings at the rate of ten per cent per year
- profits and losses are shared equally

The following financial information which follows is for the year ended 31 March 1998:

- At 1 April 1997 (the start of the year), the partners had the following balances:

	Able	*Baker*
	£	£
Capital account	20,000 Cr	15,000 Cr
Current account	2,400 Cr	200 Cr

- On 30 September 1997 (half-way through the financial year) Able withdrew £5,000 of capital and Baker subscribed £5,000 of additional capital (both transactions were by cheque).
- On 30 September 1997, partners' drawings were made: Able £9,000, Baker £12,000.
- During the year, the following partnership transactions took place:

	Able	*Baker*
	£	£
Interest allowed on partners' capital	875	875
Partnership salary	–	8,000
Interest charged on partners' drawings	450	600
Share of profits after partnership transactions	5,625	5,625

Show the partners' capital and current accounts for the year ended 31 March 1998.

solution

Partners' Capital Accounts

Dr		Able	Baker			Able	Baker
1997/98		£	£	1997/98		£	£
30 Sep	Bank	5,000	–	1 Apr	Balances b/d	20,000	15,000
31 Mar	Balances c/d	15,000	20,000	30 Sep	Bank	–	5,000
		20,000	20,000			20,000	20,000
1998/99				1998/99			
				1 Apr	Balances b/d	15,000	20,000

Cr

Dr **Partners' Current Accounts** Cr

		Able	Baker			Able	Baker
1997/98		£	£	1997/98		£	£
30 Sep	Drawings	9,000	12,000	1 Apr	Balances b/d	2,400	200
31 Mar	Interest on drawings	450	600		Salary	–	8,000
31 Mar	Balance c/d	–	2,100	31 Mar	Interest on capital	875	875
				31 Mar	Share of profits	5,625	5,625
				31 Mar	Balance c/d	550	–
		9,450	14,700			9,450	14,700
1998/99				1998/99			
1 Apr	Balance b/d	550	–	1 Apr	Balance b/d	–	2,100

Note that Able has drawn more out of the current account than the balance of the account; accordingly, at the end of the year, Able has a debit balance of £550 on account with the partnership. By contrast, Baker has a credit balance of £2,100 on current account.

PARTNERSHIP FINAL ACCOUNTS FROM THE TRIAL BALANCE

Final accounts for a partnership can be prepared using the extended trial balance method and will then be displayed in conventional format.

The procedures are exactly the same as for sole traders. The only differences to note are that both partners' capital and current accounts are shown in the balance sheet, and the net profit/loss is shared amongst the partners in their agreed ratios. An example of a partnership extended trial balance is shown on the next page (note that the partners share profits and losses equally). The current accounts of the partners – Exe and Wye – will appear in the book-keeping system as follows:

Dr **Partners' Current Accounts** Cr

	Exe	**Wye**			**Exe**	**Wye**
1999	£	£	1999		£	£
31 Dec Drawings	6,000	4,500	1 Jan	Balances b/d	3,000	500
31 Dec Balances c/d	2,000	1,000	31 Dec	Share of profits	5,000	5,000
	8,000	5,500			8,000	5,500
2000			2000			
			1 Jan	Balances b/d	2,000	1,000

EXTENDED TRIAL BALANCE **EXE AND WYE** **31 DECEMBER 1999**

Description	Ledger balances		Adjustments		Profit and loss		Balance sheet	
	Dr £	*Cr* £	*Dr* £	*Cr* £	*Dr* £	*Cr* £	*Dr* £	*Cr* £
Stock at 1 Jan 1999	5,000				5,000			
Sales		50,000				50,000		
Purchases	30,000				30,000			
Vehicles	20,000						20,000	
Provision for depreciation: vehicles		8,000		4,000				12,000
Office equipment	5,000						5,000	
Provision for depreciation: office equipment		2,000		1,000				3,000
Expenses	10,000				10,000			
Debtors	6,000						6,000	
Creditors		4,000						4,000
Value Added Tax		1,000						1,000
Bank	2,000						2,000	
Capital account: Exe		10,000						10,000
Capital account: Wye		10,000						10,000
Current account: Exe		3,000						3,000
Current account: Wye		500						500
Drawings: Exe	6,000						6,000	
Drawings: Wye	4,500						4,500	
Closing stock: Profit and loss				10,000		10,000		
Closing stock: Balance sheet			10,000				10,000	
Depreciation			5,000		5,000			
Net profit/loss: Exe					5,000			5,000
Net profit/loss: Wye					5,000			5,000
	88,500	88,500	15,000	15,000	60,000	60,000	53,500	53,500

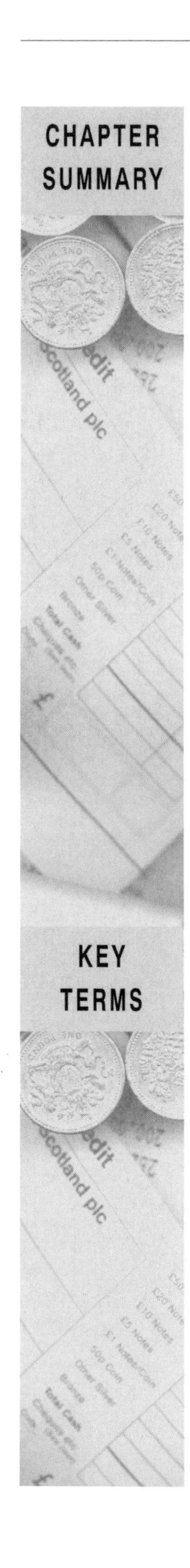

CHAPTER SUMMARY

- A partnership is formed when two or more (usually up to a maximum of twenty) people set up in business.
- The Partnership Act 1890 states certain accounting rules, principally that profits and losses must be shared equally.
- Many partnerships over-ride the accounting rules of the Act by making a partnership agreement which covers:
  - division of profits and losses between partners
  - partners' salaries/commissions
  - whether interest is to be allowed on capital, and at what rate
  - whether interest is to be charged on partners' drawings, and at what rate
- The usual way to account for partners' capital is to maintain a fixed capital account for each partner. This is complemented by a fluctuating current account which is used as a working account for share of profits, drawings, etc.
- The final accounts of partnerships are similar to those of sole traders, but incorporate:
  - an appropriation section, as a continuation of the profit and loss account, to show the share of profits and losses
  - individual capital and current accounts for each partner shown in the balance sheet

KEY TERMS

partnership the relation which subsists between persons carrying on a business in common with a view of profit

Partnership Act 1890 legislation which includes the accounting rules of partnerships

partnership agreement agreement between the partners which, amongst other things, often varies the accounting rules of the Partnership Act

capital account account which records the amount of capital contributed by a partner; usually for a fixed amount, which only alters where a permanent increase or decrease takes place

current account a fluctuating account to which is credited: share of profits, salary (if any), interest allowed on capital, and to which is debited: share of losses, drawings and interest charged on partner's drawings

appropriation section section of the profit and loss account which shows how the net profit is shared amongst the partners

STUDENT ACTIVITIES

The answers to these Student Activities are printed in the back of this book. Further questions and more fully extended Student Activities and Assessments are to be found in the accompanying Osborne Books' text *Financial Accounting Workbook*.

14.1 In the absence of a partnership agreement, which one of the following contravenes the provisions of the Partnership Act 1890?

(a) no partner is entitled to a salary

(b) profits and losses are to be shared in proportion to capital

(c) partners are not entitled to receive interest on their capital

(d) interest is not to be charged on partners' drawings

Answer (a) or (b) or (c) or (d)

14.2 The current account of a partner, Tara Shah, has a balance at the beginning of the financial year of £550 debit. During the year, the following transactions pass through her current account:

- interest on capital account, £900
- salary, £10,000
- drawings, £14,000
- interest on drawings,£275
- share of profits, £4,230

What is the balance of Tara Shah's current account at the end of the financial year?

(a) £305 Cr

(b) £855 Cr

(c) £1,405 Cr

(d) £1,495 Cr

Answer (a) or (b) or (c) or (d)

14.3 Lysa and Mark are in partnership and own a shop, 'Trends', which sells fashionable teenage clothes. The following figures are extracted from their accounts for the year ended 31 December 1998:

	£	
Capital accounts at 1 January 1998:		
Lysa	50,000	Cr
Mark	40,000	Cr
Current accounts at 1 January 1998:		
Lysa	420	Cr
Mark	1,780	Cr
Drawings for the year:		
Lysa	13,000	
Mark	12,250	
Interest on capital for the year:		
Lysa	2,500	
Mark	2,000	

Share of profits for the year:	
Lysa	9,300
Mark	9,300

Notes:

- no partner is entitled to a salary
- there is no interest charged on drawings

You are to show the partners' capital and current accounts for the year ended 31 December 1998.

14.4 John James and Steven Hill are in partnership and own a wine shop called 'Grapes'. The following trial balance has been taken from their accounts for the year ended 31 December 1998, after the calculation of gross profit:

	Dr	*Cr*
	£	£
Capital accounts:		
James		38,000
Hill		32,000
Current accounts:		
James	3,000	
Hill		1,000
Drawings:		
James	14,000	
Hill	18,000	
Gross profit		89,000
Rent and rates	7,500	
Advertising	12,000	
Heat and light	3,500	
Wages and salaries	18,000	
Sundry expenses	4,000	
Shop fittings at cost	20,000	
*Stock at 31 December 1998	35,000	
Bank	29,000	
Debtors	6,000	
Creditors		8,000
Value Added Tax		2,000
	170,000	170,000

* Closing stock is included in the trial balance because gross profit for the year has already been calculated.

Notes at 31 December 1998:

- profits and losses are to be shared equally
- depreciation is to be charged on the shop fittings at 10% per year

You are to:

(a) prepare the figures for the partnership final accounts for the year ended 31 December 1998, using the extended trial balance method

(b) show the partners' capital and current accounts for the year ended 31 December 1998

15 MANUFACTURING ACCOUNTS

this chapter covers . . .

In previous chapters we have concerned ourselves with the accounts of businesses that trade, ie buy and sell goods without carrying out a manufacturing process. However, many firms buy raw materials and manufacture products which are then sold as finished goods. The final accounts for a manufacturer include a manufacturing account which brings together all the elements of cost making up the production cost. In this chapter we will:

- *consider the manufacturing process*
- *study the elements of cost*
- *prepare a manufacturing account*

NVQ PERFORMANCE CRITERIA COVERED

unit 4: MAINTAINING FINANCIAL RECORDS AND PREPARING ACCOUNTS

element 3

collect and collate information for the preparation of final accounts

❏ *all relevant information is correctly identified and recorded*

❏ *the organisation's policies, regulations, procedures and timescales relating to preparing final accounts are observed*

element 4

prepare the extended trial balance

❏ *an agreed valuation of closing stock is correctly entered on the extended trial balance*

❏ *the extended trial balance is accurately extended and totalled*

THE MANUFACTURING PROCESS AND ELEMENTS OF COST

The diagram below shows, in outline, the manufacturing process and the costs incurred at each stage.

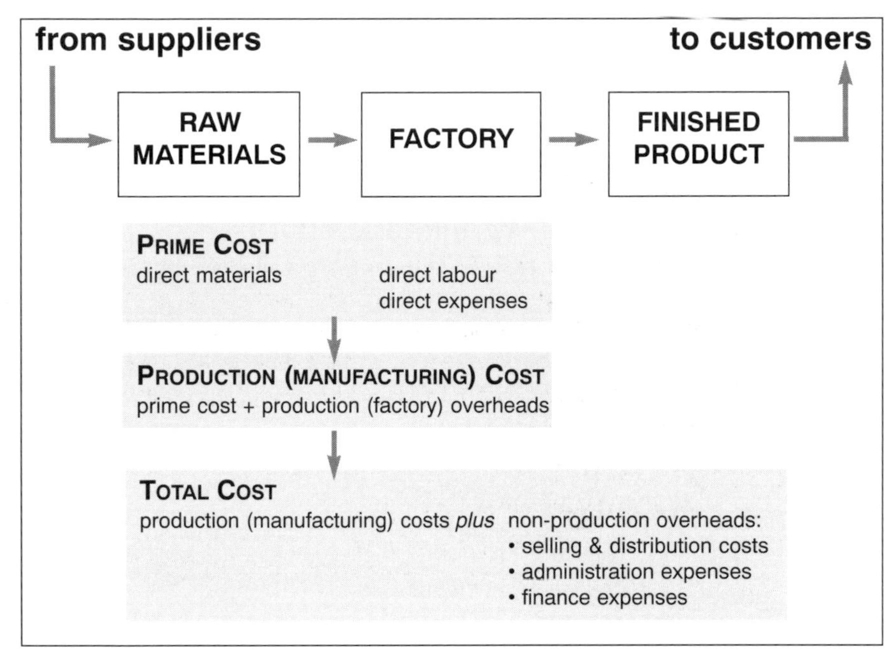

the manufacturing process and the costs incurred at each stage

Note that there are four main elements of cost which make up the manufacturing (or production) cost for a manufacturer:

1 **direct materials** – these are the raw materials that are required in manufacturing the finished product

2 **direct labour** – this is the cost of the workforce engaged in production, eg machine operators (note that the wages of factory supervisors are a production overhead expense and are usually described as 'indirect labour')

3 **direct expenses** – these include any special costs that can be identified with each unit produced, eg a royalty payable to the designer of the product for each unit made, or the hire of specialist machinery to carry out a particular manufacturing task

4 **production (factory) overheads** – all the other costs of manufacture, eg wages of supervisors, rent of factory, depreciation of factory machinery, heating and lighting of factory

Prime cost is the basic cost of manufacturing a product before the addition of production overheads. It consists of the first three costs, ie

direct materials + direct labour + direct expenses = prime cost

Production cost is the factory cost of making the product after the addition of production overheads, and is:

prime cost + production (factory) overheads = production (or manufacturing) cost

MANUFACTURING ACCOUNT

The final accounts of a manufacturer are structured as follows:

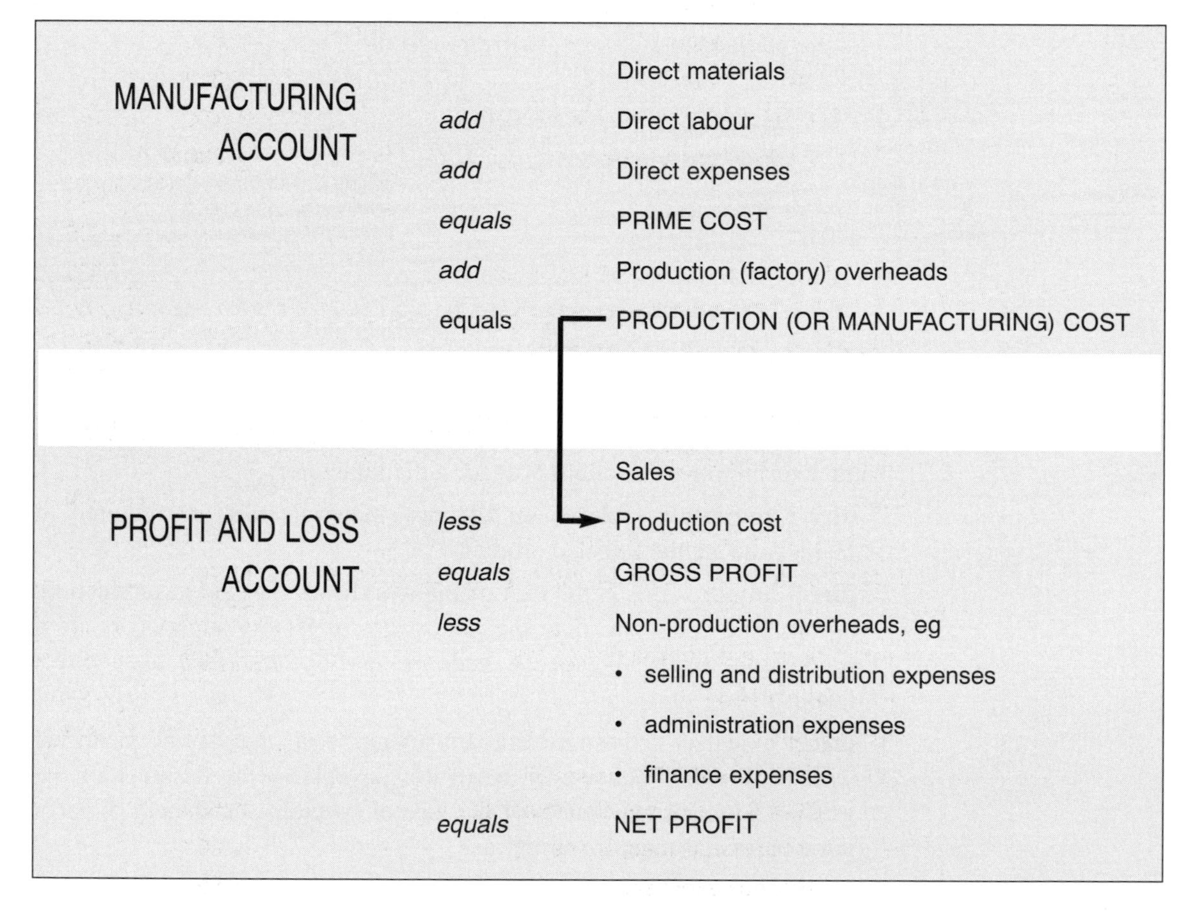

The layout of a manufacturing and profit and loss account (with figures) is shown on the next page. Study the format and read the notes that follow.

ALPHA MANUFACTURING COMPANY

MANUFACTURING AND PROFIT AND LOSS ACCOUNT

for the year ended 31 December 1999

	£	£
Opening stock of raw materials		5,000
Add Purchases of raw materials		50,000
		55,000
Less Closing stock of raw materials		6,000
COST OF RAW MATERIALS USED		49,000
Direct labour		26,000
Direct expenses		2,500
PRIME COST		77,500
Add Production (factory) overheads:		
Indirect materials	2,000	
Indirect labour	16,000	
Rent of factory	5,000	
Depreciation of factory machinery	10,000	
Factory light and heat	4,000	
		37,000
		114,500
Add Opening stock of work-in-progress		4,000
		118,500
Less Closing stock of work-in-progress		3,000
PRODUCTION (OR MANUFACTURING) COST OF GOODS COMPLETED		115,500
Sales		195,500
Opening stock of finished goods	6,500	
Production (or manufacturing) cost of goods completed	115,500	
	122,000	
Less Closing stock of finished goods	7,500	
COST OF SALES		114,500
Gross profit		81,000
Less Non-production overheads:		
Selling and distribution expenses	38,500	
Administration expenses	32,000	
Finance expenses	3,500	
		74,000
Net profit		7,000

notes

- *Production cost (or manufacturing cost)* is the final figure of the manufacturing account.
- A manufacturing account forms one part of the year-end accounts for a manufacturing business, and precedes profit and loss account. The latter is prepared in the usual way except that production cost takes the place of purchases. However, some businesses both manufacture goods and buy in finished goods, in which case the figures will be shown for both production cost and purchases of goods for resale.
- In the profit and loss account, the opening and closing stocks are the *finished goods* held by a business.
- Manufacturing businesses usually hold stocks of goods in three different forms:
  - *raw materials:* commodities and components purchased from suppliers required in manufacturing the finished product
  - *work-in-progress:* products in course of manufacture at a particular moment in time
  - *finished goods:* products on which the manufacturing process has been completed and which are ready for sale

  Note that, with raw materials, there may be the cost of *carriage in* to be added, and an amount for *purchases returns* to be deducted.

  The first two stocks appear in the manufacturing account, while finished goods stock is in the profit and loss account.
- Certain expenses might be apportioned between the manufacturing account and the profit and loss account – for example, rates might be apportioned two-thirds to the factory (production overhead) and one-third to the office (non-production overhead).
- The balance sheet follows on from the manufacturing and profit and loss account and includes the closing stock valuation of *all three* forms of stock.

extended trial balance format

Final accounts for a manufacturer can also be prepared in extended trial balance format. The procedures are exactly the same as we have followed for sole traders; however, note the following:

- it is advisable to create a separate column for manufacturing account (which goes before profit and loss)
- stocks of raw materials and work-in-progress are shown in the manufacturing account and balance sheet columns
- stocks of finished goods are shown in the profit and loss and balance sheet columns

- the credit figure which balances the manufacturing account column is the production cost of goods completed; this is transferred into the profit and loss debit column
- the profit and loss column is completed as we have seen previously

unit cost of goods manufactured

When the production cost has been ascertained, the unit cost can be calculated as follows:

$$\textit{Unit cost} = \frac{\textit{Production cost of goods completed}}{\textit{Number of units completed}}$$

For example, if the manufacturing account on page 233 represented production of 200,000 units, the unit cost for the year was:

$$\textit{Unit cost} = \frac{\pounds 115{,}500}{200{,}000} = \pounds 0.58 \textit{ per unit}$$

closing stock valuation for a manufacturer

We saw earlier (Chapter 8) that, under SSAP 9, stock is normally valued *at the lower of cost and net realisable value.* This principle applies to a manufacturer for the three types of stock that may be held at the year-end:

- raw materials
- work-in-progress
- finished goods

For *raw materials*, the comparison is made between cost (which can be found using techniques such as FIFO, LIFO, or AVCO – see page 125) and net realisable value.

For stocks of both *work-in-progress* and *finished goods*, SSAP 9 requires that the cost valuation includes expenditure not only on direct materials but also on direct labour, direct expenses and production overheads. Thus for work-in-progress and finished goods, 'cost' comprises:

- direct materials
- direct labour
- direct expenses
- production overheads (to bring the product to its present location or condition)

Such 'cost' is then compared with net realisable value, and the lower figure is taken as the stock valuation (remember that different items or groups of stock are compared separately).

STOCK VALUATION – XYZ MANUFACTURING

situation

XYZ Manufacturing started in business on 1 July 1998 producing security devices for doors and windows. During the first year 2,000 units were sold and at the end of the year, on 30 June 1999, there were 200 finished units in stock and 20 units which were exactly half-finished as regards direct materials, direct labour and production overheads.

Costs for the first year were:

	£
Direct materials used	18,785
Direct labour	13,260
Production overheads	8,840
Non-production overheads	4,420
TOTAL COST FOR YEAR	45,305

At 30 June 1999 it was estimated that the net realisable value of each completed security device was £35. At the same date, the company holds stocks of raw materials as follows:

	cost	*net realisable value*
	£	£
Material X	1,400	1,480
Material Y	400	360
Material Z	260	280

Calculate the stock valuation at 30 June 1999 for:

- raw materials
- work-in-progress
- finished goods

solution

RAW MATERIALS

Using the SSAP 9 rule of 'the lower of cost and net realisable value' the total value is:

	£	
Material X	1,400	(cost)
Material Y	360	(net realisable value)
Material Z	260	(cost)
	2,020	

WORK-IN-PROGRESS

To calculate the value of work-in-progress and finished goods we need to know the production cost, ie direct materials, direct labour and production overheads. This is:

	£
Direct materials used	18,785
Direct labour	13,260
Production overheads	8,840
PRODUCTION COST FOR YEAR	40,885

All these costs must be included because they have been incurred in bringing the product to its present location or condition. Non-production overheads are not included because they are not directly related to production. Thus, a production cost of £40,885 has produced:

Units sold	2,000
Closing stock of completed units	200
Closing stock of work-in-progress –	
20 units exactly half-finished equals	
10 completed units	10
PRODUCTION FOR YEAR	2,210

The **cost per unit** is: $\frac{£40,885}{2,210}$ = **£18.50 per unit**

The 20 half-finished units have a cost of (20 ÷ 2) x £18.50 = **£185.** They have a net realisable value of (20 ÷ 2) x £35 = £350. The value of work-in-progress will, therefore, be shown in the accounts as £185, which is the lower of cost and net realisable value.

FINISHED GOODS

The completed units in stock at the end of the year have a production cost of 200 x £18.50 = £3,700, compared with a net realisable value of 200 x £35 = £7,000. Applying the rule of lower of cost and net realisable value, finished goods stock will be valued at **£3,700.**

TRANSFER PRICES AND FACTORY PROFIT

Some manufacturing businesses transfer completed goods from the factory to the warehouse at, for example, 'factory cost plus ten per cent' (the transfer price). The objective in doing this is for the factory to make a notional profit which is added into net profit at a later stage. This might enable the unit cost of goods manufactured to be compared with the cost of buying in completed goods from an outside source. Also, by showing a factory profit, the profit (or loss) from trading activities (as distinct from manufacturing) can be identified separately.

Referring back to the manufacturing account on page 233 and amending the figures to allow for a factory 'profit' of ten per cent, the final part of the manufacturing account, and the profit and loss account appear as follows:

	£	£
PRODUCTION COST		115,500
Factory profit of ten per cent		11,550
PRODUCTION COST OF GOODS COMPLETED (including profit)		127,050
Sales		195,500
Opening stock of finished goods	6,500	
Production (or manufacturing) cost of goods completed	127,050	
	133,550	
Less Closing stock of finished goods	7,500	
COST OF SALES		126,050
Gross profit		69,450
Less Non-production overheads:		
Selling and distribution expenses	38,500	
Administration expenses	32,000	
Finance expenses	3,500	
		74,000
Loss from trading		(4,550)
Add Factory profit		11,550
Net profit		7,000

Note that the final net profit is unchanged, but the manufacturing cost is higher, and gross profit is lower. The factory profit is added back in the profit and loss account, after showing separately the profit or loss from trading. The reason for doing this is to make the factory and the warehouse into separate profit centres.

provision for unrealised profit on finished goods stocks

A business using the 'factory profit' method may choose to value stocks of finished goods at *manufacturing cost plus manufacturing profit.* For example, the business whose manufacturing account is shown above, might value finished goods stocks as:

Opening stock

manufacturing cost (£6,500) + manufacturing profit of 10 per cent (£650) = £7,150

Closing stock

manufacturing cost (£7,500) + manufacturing profit of 10 per cent (£750) = £8,250

The logic behind valuing finished goods stocks in this way is to show more clearly the profit from the separate sections of the business, ie manufacturing and trading. It will apply particularly where goods are both manufactured *and* bought in as finished goods from outside manufacturers. The profit and loss account now compares 'like with like', ie own-manufactured goods are priced to include a profit, while the bought-in goods include the supplier's profit. At the end of the financial year the closing stock of own-manufactured goods includes an element of *unrealised profit.*

SSAP 9 requires that stocks should be shown in the balance sheet at cost price if purchased, or cost of production if manufactured. (Note that if realisable value is lower than cost, then this will be used instead.) In order to comply with SSAP 9, it is necessary to account for the element of unrealised profit included in the finished goods stock valuation. This is done through an account called *provision for unrealised profit,* which is used to adjust downwards the closing stock figure in the balance sheet to cost price.

For example, using the adjusted finished goods opening and closing stock figures of £7,150 (above) and £8,250 (which include manufacturing profits of £650 and £750 respectively), the provision for unrealised profit account appears as:

Dr	**Provision for Unrealised Profit Account**				Cr
1999		£	1999		£
31 Dec	Balance c/d (adjustment in respect of closing stock)	750	1 Jan	Balance b/d (adjustment in respect of opening stock)	650
			31 Dec	Profit and loss account	100
		750			750
2000			2000		
			1 Jan	Balance b/d	750

Note that the *increase* in provision for unrealised profit of £100 is shown as an expense in profit and loss account. It is recorded as a *deduction* from factory profit shown in the profit and loss account, eg

	£	£
Factory profit	11,550	
Less increase in provision for unrealised profit	100	
		11,450

If there is a fall in the value of finished goods stock during the year, then there will be a decrease in the provision for unrealised profit, and this will be *added* to the factory profit shown in the profit and loss account.

Stock account uses the finished goods stock valuations which include the manufacturing profit, as follows:

Stock Account

Dr					Cr
1999		£	1999		£
1 Jan	Balance b/d (opening stock)	7,150	31 Dec	Profit and loss account	7,150
31 Dec	Profit and loss account (closing stock)	8,250	31 Dec	Balance c/d	8,250
2000			2000		
1 Jan	Balance b/d	8,250			

The balance sheet figure at 31 December 1999 for finished goods stocks shows the net value, ie

	£
Finished goods stocks	8,250
Less Provision for unrealised profit	750
Net value	7,500

As can be seen this reduces the closing stock value of finished goods to cost price, and enables the balance sheet valuation to comply with SSAP 9.

CHAPTER SUMMARY

- A manufacturing account brings together all the elements of cost which make up production (or manufacturing) cost.
- A manufacturing account shows prime cost and the production (or manufacturing) cost.
- A manufacturer usually holds stock in three different forms:
  - raw materials, used in the calculation of cost of raw materials used
  - work-in-progress, used in the calculation of manufacturing (or production) cost
  - finished goods, used in the calculation of cost of sales
- Profit and loss account shows the non-production overheads.
- The stock valuation for a manufacturer is based on the SSAP 9 principle of 'at the lower of cost and net realisable value'. For work-in-progress and finished goods 'cost' will include production overheads.

- A transfer price is sometimes used to enable a factory to earn a notional profit.

  Manufacturing accounts provide an introduction to cost accounting. This type of accounting is covered in a further Unit of level 3 of NVQ Accounting, and by Osborne Books' *Costing, Reports & Returns Tutorial.*

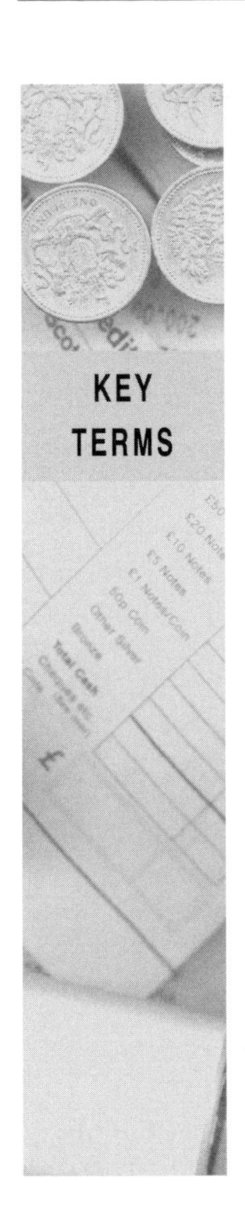

direct materials	the raw materials that are required in manufacturing the finished product
direct labour	the cost of the workforce engaged in production
direct expenses	special costs that can be identified with each unit produced
prime cost	direct materials + direct labour + direct expenses
production overheads	manufacturing costs other than prime cost
production (or manufacturing) cost	prime cost + production overheads
gross profit	sales – manufacturing cost
net profit	gross profit – non-production overheads
unit cost	manufacturing cost ÷ number of completed units
transfer price	price at which goods are transferred from the factory
factory profit	notional profit made by the factory when goods are transferred to the warehouse at above factory cost
unrealised profit	factory profit element of the valuation of finished goods stocks

STUDENT ACTIVITIES

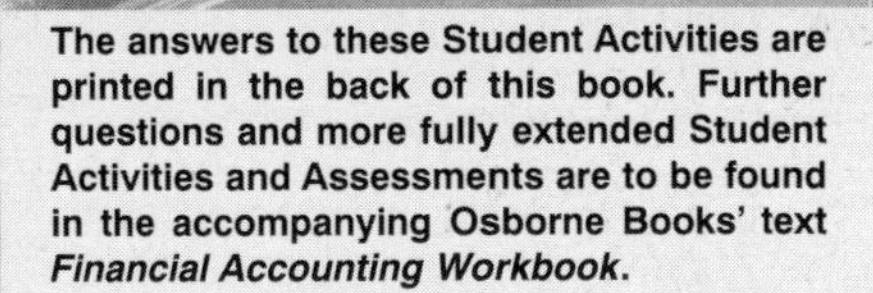

15.1 In manufacturing, direct materials + direct labour + direct expenses equals:

(a) production overheads

(b) prime cost

(c) production cost

(d) administration costs

Answer (a) or (b) or (c) or (d)

15.2 Which one of the following does not appear in a manufacturing account?

(a) depreciation of factory machinery

(b) supervisors' wages

(c) depreciation of office equipment

(d) factory heating and lighting

Answer (a) or (b) or (c) or (d)

15.3 For a manufacturing business, which type of stock is recorded in the profit and loss account?

(a) raw materials

(b) work-in-progress

(c) partly manufactured goods

(d) finished goods

Answer (a) or (b) or (c) or (d)

15.4 A business has the following unit costs for making its products:

Direct materials	£2.00 per unit
Direct labour	£3.00 per unit
Production overheads	£1.00 per unit
Non-production overheads	£1.00 per unit

Each unit sells for £15.

What is the correct valuation for completed units held in stock?

(a) £2

(b) £6

(c) £7

(d) £15

Answer (a) or (b) or (c) or (d)

15.5 Allocate the following costs to

- manufacturing account
- profit and loss account

(a) factory rent

(b) production supervisors' wages

(c) insurance of factory buildings

(d) depreciation of office photocopier

(e) sales commission

(f) raw materials purchased

(g) advertising

15.6 The following figures relate to the accounts of Barbara Francis, who operates a furniture manufacturing business, for the year ended 31 December 1998:

	£
Stocks of raw materials, 1 January 1998	31,860
Stocks of raw materials, 31 December 1998	44,790
Stocks of finished goods, 1 January 1998	42,640
Stocks of finished goods, 31 December 1998	96,510
Purchases of raw materials	237,660
Sale of finished goods	796,950
Rent and rates	32,920
Manufacturing wages	234,630
Manufacturing power	7,650
Manufacturing heat and light	2,370
Manufacturing sundry expenses and maintenance	8,190
Salaries	138,700
Advertising	22,170
Office expenses	7,860
Depreciation of manufacturing plant and machinery	7,450

Three-quarters of the rent and rates is to be treated as a manufacturing charge.

You are to prepare manufacturing and profit and loss accounts for the year-ended 31 December 1998, to show clearly:

- the cost of raw materials used
- prime cost
- cost of production (factory) overheads
- production cost of goods completed
- cost of sales
- gross profit for the year
- net profit for the year

Explain, by memorandum, to Miss Francis why you have presented the accounts in such a form, and what they show.

15.7 A manufacturer values the closing stock of finished goods at factory cost plus 20 per cent. For 1999 the opening and closing stocks (including profit of 20 per cent) were £12,000 and £18,000 respectively. Show the transactions on provision for unrealised profit account for the year ended 31 December 1999.

16 ACCOUNTING FOR CAPITAL TRANSACTIONS

this chapter covers . . .

Capital transactions concern all aspects of the acquisition and disposal of fixed assets. Because of the nature of capital transactions – their high cost and long-term use within the business – management keeps careful control over them. We will examine:

- *accounting entries to record acquisition, depreciation, and disposal of fixed assets*
- *the importance of distinguishing between capital expenditure and revenue expenditure*
- *acquisition and control of fixed assets, including the use of a fixed asset register*
- *accounting for research and development expenditure*
- *methods of financing capital expenditure*

NVQ PERFORMANCE CRITERIA COVERED

unit 4: MAINTAINING FINANCIAL RECORDS AND PREPARING ACCOUNTS

element 1

maintain records relating to capital acquisition and disposal

- ❑ *relevant details relating to capital expenditure are correctly entered in the appropriate records*
- ❑ *the organisation's records agree with the physical presence of capital items*
- ❑ *all acquisition and disposal costs and revenues are correctly identified and recorded in the appropriate records*
- ❑ *depreciation charges and other necessary entries and adjustments are correctly calculated and recorded in the appropriate records*
- ❑ *the records clearly show the prior authority for capital expenditure and disposal and indicate the approved method of funding and disposal*
- ❑ *profit and loss on disposal is correctly calculated and recorded in the appropriate records*
- ❑ *the organisation's policies and procedures relating to the maintenance of capital records are adhered to*
- ❑ *lack of agreement between physical items and records are identified and either resolved or referred to the appropriate person*
- ❑ *when possible, suggestions for improvements in the way the organisation maintains its capital records are made to the appropriate person*

CAPITAL TRANSACTIONS

Capital transactions concern all aspects of fixed assets – through purchasing, control and final disposal.

Fixed assets are described in FRS 15, 'Tangible fixed assets', as assets which "are held for use in the production or supply of goods or services . . . on a continuing basis in the reporting entity's activities." Examples of fixed assets include land, premises, vehicles, machinery, office, equipment, etc. These are *tangible fixed assets* which have a physical existence, ie they can be touched and felt. Assets which have no physical form are called *intangible fixed assets*; examples include:

- *goodwill* – the difference between the value of a business as a whole and the total value of its separate assets and liabilities (for example, an existing business is bought for £500,000, with the separate assets and liabilities being worth £450,000; goodwill is, therefore, £50,000); goodwill is the purchase cost of the connections and reputations of a business being acquired
- *development costs* – money that has been spent on developing new or improved products (can only be shown as a fixed asset if it is reasonably certain that the product will produce profits in the future – see also page 256)

Because of the nature of fixed assets – their high cost and long-term use within the business – management will keep careful control over capital transactions. For example, the purchase of a new computer system costing £50,000 will be authorised by a meeting of senior management; by contrast the purchase of new wastepaper baskets for the office at a cost of £50 will be authorised by the office supervisor.

Before we study the procedures for authorising the purchase, control and final disposal of fixed assets, we will look at a Case Study which shows the accounting entries to record the life of a fixed asset.

ACCOUNTING FOR FIXED ASSETS

situation

Eveshore Growers Limited is a co-operative venture which sells fruit, vegetables and flowers grown by its members in the Vale of Eveshore. The company's financial year end is 31 December.

On 4 January 1996 the company buys a Supra XG 5000 computer for use in the administration office. The cost is £2,000 + VAT at 17.5% (Eveshore Growers Limited is registered for VAT); the amount is paid by cheque.

The computer is depreciated using the straight-line method at a rate of 25 per cent each year. It is company policy to charge a full year's depreciation in the year of purchase, but none in the year of sale.

By mid-1999 the computer is beginning to show its age and it is decided to replace it by a more up-to-date model. The old computer is sold on 12 July 1999 for £400 + VAT at 17.5%, a cheque being received.

Show the journal and accounting entries to record:

- acquisition of the computer
- depreciation
- disposal

solution

The cost of the fixed asset is £2,000 + VAT (at 17.5%) of £350. This is entered in the journal as the primary accounting record and recorded in the double-entry accounts:

Date	Details	Folio	Dr	Cr
1996			£	£
4 Jan	Computer	GL	2,000	
	VAT	GL	350	
	Bank	CB		2,350
			2,350	2,350
	Purchase of Supra XG 5000 computer for use in the administration office; capital expenditure authorisation number 001/96			

Computer Account

Dr			Cr		
1996		£	1996		£
4 Jan	Bank	2,000			

Value Added Tax Account

Dr			Cr		
1996		£	1996		£
4 Jan	Bank	350			

Cash Book (payments)

		Cash	Bank	VAT	Purchases ledger	Sundry
1996		£	£	£	£	£
4 Jan	Computer		2,350	350		2,000

Note that, as Eveshore Growers Limited is registered for VAT, it will debit its VAT account with the tax. The amount is then included with VAT paid on inputs (purchases and expenses) and set-off against VAT charged on outputs (sales and services).

DEPRECIATION

Depreciation at 25 per cent straight-line per year is as follows:

year ended 31 December 1996	£500	(full year's depreciation)
year ended 31 December 1997	£500	
year ended 31 December 1998	£500	

Note that, following company policy, no depreciation is charged in 1999, being the year of sale.

Depreciation is recorded in the journal (first year only shown) and in the depreciation account, provision for depreciation and profit and loss accounts as follows:

Date	Details	Folio	Dr	Cr
1996			£	£
31 Dec	Profit and loss	GL	500	
	Depreciation	GL		500
	Depreciation charge for year on Supra XG 5000 computer			
31 Dec	Depreciation	GL	500	
	Provision for depreciation account – computer	GL		500
	Transfer of depreciation charge for year to provision for depreciation account			

Depreciation Account – Computer

Dr					Cr
1996		£	1996		£
31 Dec	Provision for dep'n	500	31 Dec	Profit and loss account	500
1997			1997		
31 Dec	Provision for dep'n	500	31 Dec	Profit and loss account	500
1998			1998		
31 Dec	Provision for dep'n	500	31 Dec	Profit and loss account	500

Provision for Depreciation Account – Computer

Dr		£			Cr £
1996		£	1996		£
31 Dec	Balance c/d	500	31 Dec	Dep'n account: computer	500
1997			1997		
31 Dec	Balance c/d	1,000	1 Jan	Balance b/d	500
			31 Dec	Dep'n account: computer	500
		1,000			1,000
1998			1998		
31 Dec	Balance c/d	1,000	1 Jan	Balance b/d	1,000
			31 Dec	Dep'n account: computer	500
		1,500			1,500
			1999		
			1 Jan	Balance b/d	1,500

PROFIT AND LOSS ACCOUNT (extracts)

	£	£
for the year ended 31 December 1996		
Depreciation – computer	500	
for the year ended 31 December 1997		
Depreciation – computer	500	
for the year ended 31 December 1998		
Depreciation – computer	500	

Notes:

- Each year's profit is reduced by the amount of the depreciation, ie £500
- The fixed asset account for the computer remains with the balance of £2,000, which is the cost price

The balance sheet shows for each year the net book value (cost, less provision for depreciation) reducing with each year's depreciation:

BALANCE SHEET (extracts)

	£ *Cost*	£ *Provision for dep'n*	£ *Net*
as at 31 December 1996			
Fixed assets			
Computer	2,000	500	1,500
as at 31 December 1997			
Computer	2,000	1,000	1,000
as at 31 December 1998			
Computer	2,000	1,500	500

DISPOSAL

The accounting entries to deal with the disposal of fixed assets have been described in Chapter 6 (page 92). The disposal account brings together

- the original cost of the computer
- provision for depreciation over the asset's life
- sale proceeds

The computer is sold for £400 + VAT at 17.5%; a cheque is received from the buyer. The transaction is recorded in the journal as the primary accounting record, and in the double-entry accounts as follows:

Date	Details	Folio	Dr	Cr
1999			£	£
12 Jul	Disposals	GL	2,000	
	Computer	GL		2,000
	Provision for depreciation account – computer	GL	1,500	
	Disposals	GL		1,500
	Bank	CB	470	
	Disposals	GL		400
	VAT	GL		70
	Profit and loss	GL	100	
	Disposals	GL		100
			4,070	4,070
	Sale of Supra XG 5000 computer; loss on sale of £100 transferred to profit and loss account			

Disposals Account – Computer

Dr			Cr		
1999		£	1999		£
12 Jul	Computer	2,000	12 Jul	Provision for dep'n	1,500
			12 Jul	Bank	400
			12 Jul	Profit and loss (loss on sale)	100
		2,000			2,000

Computer Account

Dr			Cr		
1999		£	1999		£
1 Jan	Balance b/d	2,000	12 Jul	Disposals	2,000

Dr		Provision for Depreciation Account – Computer			Cr
1999		£	1999		£
12 Jul	Disposals	1,500	1 Jan	Balance b/d	1,500

Dr		Value Added Tax Account			Cr
1999		£	1999		£
			12 Jul	Bank	70

Cash Book (receipts)

		Cash	Bank	VAT	Sales ledger	Sundry
1999		£	£	£	£	£
12 Jul	Disposals – computer		470	70		400

PROFIT AND LOSS ACCOUNT (extract)
for the year ended 31 December 1999

	£	£
Loss on sale of computer	100	

Notes:

- The 'loss on sale' of the computer (more correctly an underprovision of depreciation) is debited to the profit and loss account for the year
- If a 'profit on sale' (or overprovision of depreciation) had been made, ie a debit entry in disposals account, it will be credited to profit and loss account

CAPITAL EXPENDITURE AND REVENUE EXPENDITURE

The importance of distinguishing between capital expenditure and revenue expenditure has been highlighted in Chapter 8 (page 128). For example, the purchase of the computer seen in the Case Study is capital expenditure, which is recorded as a fixed asset of the business. Certain costs associated with the delivery and installation of the fixed asset can be capitalised (ie included in the cost of the fixed asset) – for guidance, see the diagram on page 129.

Most fixed assets are depreciated – thus the costs of the assets are spread over the period during which they are used by the business.

The sale proceeds, or part exchange value, must be accounted for correctly through disposals account (see page 92). At the same time, the fixed asset register must be updated to record the disposal, and any profit or loss on sale taken to profit and loss account.

FRS 15 'TANGIBLE FIXED ASSETS'

In accounting for fixed assets, most businesses follow the requirements of FRS 15, the main points of which are:

- all fixed assets having a known useful economic life are to be depreciated (freehold land is not usually depreciated – unless it is a mine or a quarry)
- any acceptable depreciation method may be used to spread the cost of the fixed asset over its estimated useful economic life
- depreciation amounts are normally based on the cost of the fixed assets; where assets are revalued (ie increased in value) depreciation is based on the revalued amount
- where an asset is thought to have fallen below its net book value (eg the asset has been superseded by new technology), it should be written down to its estimated value and then depreciated over its remaining useful life
- a change in the method of calculating depreciation (eg from reducing balance to straight-line) can be implemented – the asset's remaining book value is to be written off over its remaining useful life
- a note to the accounts must show the depreciation method used for each class of fixed asset, together with the depreciation method used, and the useful economic life or depreciation rates used

SSAP 13 'ACCOUNTING FOR RESEARCH AND DEVELOPMENT'

The accounting treatment of research and development expenditure can lead to the creation of an intangible fixed asset when it is not fully written off to profit and loss account in the year in which it is incurred.

SSAP 13 sets out three categories of research and development expenditure:

- *pure research* – experimental or theoretical work undertaken to acquire knowledge for its own sake rather than directed to a specific aim or application
- *applied research* – investigation undertaken to gain new knowledge which is directed to a specific practical aim or objective
- *development* – the use of knowledge to develop new or improved products

SSAP 13 requires that expenditure on pure and applied research is to be written off to profit and loss account as revenue expenditure. However, capital expenditure on fixed assets – such as a new research laboratory – is to be recorded as fixed assets and depreciated over the useful lives of the assets.

Development expenditure should, generally, be written off to profit and loss account as it is incurred. It may, however, be *capitalised* and treated as an intangible fixed asset if it relates to an ultimately profitable project. The criteria for this are:

- there is a clearly defined project
- the related expenditure is separately identifiable
- the outcome of such a project has been examined for its technical feasibility and its ultimate commercial viability

Provided these criteria can be established, the development expenditure can be capitalised as an intangible fixed asset and recorded on the balance sheet. The asset will then be amortised (depreciated down to zero) in proportion to sales of the product as they materialise.

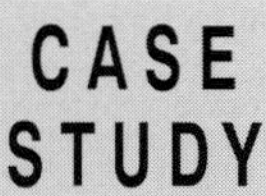

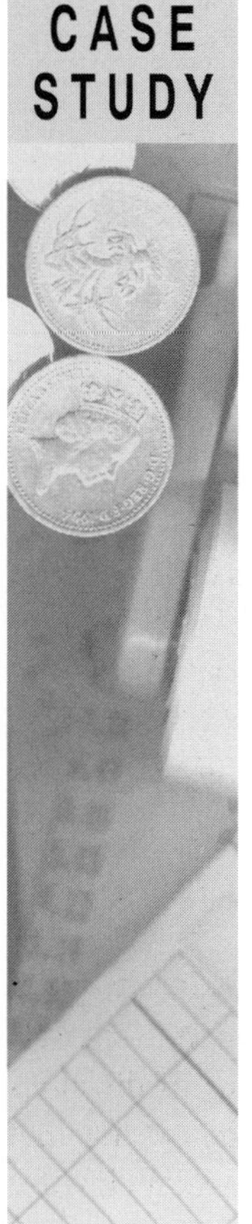

RESEARCH AND DEVELOPMENT

situation

Wyvern Agrochemical Company Limited has the following account in its book-keeping system:

Dr	**Research and Development Expenditure Account**			Cr
1998		£	1998	£
24 Mar	Bank (research)	24,000		
18 Nov	Bank (development)	40,000		

The development costs have been incurred in respect of a new agricultural chemical, WACL X123. This product has been on sale since 1 January 1999 and sales in the first few weeks look very promising.

It is now February 1999 and you are preparing the company's accounts for the financial year ended 31 December 1998. How will you deal with the research and development expenditure?

solution

The research expenditure of £24,000 will be charged as an overhead in the profit and loss account for the year ended 31 December 1998.

The development expenditure of £40,000 should be charged to profit and loss account unless it meets the criteria set out in SSAP 13. Here, the development of the new chemical does appear to be a clearly defined project, for which the related expenditure is separately identifiable, and for which the outcome is technically feasible and has commercial viability. Thus, the development expenditure can be capitalised and shown on Wyvern's balance sheet as an intangible fixed asset with a value of £40,000 at 31 December 1998. As the new chemical is now in production, the asset must now be amortised over its expected life, so the question for the following year's accounts will be to decide how long sales of the product will last – this will determine the amount of amortisation to be shown in the profit and loss account for the year ended 31 December 1999, and the reduced value of the intangible fixed asset for the year end balance sheet.

FINANCING CAPITAL EXPENDITURE

An important consideration with capital transactions is the way in which they are to be financed. Methods of raising the finance include:

- cash flow from retained profits
- sale of surplus assets
- part exchange of old assets
- capital/share issue
- bank overdrafts and loans
- hire purchase
- leasing

cash flow from retained profits

A business that is able to generate surplus cash from its trading activities may be able to fund part or all of capital expenditure requirements. However, this will reduce the amount of cash available for the payment of drawings or dividends to the owners/shareholders. Nevertheless, it is good financial management for some part of the costs of capital expenditure to be financed in this way.

sale of surplus assets

There is often scope to raise funds from the sale of surplus assets – ranging from the sale proceeds of old machinery and equipment, through to the sale of unused factory or office accommodation, and the sale of major divisions of the business as going concerns. Whilst the sale of old equipment may not realise much cash, a major reorganisation of the business may involve substantial income which can be used to fund capital expenditure programmes. Clearly, before it sells surplus assets, a business must ensure that it is not going to want to make use of them again in the future – when it would be much more expensive to buy them back again.

part exchange of old assets

There is often scope to raise funds from the part exchange of old assets. Whilst old assets may not be worth very much, they may be able to provide a deposit to enable new assets to be bought by means of a bank loan or hire purchase; indeed old assets may be worth more as a part exchange than as a sale on the open market. By using old assets as a deposit (or part deposit), the business can acquire new assets for minimal cash outlay, and will then be able to generate cash from increased output to meet the financing costs.

capital/share issue

Sole trader and partnership businesses might be able to increase their capital in order to fund capital expenditure. This means that the owner(s) must pay cash into the business from private savings or resources. In reality many sole traders and partners do not have spare cash to invest in their businesses.

For a limited company, capital can be increased by means of a further share issue. Typically, this will take the form of a *rights issue* by means of which shareholders are offered extra shares at a favourable price (usually a little below the current market price); the extra shares are offered in proportion to the shareholders' existing holding. The shareholder may take up the rights by subscribing for the shares offered; alternatively the rights can often be sold to other potential shareholders.

The disadvantage of increasing capital/share capital is that the money will be invested in the business on a semi-permanent basis (although it is possible to withdraw capital and to repay some types of shares). Instead, what is often needed for capital expenditure projects, is an initial contribution of cash which can then be repaid as the cash flow benefits of the project are received.

bank overdrafts and loans

Bank overdrafts are a relatively cheap source of short-term borrowing on a bank current account. They are not a suitable form of finance for long-term capital expenditure but, nevertheless, might be used to cover a short-term 'gap' between paying for capital expenditure and the receipt of the proceeds of the sale of surplus assets or a share issue. In final accounts, the interest charged each year by the bank on the overdraft is shown as an overhead in profit and loss account; the amount of the overdraft outstanding at the end of the financial year is shown as a current liability in the balance sheet.

A loan, or a commercial mortgage for the purchase of property, is more commonly used to fund capital expenditure. Facilities are available from banks, building societies, insurance companies, finance houses, and other providers.

Such a loan is available for a fixed amount of money for a medium-term, typically for between 3 and 10 years. It is used for the purchase of machinery or equipment. Interest is charged – usually at a fixed rate – and repayments are made by monthly or quarterly (three-monthly) instalments.

Business premises are usually bought by means of a commercial mortgage. The mortgage can be for up to 80% of the value of the property, repayable over a period of up to 25 years. The property is taken as security for the loan by the lender: this means that, if the business fails, the premises will be sold to repay the lender.

The interest charged each year by the lender for loans and commercial mortgages is shown as an overhead in profit and loss account. The amount of the debt outstanding at the end of the financial year is shown in the balance sheet – mostly as a long-term liability, but repayments of capital due within the next 12 months are shown as a current liability.

hire purchase

A hire purchase (HP) agreement from a finance company enables a business (the hirer) to have the use of a fixed asset on payment of a deposit. Regular instalment payments – monthly, quarterly or half-yearly – are made which pay back the cost plus interest over a set period. At the end of the hire purchase period, ownership of the asset passes from the finance company to the business. HP is often used to finance fixed assets such as vehicles, machinery, computers and office equipment.

In the accounts of the hirer, an asset being bought under an HP agreement is shown as a fixed asset on the balance sheet of the hirer, despite that, in legal terms, the owner is the finance company. The asset being bought on hire purchase is treated as a capital cost (capitalised) so that the hirer's final accounts show:

- in the balance sheet, the cost of the fixed asset (excluding interest), less provision for depreciation
- in the profit and loss account, interest due for the year to the HP company, together with depreciation for the year
- in the balance sheet a liability for future HP payments (excluding interest), divided between the current liabilities and long-term liabilities sections

leasing

Leasing arrangements are also used to finance fixed assets such as vehicles, machinery, computers and office equipment. With a leasing agreement, a business (the lessee) has the use of an asset bought by a finance company (the lessor). The lessee makes regular hire or rental payments to the lessor over the period of the lease, which might be up to seven years. Ownership of the asset never passes to the lessee.

There are two main types of lease:

- *operating lease* – a short-term lease under which the asset is likely to be hired to several lessees
- *finance lease* – a long-term lease under which the asset is likely to be rented to only one lessee

In the accounts of the lessee, with an operating lease the hire payments are shown in the profit and loss account as revenue expenditure. For finance leases, as with hire purchase contracts, the asset being leased is treated as a capital cost (capitalised) so that the lessee's final accounts show:

- in the balance sheet, the cost of the fixed asset (excluding interest), less provision for depreciation
- in the profit and loss account, interest due for the year to the lessor, together with depreciation for the year
- in the balance sheet a liability for future leasing payments (excluding interest) divided between current and long-term liabilities

CASE STUDY

ROCKET ENTERPRISES

situation

Jason Smythe runs a firework manufacturing business, Rocket Enterprises. At the end of his financial year on 31 December 1998, he has the following loans and overdraft:

- *commercial mortgage* – balance outstanding £55,250, of which he expects to repay capital of £1,750 in 1999; interest paid on the mortgage in 1998 was £4,450
- *bank loan* – balance outstanding £8,000, of which he expects to repay capital of £2,400 in 1999; interest paid on the loan in 1998 was £860
- *bank overdraft* – balance outstanding £4,850; interest paid on the overdraft in 1998 was £375

Show how the interest and loans will be recorded in the final accounts of Rocket Enterprises for the year ended 31 December 1998.

solution

PROFIT AND LOSS ACCOUNT (extract)
for the year ended 31 December 1998

	£	£
Overheads:		
Interest on commercial mortgage	4,450	
Interest on bank loan	860	
Interest on bank overdraft	375	

BALANCE SHEET (extract)
as at 31 December 1998

	£	£
Current liabilities		
Bank overdraft	4,850	
Commercial mortgage (1999 repayment)	1,750	
Bank loan (1999 repayment)	2,400	
Long-term liabilities		
Commercial mortgage (£55,250 – £1,750)	53,500	
Bank loan (£8,000 – £2,400)	5,600	

CHAPTER SUMMARY

- Capital transactions concern all aspects of fixed assets – through purchasing, control and final disposal.
- Tangible fixed assets – such as premises, vehicles, equipment – have a physical existence; intangible fixed assets – such as goodwill and development costs – have no physical form.
- A fixed asset register is often used to record details of fixed assets.
- Expenditure on pure and applied research is written off to profit and loss account as it is incurred.
- Development expenditure is *either* written off to profit and loss account as it is incurred *or* capitalised and treated as an intangible fixed asset.

  In the latter case certain criteria must be met; the asset will then be amortised in proportion to sales of the product as they materialise.
- Capital transactions can be financed from a variety of sources, including:

  cash flow from retained profits, sale of surplus assets, part exchange of old assets, capital/share issues, bank overdrafts and loans, hire purchase and leasing.

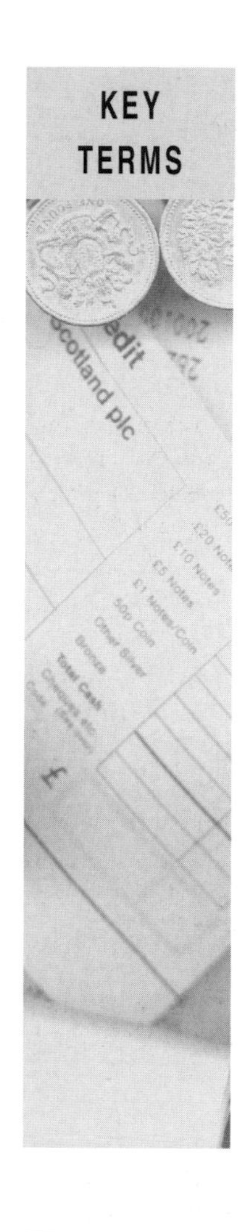

fixed assets	assets which "are held for use in the production or supply of goods or services . . . on a continuing basis in the reporting entity's activities" (FRS 15)
goodwill	the purchase cost of the connections and reputations of a business being acquired
fixed asset register	used for control purposes; records details of purchase, depreciation, disposal of all fixed assets owned by a business
pure research	experimental or theoretical work undertaken to acquire knowledge for its own sake
applied research	investigation undertaken to gain new knowledge directed to a specific practical aim or objective
development	the use of knowledge to develop new or improved products
amortisation	writing down fixed assets to zero over their life
hire purchase	agreement between a finance company and a hirer which enables the hirer to have the use of a fixed asset against a deposit and regular instalment payments
leasing	agreement between a finance company (lessor) and a business (lessee) which enables the lessee to have the use of a fixed asset against regular hire or rental payments
operating lease	a short-term lease under which the asset is likely to be hired to several lessees
finance lease	a long-term lease under which the asset is likely to be rented to only one lessee

STUDENT ACTIVITIES

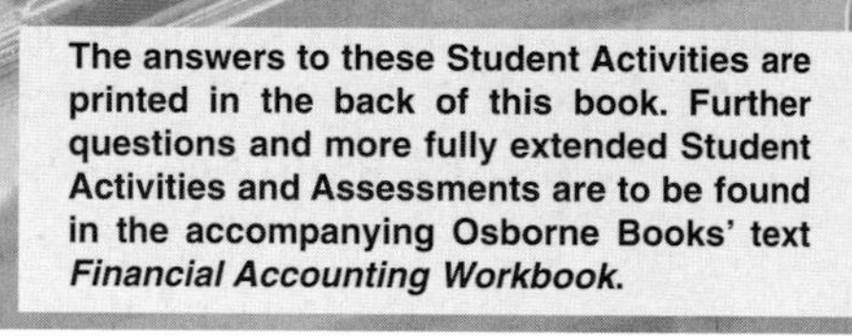

The answers to these Student Activities are printed in the back of this book. Further questions and more fully extended Student Activities and Assessments are to be found in the accompanying Osborne Books' text *Financial Accounting Workbook.*

16.1 Which one of the following is a tangible fixed asset?

(a) goodwill

(b) premises

(c) commercial mortgage

(d) development costs

Answer (a) or (b) or (c) or (d)

16.2 A finance lease is

(a) a short-term lease under which the asset is likely to be hired to several lessees

(b) a long-term lease under which the asset is likely to be rented to only one lessee

(c) a long-term lease over land

(d) a type of hire purchase contract

Answer (a) or (b) or (c) or (d)

16.3 Wyvern Alarms Limited is considering leasing a photocopier for use in the business. The managing director, Jemima Tomkinson, understands that leases are classified as operating leases or finance leases and that the two types affect the accounts of a business in different ways. She asks you "Which type of lease would have to be treated as a capital cost in the company's accounts?"

(a) finance lease

(b) operating lease

(c) both a finance lease and an operating lease

(d) neither a finance lease nor an operating lease

Answer (a) or (b) or (c) or (d)

16.4 (a) An extract from the fixed asset register of Wyvern Building Supplies is shown on the next page. You are to complete the register with depreciation on the fixed asset for the year ended 31 December 1998.

(b) The fixed asset is sold on 10 February 1999 for £500 (net of VAT); it is company policy not to charge depreciation in the year of sale. You are to complete the fixed asset register showing the profit or loss on sale.

16.5 QuickPrint Limited is a photographic processing company with a financial year end of 31 December. On 10 January 1997 it buys an automated machine to develop and print films; the cost is £32,000 (paid by cheque). The machine is expected to last for five years, after which its estimated value will be £2,500. Depreciation is charged at 40% each year, using the reducing balance method. It is company policy to charge a full year's depreciation in the year of purchase, but none in the year of sale.

The printing and developing machine works well but it is decided to replace it in 2000 by a more up-to-date model. The old machine is sold on 17 August 2000 for a part-exchange price of £5,000.

(a) You are to show the journal and accounting entries (cash book not required) to record the machine's:

- acquisition
- depreciation
- disposal

Note: VAT is to be ignored

(b) Draw up the page from the fixed asset register to show the machine's acquisition, depreciation and disposal. (A photocopiable register page is reproduced on page 309).

FIXED ASSET RECORD

No 67462874

Description Computer, Supra ML 6500

Location Office

Supplier Eveshore Computers Ltd

Date	Cost (net of VAT) £	Expected useful life	Estimated scrap value £	Depreciation method SL or RB	Percentage per annum	Depreciation for year £	Provision for dep'n £	Net book value £	Disposal proceeds (net of VAT) £	Profit/loss on sale £
1996										
12 Mar	*3,000*	*4 years*	*350*	*RB*	*50*					
31 Dec						*1,500*	*1,500*	*1,500*		
1997										
31 Dec						*750*	*2,250*	*750*		

16.6 John Aziz runs a taxi company called Silver Link Cabs. He started in business on 24 January 1996 when he bought two taxis, registration numbers N704 ZNP and N705 ZNP, at a cost of £15,000 each (paid by cheque).

John charges depreciation at the rate of 30 per cent each year, using the straight-line method. He charges a full year's depreciation in the year of purchase, but none in the year of sale.

On 17 February 1998 he buys another taxi, registration number R81 ZUY, at a cost of £17,500 (paid by cheque). On 13 October 1998 he sells N704 ZNP for £6,500 (a cheque being received).

You are to show the accounting entries (journal and cash book not required) to record the acquisition, depreciation and disposal of his taxis for the years ended 31 December 1996, 1997 and 1998.

Notes:

- VAT is to be ignored
- use one fixed asset account for all three taxis, one depreciation account, and one provision for depreciation account

16.7 The following information is taken from the accounting records of Wyvern Pharmaceutical Limited for the year ended 31 December 1998:

Revenue expenditure	£000s
• pure research	45
• applied research	172
• development	49

You are to:

(a) Define the terms

- pure research
- applied research
- development

in the context of standard accounting practice

(b) Show how each of the above items should be accounted for by Wyvern Pharmaceutical Ltd in its year-end accounts, in order to comply with standard accounting practice. Show any alternative permissible accounting treatments, and explain their effect on profit in the year ended 31 December 1998 and in future years.

ANSWERS TO STUDENT ACTIVITIES

CHAPTER 1: THE ACCOUNTING SYSTEM

1.1 (a) ledger (b) debtor (c) creditor (d) sales day book
(e) cash book (f) general nominal ledger (g) assets minus liabilities equals capital

1.2 (a) assets – items owned by a business; liabilities – items owed by a business
(b) debtors – individuals or businesses who owe money in respect of goods or services supplied by the business; creditors – individuals or businesses to whom money is owed by the business
(c) purchases – goods bought, either on credit or for cash, which are intended to be resold later; sales – the sale of goods, whether on credit or for cash, in which the business trades
(d) credit purchases – goods bought, with payment to be made at a later date; cash purchases – goods bought and paid for immediately

1.3 (a) asset of bank increases by £8,000
capital increases by £8,000
asset £8,000 – liability £0 = capital £8,000

(b) asset of computer increases by £4,000
asset of bank decreases by £4,000
asset £8,000 – liability £0 = capital £8,000

(c) asset of bank increases by £3,000
liability of loan increases by £3,000
asset £11,000 – liability £3,000 = capital £8,000

(d) asset of van increases by £6,000
asset of bank decreases by £6,000
asset £11,000 – liability £3,000 = capital £8,000

1.4

(a)	capital	£20,000
(b)	capital	£10,000
(c)	liabilities	£7,550
(d)	assets	£14,100
(e)	liabilities	£18,430
(f)	assets	£21,160

1.5 (a) Owner started in business with capital of £10,000 in the bank
(b) Bought office equipment for £2,000, paying by cheque
(c) Received a loan of £6,000 by cheque
(d) Bought a van for £10,000, paying by cheque
(e) Owner introduces £2,000 additional capital by cheque
(f) Loan repayment of £3,000 made by cheque

CHAPTER 2: DOUBLE-ENTRY BOOK-KEEPING

2.1 (d) **2.2** (b) **2.3** (d)

2.4 **JAMES ANDERSON (summary of transactions)**

Account	Dr 1998		£	Cr 1998		£
Capital Account				2 Feb	Bank	7,500
Computer	6 Feb	Bank	2,000			
Rent Paid	9 Feb	Bank	750			
Wages	12 Feb	Bank	425			
	25 Feb	Bank	380			
Bank Loan				13 Feb	Bank	2,500
Commission Rec'd				20 Feb	Bank	145
Drawings	23 Feb	Bank	200			
Van	27 Feb	Bank	6,000			

CHAPTER 3: BALANCING ACCOUNTS AND THE TRIAL BALANCE

3.1 (c) **3.2** (b) **3.3** (c)

3.4 (a) and (c) **ANDREW JOHNSTONE**

Bank Account

Dr 1999		£	Cr 1999		£
1 Jan	Capital	10,000	4 Jan	Rent paid	500
11 Jan	Sales	1,000	5 Jan	Shop fittings	1,500
12 Jan	Sales	1,250	20 Jan	Comp Supplies Ltd	5,000
22 Jan	Sales	1,450	31 Jan	Balance c/d	6,700
		13,700			13,700
1 Feb	Balance b/d	6,700	2 Feb	Rent paid	500
4 Feb	Sales	1,550	15 Feb	Shop fittings	850
10 Feb	Sales	1,300	27 Feb	Comp Supplies Ltd	6,350
12 Feb	Rowcester College	750	28 Feb	Balance c/d	5,300
19 Feb	Sales	1,600			
25 Feb	Sales	1,100			
		13,000			13,000
1 Mar	Balance b/d	5,300			

Capital Account

Dr 1999		£	Cr 1999		£
			1 Jan	Bank	10,000

Rent Paid Account

Dr 1999		£	Cr 1999		£
4 Jan	Bank	500	28 Feb	Balance c/d	1,000
2 Feb	Bank	500			
		1,000			1,000
1 Mar	Balance b/d	1,000			

Shop Fittings Account

Dr			Cr		
1999		£	1999		£
5 Jan	Bank	1,500	28 Feb	Balance c/d	2,350
15 Feb	Bank	850			
		2,350			2,350
1 Mar	Balance b/d	2,350			

Purchases Account

Dr			Cr		
1999		£	1999		£
7 Jan	Comp Supplies Ltd	5,000	31 Jan	Balance c/d	11,500
25 Jan	Comp Supplies Ltd	6,500			
		11,500			11,500
1 Feb	Balance b/d	11,500	28 Feb	Balance c/d	17,000
24 Feb	Comp Supplies Ltd	5,500			
		17,000			17,000
1 Mar	Balance b/d	17,000			

Comp Supplies Limited

Dr			Cr		
1999		£	1999		£
20 Jan	Bank	5,000	7 Jan	Purchases	5,000
31 Jan	Balance c/d	6,500	25 Jan	Purchases	6,500
		11,500			11,500
5 Feb	Purchases returns	150	1 Feb	Balance b/d	6,500
27 Feb	Bank	6,350	24 Feb	Purchases	5,500
28 Feb	Balance c/d	5,500			
		12,000			12,000
			1 Mar	Balance b/d	5,500

Sales Account

Dr			Cr		
1999		£	1999		£
31 Jan	Balance c/d	4,550	11 Jan	Bank	1,000
			12 Jan	Bank	1,250
			16 Jan	Rowcester College	850
			22 Jan	Bank	1,450
		4,550			4,550
28 Feb	Balance c/d	11,150	1 Feb	Balance b/d	4,550
			4 Feb	Bank	1,550
			10 Feb	Bank	1,300
			19 Feb	Bank	1,600
			25 Feb	Bank	1,100
			26 Feb	Rowcester College	1,050
		11,150			11,150
			1 Mar	Balance b/d	11,150

Dr		Rowcester College			Cr
1999		£	1999		£
16 Jan	Sales	850	27 Jan	Sales returns	100
			31 Jan	Balance c/d	750
		850			850
1 Feb	Balance b/d	750	12 Feb	Bank	750
26 Feb	Sales	1,050	28 Feb	Balance c/d	1,050
		1,800			1,800
1 Mar	Balance b/d	1,050			

Dr		Sales Returns Account			Cr
1999		£	1999		£
27 Jan	Rowcester College	100			

Dr		Purchases Returns Account			Cr
1999		£	1999		£
			5 Feb	Comp Supplies Ltd	150

(b) **Trial balance as at 31 January 1999**

	Dr	*Cr*
	£	£
Bank	6,700	
Capital		10,000
Rent paid	500	
Shop fittings	1,500	
Purchases	11,500	
Comp Supplies Limited		6,500
Sales		4,550
Rowcester College	750	
Sales returns	100	
	21,050	21,050

(d) **Trial balance as at 28 February 1999**

	Dr	*Cr*
	£	£
Bank	5,300	
Capital		10,000
Rent paid	1,000	
Shop fittings	2,350	
Purchases	17,000	
Comp Supplies Limited		5,500
Sales		11,150
Rowcester College	1,050	
Sales returns	100	
Purchases returns		150
	26,800	26,800

CHAPTER 4: FINAL ACCOUNTS – THE EXTENDED TRIAL BALANCE

4.1 (b) **4.2** (d)

4.3 Business A: net profit £40,000; capital £100,000
Business B: expenses £70,000; liabilities £100,000
Business C: income £70,000; assets £90,000
Business D: expenses £75,000; liabilities £60,000
Business E: net loss £10,000; assets £100,000

4.4

				FINAL ACCOUNTS			
		TRIAL BALANCE		PROFIT & LOSS		BALANCE SHEET	
		Debit	Credit	Debit	Credit	Debit	Credit
(a)	Salaries	✓		✓			
(b)	Purchases	✓		✓			
(c)	Debtors	✓				✓	
(d)	Sales returns	✓		✓			
(e)	Discount received		✓		✓		
(f)	Motor vehicle	✓				✓	
(g)	Capital		✓				✓

4.5 EXTENDED TRIAL BALANCE NICK JOHNSON 31 DECEMBER 1998

Description	Ledger balances		Adjustments		Profit and loss		Balance sheet	
	Dr £	Cr £	Dr £	Cr £	Dr £	Cr £	Dr £	Cr £
Stocks at 1 Jan 1998	25,000				25,000			
Purchases	210,000				210,000			
Sales		310,000				310,000		
Administration expenses	12,400				12,400			
Wages	41,000				41,000			
Rent paid	7,500				7,500			
Telephone	1,000				1,000			
Interest paid	9,000				9,000			
Travel expenses	1,100				1,100			
Premises	200,000						200,000	
Machinery	40,000						40,000	
Debtors	31,000						31,000	
Bank	900						900	
Cash	100						100	
Capital		150,000						150,000
Drawings	14,000						14,000	
Loan from bank		100,000						100,000
Creditors		29,000						29,000
Value Added Tax		4,000						4,000
Closing stock: Profit & loss				21,000		21,000		
Closing stock: Balance sheet			21,000				21,000	
Net profit/loss					24,000			24,000
	593,000	593,000	21,000	21,000	331,000	331,000	307,000	307,000

4.6 EXTENDED TRIAL BALANCE **ALAN HARRIS** **30 JUNE 1998**

Description	Ledger balances		Adjustments		Profit and loss		Balance sheet	
	Dr £	Cr £	Dr £	Cr £	Dr £	Cr £	Dr £	Cr £
Stocks at 1 July 1997	13,250				13,250			
Capital		70,000						70,000
Premises	65,000						65,000	
Motor vehicle	5,250						5,250	
Purchases	55,000				55,000			
Sales		85,500				85,500		
Administration expenses	850				850			
Wages	9,220				9,220			
Rent paid	1,200				1,200			
Telephone	680				680			
Interest paid	120				120			
Travel expenses	330				330			
Debtors	1,350						1,350	
Creditors		6,400						6,400
Value Added Tax		1,150						1,150
Bank	2,100						2,100	
Cash	600						600	
Drawings	8,100						8,100	
Closing stock: Profit & loss				18,100		18,100		
Closing stock: Balance sheet			18,100				18,100	
Net profit/loss					22,950			22,950
	163,050	163,050	18,100	18,100	103,600	103,600	100,500	100,500

CHAPTER 5: ACCRUALS AND PREPAYMENTS

5.1 (d) **5.2** (c)

5.3

Vehicle Expenses Account

Dr			Cr		
1999		£	1999		£
31 Dec	Balance b/d	1,680	31 Dec	Drawings	420
			31 Dec	Profit and loss account	1,260
		1,680			1,680

5.4

Insurance Claims Account

Dr			Cr		
1999		£	1998		£
17 Dec	Purchases	845			

Purchases

Dr			Cr		
1999		£	1998		£
			17 Dec	Insurance claims	845

If the amount is not paid by 31 December 1998, the balance sheet will show the amount of insurance claims account as a current asset.

5.5 (a) Overhead in profit and loss account of £56,760; balance sheet shows accruals account (current liability) of £1,120.

(b) Overhead in profit and loss account of £2,852 (ie £3,565 – £713); balance sheet shows prepayments account (current asset) of £713.

(c) Overhead in profit and loss account of £1,800; balance sheet shows prepayments account (current asset) of £150.

5.6 EXTENDED TRIAL BALANCE DON SMITH 31 DECEMBER 1998

Description	Ledger balances		Adjustments		Profit and loss		Balance sheet	
	Dr £	Cr £	Dr £	Cr £	Dr £	Cr £	Dr £	Cr £
Debtors	24,325						24,325	
Creditors		15,408						15,408
Value Added Tax		4,276						4,276
Capital		30,000						30,000
Bank		1,083						1,083
Rent and rates	10,862			250	10,612			
Electricity	2,054		110		2,164			
Telephone	1,695				1,695			
Salaries	55,891		365		56,256			
Motor vehicles	22,250						22,250	
Office equipment	7,500						7,500	
Motor vehicle expenses	10,855				10,855			
Drawings	15,275						15,275	
Discount allowed	478				478			
Discount received		591				591		
Purchases	138,960				138,960			
Sales		257,258				257,258		
Stock at 1 Jan 1998	18,471				18,471			
Closing stock: Profit & loss				14,075		14,075		
Closing stock: Balance sheet			14,075				14,075	
Accruals				475				475
Prepayments			250				250	
Net profit/loss					32,433			32,433
	308,616	308,616	14,800	14,800	271,924	271,924	83,675	83,675

5.7 EXTENDED TRIAL BALANCE JOHN BARCLAY 30 JUNE 1999

Description	Ledger balances		Adjustments		Profit and loss		Balance sheet	
	Dr £	Cr £	Dr £	Cr £	Dr £	Cr £	Dr £	Cr £
Sales		864,321				864,321		
Purchases	600,128			250	599,878			
Sales returns	2,746				2,746			
Purchases returns		3,894				3,894		
Office expenses	33,947			346	33,601			
Salaries	122,611				122,611			
Motor vehicle expenses	36,894		1,250		38,144			
Discount allowed	3,187				3,187			
Discount received		4,951				4,951		
Debtors and creditors	74,328	52,919					74,328	52,919
Value Added Tax		10,497						10,497
Stock at 1 July 1998	63,084				63,084			
Motor vehicles	83,500						83,500	
Office equipment	23,250						23,250	
Land and buildings	100,000						100,000	
Bank loan		75,000						75,000
Bank	1,197						1,197	
Capital		155,000						155,000
Drawings	21,710						21,710	
Closing stock: Profit & loss				66,941		66,941		
Closing stock: Balance sheet			66,941				66,941	
Accruals				1,250				1,250
Prepayments			346				346	
Drawings			250				250	
Net profit/loss					76,856			76,856
	1,166,582	1,166,582	68,787	68,787	940,107	940,107	371,522	371,522

CHAPTER 6: DEPRECIATION OF FIXED ASSETS

6.1 (a) **6.2** (c) **6.3** (c)

6.4 A letter incorporating the following points

- Straight-line method at 20% per year = depreciation of £200 per year
- Reducing balance method at 50% per year = depreciation of £500 for year 1, £250 for year 2, £125 for year 3, £62 for year 4, and £31 for year 5, leaving a small residual value of £32
- Either method acceptable
- The straight-line method will give larger profits for the first two years
- The cash position is not affected, as depreciation is a non-cash expense (this point should be stressed)

6.5

- With reducing balance depreciation a fixed percentage is written off the reduced balance of the asset each year.
- When compared with straight-line depreciation, reducing balance needs a much higher percentage to be written off each year to achieve the same residual value.
- Thus the money amounts for reducing balance are greater in the early years and smaller in the later years when compared with straight-line depreciation.

- As delivery vans depreciate more in the early years and are unlikely to be kept for the whole of their expected lives, reducing balance depreciation is a more accurate reflection of their worth than is straight-line depreciation.
- The depreciation charge will be high in the early years but smaller in the later years; by contrast repair costs are likely to be low early on but will increase in later years. By using reducing balance depreciation, the total charge to profit and loss account for both depreciation and repair costs is likely to be similar throughout the assets' lives.

6.6 (a)

Provision for Depreciation Account – Car

Dr					Cr
1998		£	1998		£
31 Dec	Balance c/d	3,000	31 Dec	Depreciation account	3,000
1999			1999		
31 Dec	Balance c/d	5,250	1 Jan	Balance b/d	3,000
			31 Dec	Depreciation account	2,250
		5,250			5,250
2000			2000		
31 Dec	Disposals account	6,937	1 Jan	Balance b/d	5,250
			31 Dec	Depreciation account	1,687
		6,937			6,937

(b)

MARTIN JACKSON
Balance sheet (extract) as at 31 December 1998

	£	£	£
	Cost	*Provision for dep'n*	*Net*
Fixed assets			
Car	12,000	3,000	9,000

Balance sheet (extract) as at 31 December 1999

	£	£	£
	Cost	*Provision for dep'n*	*Net*
Fixed assets			
Car	12,000	5,250	6,750

(c)

Disposals Account

Dr					Cr
2000		£	2000		£
31 Dec	Car account	12,000	31 Dec	Prov for dep'n account	6,937
31 Dec	Profit and loss account		31 Dec	Bank	5,500
	(profit on sale)	437			
		12,437			12,437

6.7 EXTENDED TRIAL BALANCE JOHN HENSON 31 DECEMBER 1998

Description	Ledger balances		Adjustments		Profit and loss		Balance sheet	
	Dr £	Cr £	Dr £	Cr £	Dr £	Cr £	Dr £	Cr £
Purchases	71,600				71,600			
Sales		122,000				122,000		
Stock at 1 Jan 1998	6,250				6,250			
Vehicle running expenses	1,480				1,480			
Rent and rates	5,650				5,650			
Office expenses	2,220				2,220			
Discount received		285				285		
Wages and salaries	18,950				18,950			
Office equipment	10,000						10,000	
Prov for dep'n: office equip				1,000				1,000
Vehicle	12,000						12,000	
Prov for dep'n: vehicle				3,000				3,000
Debtors	5,225						5,225	
Creditors		3,190						3,190
Value Added Tax		1,720						1,720
Capital		20,000						20,000
Drawings	13,095						13,095	
Bank	725						725	
Closing stock: Profit & loss				8,500		8,500		
Closing stock: Balance sheet			8,500				8,500	
Depreciation			4,000		4,000			
Net profit/loss					20,635			20,635
	147,195	147,195	12,500	12,500	130,785	130,785	49,545	49,545

6.8 EXTENDED TRIAL BALANCE HAZEL HARRIS 31 DECEMBER 1998

Description	Ledger balances		Adjustments		Profit and loss		Balance sheet	
	Dr £	Cr £	Dr £	Cr £	Dr £	Cr £	Dr £	Cr £
Bank loan		75,000						75,000
Capital		125,000						125,000
Purchases and sales	465,000	614,000			465,000	614,000		
Building repairs	8,480				8,480			
Motor vehicle	12,000						12,000	
Prov for dep'n: vehicle		2,400		2,400				4,800
Motor expenses	2,680				2,680			
Land and buildings	100,000						100,000	
Bank		2,000						2,000
Furniture and fittings	25,000						25,000	
Prov for dep'n: furn & fitts		2,500		2,500				5,000
Wages and salaries	86,060		3,180		89,240			
Discounts	10,610	8,140			10,610	8,140		
Drawings	24,000						24,000	
Rates and insurance	6,070			450	5,620			
Debtors and creditors	52,130	36,600					52,130	36,600
Value Added Tax		5,250						5,250
General expenses	15,860				15,860			
Stock at 1 Jan 1998	63,000				63,000			
Closing stock: Profit & loss				88,000		88,000		
Closing stock: Balance sheet			88,000				88,000	
Accruals				3,180				3,180
Prepayments			450				450	
Depreciation			4,900		4,900			
Net profit/loss					44,750			44,750
	870,890	870,890	96,530	96,530	710,140	710,140	301,580	301,580

CHAPTER 7: BAD DEBTS AND PROVISION FOR BAD DEBTS

7.1 (a)

7.2 (c)

7.3

- *Profit and loss account*
  debit bad debts written off, £210
  debit provision for bad debts: adjustment, £500
- *Balance sheet*
  debtors £20,000, less provision for bad debts £500, net debtors £19,500

7.4

Provision for Bad Debts Account

Dr		£			Cr £
1998/99		£	1998/99		£
30 Jun	Balance c/d	400	1 Jul	Balance b/d	300
			30 Jun	Prov for bad debts: adjustment *(increase in provision)*	100
		400			400
1999/2000			1999/2000		
30 Jun	Prov for bad debts: adjustment *(decrease in provision)*	50	1 Jul	Balance b/d	400
30 Jun	Balance c/d	350			
		400			400
2000/01			2000/01		
			1 Jul	Balance b/d	350

1999 *Extracts from final accounts produced for year ended 30 June:*

Profit and loss account: overhead cost of £100

Balance sheet: debtors £8,000 - £400 = £7,600

2000 *Extracts from final accounts produced for year ended 30 June:*

Profit and loss account: income of £50

Balance sheet: debtors £7,000 - £350 = £6,650

7.5 EXTENDED TRIAL BALANCE PAUL SANDERS 31 DECEMBER 1998

Description	Ledger balances		Adjustments		Profit and loss		Balance sheet	
	Dr £	Cr £	Dr £	Cr £	Dr £	Cr £	Dr £	Cr £
Purchases and sales	51,225	81,762			51,225	81,762		
Returns	186	254			186	254		
Stock at 1 Jan 1998	6,031				6,031			
Discounts	324	438			324	438		
Motor expenses	1,086				1,086			
Wages and salaries	20,379				20,379			
Electricity	876		102		978			
Telephone	1,241				1,241			
Rent and rates	4,565			251	4,314			
sundry expenses	732				732			
Bad debts written off	219				219			
Debtors and creditors	1,040	7,671					1,040	7,671
Value Added Tax		1,301						1,301
Bank	3,501						3,501	
Cash	21						21	
Motor vehicles	15,000						15,000	
Prov for dep'n: vehicles		3,000		3,000				6,000
Office equipment	10,000						10,000	
Prov for dep'n: equipment		5,000		1,000				6,000
Capital		25,000						25,000
Drawings	8,000						8,000	
Provision for bad debts				52				52
Closing stock: Profit & loss				8,210		8,210		
Closing stock: Balance sheet			8,210				8,210	
Accruals				102				102
Prepayments			251				251	
Depreciation			4,000		4,000			
Prov for bad debts:adjustment			52		52			
Net profit/loss						103	103	
	124,426	124,426	12,615	12,615	90,767	90,767	46,126	46,126

7.6 EXTENDED TRIAL BALANCE JAMES JENKINS 30 JUNE 1999

Description	Ledger balances		Adjustments		Profit and loss		Balance sheet	
	Dr £	Cr £	Dr £	Cr £	Dr £	Cr £	Dr £	Cr £
Capital		36,175						36,175
Drawings	19,050						19,050	
Purchases and sales	105,240	168,432			105,240	168,432		
Stock at 1 July 1998	9,427				9,427			
Debtors and creditors	3,840	5,294					3,840	5,294
Value Added Tax		1,492						1,492
Returns	975	1,237			975	1,237		
Discounts	127	643			127	643		
Wages and salaries	30,841				30,841			
Motor vehicle expenses	1,021		55		1,076			
Rent and rates	8,796			275	8,521			
Heating and lighting	1,840				1,840			
Telephone	355				355			
General expenses	1,752				1,752			
Bad debts written off	85				85			
Motor vehicle	8,000						8,000	
Prov for dep'n: vehicle		3,500		1,125				4,625
Shop fittings	6,000						6,000	
Prov for dep'n: shop fittings		2,000		600				2,600
Provision for bad debts		150	54					96
Cash	155						155	
Bank	21,419						21,419	
Closing stock: Profit & loss				11,517		11,517		
Closing stock: Balance sheet			11,517				11,517	
Accruals				55				55
Prepayments			275				275	
Depreciation			1,725		1,725			
Prov for bad debts:adjustment				54		54		
Net profit/loss					19,919			19,919
	218,923	218,923	13,626	13,626	181,883	181,883	70,256	70,256

CHAPTER 8: THE REGULATORY FRAMEWORK OF ACCOUNTING

8.1 (d)

8.2 (a) Prudence: by making a provision for bad debts the business is recording the possibility that the debtor may not pay.

(b) Materiality: although the video tapes will be kept for a number of years they are not treated as a fixed asset and depreciated because their cost is not material to the business.

(c) Consistency: the owner of the business should use the most appropriate depreciation method for the type of asset, and apply it consistently from year-to-year. In this way the accounts of different years are comparable; the accounting policy can be changed – for example, from one method of depreciation to another – provided there are good reasons for so doing, with a note to the final accounts explaining what has happened.

(d) Accruals (or matching): here the expense of electricity is being matched to the time period in which the cost was incurred.

8.3 (a) Consistency concept: he should continue to use reducing balance method (it won't make any difference to the bank manager anyway).

(b) Prudence concept: stock valuation should be at lower of cost and net realisable value, ie £10,000 in this case.

(c) Business entity concept: car is an asset of John's firm, not a personal asset (in any case personal assets, for sole traders and partnerships, might well be used to repay debts of firm).

(d) Prudence concept: the bad debt should be written off as a bad debt in profit and loss account (so reducing net profit), and the balance sheet figure for debtors should be £27,500 (which is closer to the amount he can expect to receive from debtors).

(e) Accruals concept: expenses and revenues must be matched, therefore it must go through the old year's accounts.

(f) Going concern concept: presumes that business will continue to trade in the foreseeable future: alternative is 'gone concern' and assets may have very different values.

8.4 (c)

8.5 (d)

8.6 (a) Sales for February: 24 tables at £50 each = £1,200

(b) Closing stock at 28 February: 6 tables at £31 each = £186

(c) Cost of sales for February:

	£
• opening stock	300
• plus purchases	632
• less closing stock	186
	746

8.7

	£	
• seeds	1,450	(selling price)
• fertilisers and insecticides	2,270	(cost price)
• tools	4,390	(cost price)
	8,110	

8.8 (a) this year's profit is overstated by £1,000

(b) next year's profit will be understated by £1,000

8.9

MEMORANDUM

Cost of computer accounting software

As the cost of the software is relatively low, I recommend that it is treated as revenue expenditure and shown amongst the overheads in profit and loss account. This is in line with the accounting concept of materiality: at a cost of £99 it is not worth recording it separately. Had the cost been much higher, the software would have been treated as a fixed asset and depreciated over its expected life.

8.10

- The first part of the statement is true – capital expenditure is money spent on fixed assets
- Whilst fixed assets are recorded in the balance sheet, there is a link with profit and loss account in that the annual depreciation will be recorded as an overhead
- As all fixed assets having a known useful economic life must be depreciated (FRS 15), there is a clear link between such fixed assets shown in the balance sheet and the annual depreciation recorded in profit and loss account
- On disposal of fixed assets the amount of over-provision or under-provision for depreciation is taken to the profit and loss account.

CHAPTER 9: CONTROL ACCOUNTS

9.1 (d)

9.2 (b)

9.3

Dr **Sales Ledger Control Account** Cr

1998		£	1998		£
1 Jun	Balances b/d	17,491	30 Jun	Sales returns	1,045
30 Jun	Credit sales	42,591	30 Jun	Payments received from debtors	39,024
			30 Jun	Cash discount allowed	593
			30 Jun	Bad debts written off	296
			30 Jun	Balances c/d	19,124
		60,082			60,082
1 Jul	Balances b/d	19,124			

9.4

Purchases Ledger Control Account

Dr			Cr		
1998		£	1998		£
30 Apr	Purchases returns	653	1 Apr	Balances b/d	14,275
30 Apr	Payments made to creditors	31,074	30 Apr	Credit purchases	36,592
30 Apr	Cash discount received	1,048			
30 Apr	Set-off: sales ledger	597			
30 Apr	Balances c/d	17,495			
		50,867			50,867
			1 May	Balances b/d	17,495

9.5 (a)

SALES LEDGER

Arrow Valley Retailers

Dr			Cr		
1998		£ p	1998		£ p
1 Feb	Balance b/d	826.40	20 Feb	Bank	805.74
3 Feb	Sales	338.59	20 Feb	Discount allowed	20.66
			28 Feb	Balance c/d	338.59
		1,164.99			1,164.99
1 Mar	Balance b/d	338.59			

B Brick (Builders) Limited

Dr			Cr		
1998		£ p	1998		£ p
1 Feb	Balance b/d	59.28	28 Feb	Bad debts written off	59.28

Mereford Manufacturing Company

Dr			Cr		
1998		£ p	1998		£ p
1 Feb	Balance b/d	293.49	24 Feb	Sales returns	56.29
3 Feb	Sales	127.48	28 Feb	Set-off: purchases ledger	364.68
		420.97			420.97

Redgrove Restorations

Dr			Cr		
1998		£ p	1998		£ p
1 Feb	Balance b/d	724.86	7 Feb	Sales returns	165.38
17 Feb	Sales	394.78	28 Feb	Balance c/d	954.26
		1,119.64			1,119.64
1 Mar	Balance b/d	954.26			

Dr		Wyvern Warehouse Limited			Cr
1998		£ p	1998		£ p
1 Feb	Balance b/d	108.40	15 Feb	Bank	105.69
17 Feb	Sales	427.91	15 Feb	Discount allowed	2.71
			28 Feb	Balance c/d	427.91
		536.31			536.31
1 Mar	Balance b/d	427.91			

(b)

Dr		Sales Ledger Control Account			Cr
1998		£ p	1998		£ p
1 Feb	Balances b/d	2,012.43	28 Feb	Sales returns	221.67
28 Feb	Credit sales	1,288.76	28 Feb	Cheques received from debtors	911.43
			28 Feb	Cash discount allowed	23.37
			28 Feb	Set-off: purchases ldgr.	364.68
			28 Feb	Bad debts written off	59.28
			28 Feb	Balances c/d	1,720.76
		3,301.19			3,301.19
1 Mar	Balances b/d	1,720.76			

(c) **Reconciliation of sales ledger control account with debtor balances**

	1 February 1998	*28 February 1998*
	£ p	£ p
Arrow Valley Retailers	826.40	338.59
B Brick (Builders) Limited	59.28	–
Mereford Manufacturing Company	293.49	nil
Redgrove Restorations	724.86	954.26
Wyvern Warehouse Limited	108.40	427.91
Sales ledger control account	2,012.43	1,720.76

CHAPTER 10: THE JOURNAL – CORRECTION OF ERRORS

10.1 (b)

10.2 (a)

10.3

Date	Details	Folio	Dr	Cr
1998			£	£
1 May	Motor vehicle	GL	6,500	
	Fixtures and fittings	GL	2,800	
	Stock	GL	4,100	
	Cash	CB	150	
	Loan from husband	GL		5,000
	Capital	GL		8,550
			13,550	13,550
	Assets and liabilities at the start of business			

10.4 (a) *error of omission*

Date	Details	Folio	Dr	Cr
			£	£
	Sales ledger control	GL	150	
	Sales	GL		150
	Sales invoice no .... omitted from the accounts: in the memorandum sales ledger – debit J Rigby £150			

(b) *mispost/error of commission*

Date	Details	Folio	Dr	Cr
			£	£
	Purchases ledger control	GL	125	
	Purchases ledger control	GL		125
	Correction of mispost – cheque no .....: in the memorandum purchases ledger – debit H Price Limited – credit H Prince			

(c) *error of principle*

Date	Details	Folio	Dr	Cr
			£	£
	Delivery van	GL	10,000	
	Vehicle expenses	GL		10,000
	Correction of error – vehicle no .... invoice no			

(d) *reversal of entries*

Date	Details	Folio	Dr	Cr
			£	£
	Postages	GL	55	
	Bank	CB		55
	Postages	GL	55	
	Bank	CB		55
			110	110
	Correction of reversal of entries on			

(e) *compensating error*

Date	Details	Folio	Dr	Cr
			£	£
	Purchases	GL	100	
	Purchases returns	GL		100
	Correction of under-cast on purchases account and purchases returns account on ....(date).......			

(f) *error of original entry*

Date	Details	Folio	Dr	Cr
			£	£
	Sales ledger control	GL	98	
	Bank	CB		98
	Bank	CB	89	
	Sales ledger control	GL		89
			187	187
	Correction of error – cheque for £89 received on ....(date).....: in the memorandum sales ledger *– debit L Johnson £98* *– credit L Johnson £89*			

10.5

	Date	Details	Folio	Dr	Cr
				£	£
(a)		Office expenses	GL	85	
		Suspense	GL		85
		Omission of entry in office expenses account – payment made by cheque no .... on			
(b)		Suspense	GL	78	
		Photocopying	GL		78
		Photocopying	GL	87	
		Suspense	GL		87
				165	165
		Payment for photocopying £87 (cheque no .... on ....) entered in photocopying account as £78 in error			
(c)		Suspense	GL	100	
		Sales returns	GL		100
		Overcast on ...(date)... now corrected			
(d)		Commission received	GL	25	
		Suspense	GL		25
		Commission received on .... entered twice in commission received account, now corrected			

Dr **Suspense Account** Cr

		£			£
1998		£	1998		£
30 Sep	Trial balance difference	19	(a)	Office expenses	85
(b)	Photocopying	78	(b)	Photocopying	87
(c)	Sales returns	100	(d)	Commission received	25
		197			197

10.6 (a)

Date	Details	Folio	Dr	Cr
1998			£	£
31 Dec	Stock	GL	22,600	
	Profit and loss	GL		22,600
	Stock valuation at 31 December 1998 transferred to profit and loss account			

(b)

Date	Details	Folio	Dr	Cr
1998			£	£
31 Dec	Profit and loss	GL	890	
	Telephone expenses	GL		890
	Transfer to profit and loss account of expenditure for the year			

(c)

Date	Details	Folio	Dr	Cr
1998			£	£
31 Dec	Profit and loss	GL	23,930	
	Salaries	GL		22,950
	Accruals	GL		980
			23,930	23,930
	Transfer to profit and loss account of expenditure for the year			

(d)

Date	Details	Folio	Dr	Cr
1998			£	£
31 Dec	Profit and loss	GL	1,160	
	Prepayments	GL	80	
	Photocopying expenses	GL		1,240
			1,240	1,240
	Transfer to profit and loss account of expenditure for the year			

(e)

Date	Details	Folio	Dr	Cr
1998			£	£
31 Dec	Drawings	GL	200	
	Motoring expenses	GL		200
	Transfer of private motoring to drawings account			

(f)

Date	Details	Folio	Dr	Cr
1998			£	£
31 Dec	Drawings	GL	175	
	Purchases	GL		175
	Goods taken for own use by the owner			

(g)

Date	Details	Folio	Dr	Cr
1998			£	£
31 Dec	Profit and loss	GL	500	
	Depreciation	GL		500
	Depreciation charge for year on fixtures and fittings			
31 Dec	Depreciation	GL	500	
	Provision for depreciation account – fixtures and fittings	GL		500
	Transfer of depreciation charge for year to provision for depreciation account			

(h)

Date	Details	Folio	Dr	Cr
1998			£	£
31 Dec	Disposals	GL	5,000	
	Machinery	GL		5,000
	Provision for depreciation account – machinery	GL	3,750	
	Disposals	GL		3,750
	Bank	CB	2,350	
	Disposals	GL		2,000
	VAT	GL		350
	Profit and loss	GL		750
	Disposals	GL	750	
			11,850	11,850
	Sale of machine no ....; profit on sale £750 transferred to profit and loss account			

(i)

Date	Details	Folio	Dr	Cr
1998			£	£
31 Dec	Bad debts written off	GL	125	
	Sales ledger control	GL		125
	Accounts written off as bad:			
	– Nick Marshall	*£55*		
	– Crabbe & Company	*£30*		
	– A Hunt	*£40*		
	Total	*£125*		
	see memo dated			
31 Dec	Profit and loss	GL	125	
	Bad debts written off	GL		125
	Transfer to profit and loss account of bad debts for the year			

(j)

Date	Details	Folio	Dr	Cr
1998			£	£
31 Dec	Profit and loss	GL		100
	Provision for bad debts: adjustment	GL	100	
	Decrease in provision for bad debts			
31 Dec	Provision for bad debts: adjustment	GL		100
	Provision for bad debts	GL	100	
	Transfer of reduction for year to provision for bad debts account			

CHAPTER 11: BANK RECONCILIATION STATEMENTS

11.1 (a) **11.2** (c)

11.3

TOM REID

BANK RECONCILIATION STATEMENT AS AT 31 DECEMBER 1999

		£
Balance at bank as per bank statement		207
Less:	unpresented cheque:	
	B Kay cheque no. 345126	20
		187
Add:	outstanding lodgement:	
	J Hill	13
Balance at bank as per cash book		200

11.4 (a)

Dr		Cash Book (bank columns)			Cr
1999		£	1999		£
1 May	Balance b/d	300	3 May	P Stone 867714	28
7 May	Cash	162	14 May	Alpha Ltd 867715	50
17 May	C Brewster	89	28 May	E Deakin 867716	110
24 May	Cash	60	17 May	Standing order: A-Z Insurance	25
28 May	Cash	40	31 May	Bank charges	10
			31 May	Balance c/d	428
		651			651
1 Jun	Balance b/d	428			

(b) **JANE DOYLE**

BANK RECONCILIATION STATEMENT AS AT 1 MAY 1999

	£
Balance at bank as per bank statement	326
Less: unpresented cheque:	
cheque no. 867713	80
	246
Add: outstanding lodgement	54
Balance at bank as per cash book	300

(c) **BANK RECONCILIATION STATEMENT AS AT 31 MAY 1999**

	£
Balance at bank as per bank statement	498
Less: unpresented cheque:	
E Deakin cheque no. 867716	110
	388
Add: outstanding lodgement:	
cash	40
Balance at bank as per cash book	428

CHAPTER 12: INCOMPLETE RECORDS

12.1 £260,000

12.2 £77,000

12.3 £21,100

12.4

		£
(a)	• receipts from sales	153,500
	• add debtors at year end	2,500
	• **sales for year**	156,000
(b)	• payments to suppliers	95,000
	• add creditors at year end	65,000
	• **purchases for year**	160,000
(c)	• payments for rent and rates	8,750
	• less rent prepaid at 31 Dec 1998	250
	• **rent and rates for year**	8,500
	• payments for wages	15,000
	• add wages accrued at 31 Dec 1998	550
	• **wages for year**	15,550

(d)

PROFIT AND LOSS ACCOUNT OF JANE PRICE
for the year ended 31 December 1998

	£	£
Sales		156,000
Purchases	160,000	
Less Closing stock	73,900	
Cost of sales		86,100
Gross profit		69,900
Less overheads:		
Advertising	4,830	
Rent and rates	8,500	
Wages	15,550	
General expenses	5,000	
Depreciation: shop fittings	10,000	
		43,880
Net profit		26,020

(e)/(f)

BALANCE SHEET OF JANE PRICE
as at 31 December 1998

	£	£	£
Fixed assets	*Cost*	*Provision for depreciation*	*Net*
Shop fittings	50,000	10,000	40,000
Current assets			
Stock		73,900	
Debtors		2,500	
Prepayment: rent		250	
Bank*		19,900	
		96,550	
Less Current liabilities			
Creditors	65,000		
Accrual: wages	550		
		65,550	
Working capital			31,000
NET ASSETS			71,000
FINANCED BY			
Capital			
Opening capital (introduced at start of year)			60,000
Add net profit			26,020
			86,020
Less drawings			15,020
Closing capital			71,000

* Cash book summary:

	£
• total receipts for year	213,500
• less total payments for year	193,600
• **balance at year end**	19,900

12.5

JAMES HARVEY
CALCULATION OF STOCK LOSS FOR THE YEAR

	£	£
Opening stock		21,500
Purchases		132,000
Cost of stock available for sale		153,500
Sales	180,000	
Less Normal gross profit margin (30%)	54,000	
Cost of sales		126,000
Estimated closing stock		27,500
Less Actual closing stock		26,000
Value of stock loss		1,500

CHAPTER 13: CLUB AND SOCIETY ACCOUNTS

13.1 (b) **13.2** (b) **13.3** (b)

13.4

Subscriptions Control Account

Dr			Cr		
1999		£	1999		£
1 Jan	Balance b/d (subscriptions owing)	2,750	1 Jan	Balance b/d (subscriptions prepaid)	1,250
31 Dec	Income and expenditure account (subscription income for year)	25,500	31 Dec	Subscriptions received in year	25,500
31 Dec	Balance c/d (subscriptions prepaid)	1,750	31 Dec	Balance c/d (subscriptions owing)	3,250
		30,000			30,000

Note: the subscription income for the year to be transferred to income and expenditure account, £25,500, is calculated as the 'missing figure'.

13.5 EXTENDED TRIAL BALANCE WESTSIDE SPORTS CLUB 30 JUNE 1999

Description	Ledger balances		Adjustments		Income & expenditure		Balance sheet	
	Dr £	Cr £	Dr £	Cr £	Dr £	Cr £	Dr £	Cr £
Subscriptions		1,540	80			1,460		
Competition entry fees		498				498		
Sale of snacks		1,108				1,108		
Equipment	1,500						1,500	
Prov for dep'n: equipment				300				300
Postage and stationery	197				197			
Rent	550		100		650			
Competition expenses	320				320			
Purchase of snacks	520				520			
Bank	59						59	
Closing stock: Inc & Exp				70		70		
Closing stock: Balance sheet			70				70	
Accruals				180				180
Depreciation			300		300			
Surplus/deficit					1,149			1,149
	3,146	3,146	550	550	3,136	3,136	1,629	1,629

13.6 EXTENDED TRIAL BALANCE HALLOW CHOIR 31 DECEMBER 1998

Description	Ledger balances		Adjustments		Income & expenditure		Balance sheet	
	Dr £	Cr £	Dr £	Cr £	Dr £	Cr £	Dr £	Cr £
Accumulated fund*		987						987
Music 875 + 450 =	1,325						1,325	
Prov for dep'n: music				200				200
Subscriptions		750	65			685		
Music festival prize		500				500		
Concert sales		825				825		
Raffles		427				427		
Concert costs	1,250				1,250			
Conductor's fee	300				300			
Printing of programmes	60		40		100			
Bank	554						554	
* Accumulated fund (1.1.98):								
Bank 112								
Music 875								
987								
Accruals				105				105
Depreciation			200		200			
Surplus/deficit					587			587
	3,489	3,489	305	305	2,437	2,437	1,879	1,879

13.7 EXTENDED TRIAL BALANCE SOUTHWICK SOCIAL CLUB 30 JUNE 1999

Description	Ledger balances		Adjustments		Income & expenditure		Balance sheet	
	Dr £	Cr £	Dr £	Cr £	Dr £	Cr £	Dr £	Cr £
Accumulated fund*		3,500						3,500
Stock at 1 July 1998	540				540			
Furn & equip 2,500 + 1,710 =	4,210						4,210	
Prov for dep'n: furn & equip				710				710
Subscriptions		2,790	210			2,580		
Bar takings		6,380				6,380		
Dinner dance ticket sales		790				790		
Bar purchases	3,975				3,975			
Dinner dance expenses	1,280				1,280			
Secretary's expenses	890				890			
Bar wages	1,530				1,530			
Rent 940 – 120 =	820		190		1,010			
Bank	215						215	
* Accumulated fund (1.7.98):								
Bank 580								
Bar stock 540								
Furn & equip 2,500								
3,620								
Rent owing 120								
3,500								
Closing stock: Inc & Exp				630		630		
Closing stock: Balance sheet			630				630	
Accruals				400				400
Prepayments								
Depreciation			710		710			
Surplus/deficit					445			445
	13,460	13,460	1,740	1,740	10,380	10,380	5,055	5,055

CHAPTER 14: PARTNERSHIP ACCOUNTS

14.1 (b) **14.2** (a)

14.3

Dr **Partners' Capital Accounts** Cr

		Lysa	Mark			Lysa	Mark
1998		£	£	1998		£	£
31 Dec	Balances c/d	50,000	40,000	1 Jan	Balances b/d	50,000	40,000
1999				1999			
				1 Jan	Balances b/d	50,000	40,000

Dr **Partners' Current Accounts** Cr

		Lysa	Mark			Lysa	Mark
1998		£	£	1998		£	£
31 Dec	Drawings	13,000	12,250	1 Jan	Balances b/d	420	1,780
31 Dec	Balance c/d	–	830	31 Dec	Interest on capital	2,500	2,000
				31 Dec	Share of profits	9,300	9,300
				31 Dec	Balance c/d	780	–
		13,000	13,080			13,000	13,080
1999				1999			
1 Jan	Balance b/d	780	–	1 Jan	Balance b/d	–	830

14.4 (a) **EXTENDED TRIAL BALANCE** **J JAMES & S HILL T/A "GRAPES"** **31 DEC. 1998**

Description	Ledger balances		Adjustments		Profit and loss		Balance sheet	
	Dr £	Cr £	Dr £	Cr £	Dr £	Cr £	Dr £	Cr £
Capital a/c: James		38,000						38,000
Capital a/c: Hill		32,000						32,000
Current a/c: James	3,000						3,000	
Current a/c: Hill		1,000						1,000
Drawings: James	14,000						14,000	
Drawings: Hill	18,000						18,000	
Gross profit		89,000				89,000		
Rent and rates	7,500				7,500			
Advertising	12,000				12,000			
Heat and light	3,500				3,500			
Wages and salaries	18,000				18,000			
Sundry expenses	4,000				4,000			
Shop fittings	20,000						20,000	
Prov for dep'n: shop fittings				2,000				2,000
Bank	29,000						29,000	
Debtors	6,000						6,000	
Creditors		8,000						8,000
Value Added Tax		2,000						2,000
Stock at 31 Dec 1998	35,000						35,000	
Depreciation			2,000		2,000			
Net profit/loss: James					21,000			21,000
Net profit/loss: Hill					21,000			21,000
	170,000	170,000	2,000	2,000	89,000	89,000	125,000	125,000

(b)

Dr **Partners' Capital Accounts** Cr

	James	Hill		James	Hill
1998	£	£	1998	£	£
31 Dec Balances c/d	38,000	32,000	1 Jan Balances b/d	38,000	32,000
1999			1999		
			1 Jan Balances b/d	38,000	32,000

Dr **Partners' Current Accounts** Cr

	James	Hill		James	Hill
1998	£	£	1998	£	£
1 Jan Balance b/d	3,000	–	1 Jan Balance b/d	–	1,000
31 Dec Drawings	14,000	18,000	31 Dec Share of profits	21,000	21,000
31 Dec Balances c/d	4,000	4,000			
	21,000	22,000		21,000	22,000
1999			1999		
			1 Jan Balances b/d	4,000	4,000

CHAPTER 15: MANUFACTURING ACCOUNTS

15.1 (b)

15.2 (c)

15.3 (d)

15.4 (b)

15.5
- (a) manufacturing account
- (b) manufacturing account
- (c) manufacturing account
- (d) profit and loss account
- (e) profit and loss account
- (f) manufacturing account
- (g) profit and loss account

15.6

Memorandum

A manufacturing account has been prepared in order to show the main elements of cost which make up the manufacturing cost. In your business, the main elements of cost are:

- *direct materials* – the raw materials used to make the product
- *direct labour* – the wages of the workforce engaged in manufacturing the product
- *production overheads* – the other costs of manufacture; here rent and rates, power, heat and light, etc

The first two of these make up *prime cost*, the basic cost of manufacturing the product. Prime cost plus production overheads gives the production cost. The figure for production cost is carried down to the profit and loss account where it is used to calculate *cost of sales*. The profit and loss account then goes on to show *gross profit* and, after deduction of non-production overheads, *net profit*.

BARBARA FRANCIS
MANUFACTURING AND PROFIT AND LOSS ACCOUNT
for the year ended 31 December 1998

	£	£
Opening stock of raw materials		31,860
Add Purchases of raw materials		237,660
		269,520
Less Closing stock of raw materials		44,790
COST OF RAW MATERIALS USED		224,730
Direct labour		234,630
PRIME COST		459,360
Add Production (factory) overheads:		
Rent and rates	24,690	
Power	7,650	
Heat and light	2,370	
Sundry expenses and maintenance	8,190	
Depreciation of plant and machinery	7,450	
		50,350
PRODUCTION (OR MANUFACTURING) COST OF GOODS COMPLETED		509,710
Sales		796,950
Opening stock of finished goods	42,640	
Production (or manufacturing) cost of goods completed	509,710	
	552,350	
Less Closing stock of finished goods	96,510	
COST OF SALES		455,840
Gross profit		341,110
Less Non-production overheads:		
Rent and rates	8,230	
Salaries	138,700	
Advertising	22,170	
Office expenses	7,860	
		176,960
Net profit		164,150

15.7

- opening stock, £10,000 plus factory profit (20 per cent) £2,000 = £12,000
- closing stock, £15,000 plus factory profit (20 per cent) £3,000 = £18,000

Dr **Provision for Unrealised Profit Account** Cr

1999		£	1999		£
31 Dec	Balance c/d	3,000	1 Jan	Balance b/d (adjustment in respect of opening stock)	2,000
			31 Dec	Profit and loss account	1,000
		3,000			3,000
2000			2000		
			1 Jan	Balance b/d	3,000

CHAPTER 16: ACCOUNTING FOR CAPITAL TRANSACTIONS

16.1 (b) **16.2** (b) **16.3** (a)

16.4

Fixed asset number	67462874
Description	Computer, Supra ML 6500
Location	Office
Supplier	Eveshore Computers Ltd

	Date	Cost (net of VAT) £	Expected useful life	Estimated scrap value £	Depreciation method SL or RB	Percentage per annum	Depreciation for year £	Provision for depreciation £	Net book value £	Disposal proceeds (net of VAT) £	Profit/(loss) on sale £
	1996 12 Mar	3,000	4 years	350	RB	50					
	31 Dec						1,500	1,500	1,500		
	1997 31 Dec						750	2,250	750		
(a)	1998 31 Dec						375	2,625	375		
(b)	1999 10 Feb									500	125 profit

16.5 (a)

Date	Details	Folio	Dr	Cr
1997			£	£
10 Jan	Machine	GL	32,000	
	Bank	CB		32,000
	Purchase of machine to develop and print films; capital expenditure authorisation number			

Machine Account

Dr		£	Cr		£
1997		£	2000		£
10 Jan	Bank	32,000	17 Aug	Disposals	32,000
2000					
17 Aug	Disposals (part exchange allowance)	5,000			

Depreciation calculations

Depreciation at 40 per cent reducing balance per year is as follows:

year ended 31 December 1997	£12,800
year ended 31 December 1998	£7,680
year ended 31 December 1999	£4,608

Note: the journal entry for the first year only is shown

Date	Details	Folio	Dr	Cr
1997			£	£
31 Dec	Profit and loss	GL	12,800	
	Depreciation	GL		12,800
	Depreciation charge for year on machine			
31 Dec	Depreciation	GL	12,800	
	Provision for depreciation account – machine	GL		12,800
	Transfer of depreciation charge for year to provision for depreciation account			

Depreciation Account – Machine

Dr					Cr
1997		£	1997		£
31 Dec	Prov for dep'n account	12,800	31 Dec	Profit and loss account	12,800
1998			1998		
31 Dec	Prov for dep'n account	7,680	31 Dec	Profit and loss account	7,680
1999			1999		
31 Dec	Prov for dep'n account	4,608	31 Dec	Profit and loss account	4,608

Provision for Depreciation Account – Machine

Dr					Cr
1997		£	1997		£
31 Dec	Balance c/d	12,800	31 Dec	Dep'n account: machine	12,800
1998			1998		
31 Dec	Balance c/d	20,480	1 Jan	Balance b/d	12,800
			31 Dec	Dep'n account: machine	7,680
		20,480			20,480
1999			1999		
31 Dec	Balance c/d	25,088	1 Jan	Balance b/d	20,480
			31 Dec	Dep'n account: machine	4,608
		25,088			25,088
2000			2000		
17 Aug	Disposals	25,088	1 Jan	Balance b/d	25,088

Date	Details	Folio	Dr	Cr
2000			£	£
17 Aug	Disposals	GL	32,000	
	Machine	GL		32,000
	Provision for depreciation account – machine	GL	25,088	
	Disposals	GL		25,088
	Machine	GL	5,000	
	Disposals	GL		5,000
	Profit and loss	GL	1,912	
	Disposals	GL		1,912
			64,000	64,000
	Part exchange of machine to develop and print films; loss on sale of £1,912 transferred to profit and loss account			

Disposals Account – Machine

Dr		£	Cr		£
2000			2000		
17 Aug	Machine	32,000	17 Aug	Provision for dep'n	25,088
			17 Aug	Machine (part exchange)	5,000
			17 Aug	Profit and loss (loss on sale)	1,912
		32,000			32,000

16.5 (b)

Fixed asset number	
Description	Automated developing and printing machine
Location	
Supplier	

Date	Cost (net of VAT) £	Expected useful life	Estimated scrap value £	Depreciation method SL or RB	Percentage per annum	Depreciation for year £	Provision for depreciation £	Net book value £	Disposal proceeds (net of VAT) £	Profit/(loss) on sale £
1997 10 Jan	32,000	5 years	2,500	RB	40					
31 Dec						12,800	12,800	19,200		
1998 31 Dec						7,680	20,480	11,520		
1999 31 Dec						4,608	25,088	6,912		
2000 17 Aug									5,000	(1,912)

16.6 Depreciation calculations:

Registration number	1996 £	1997 £	1998 £	TOTAL £
N704 ZNP	4,500	4,500	–	9,000
N705 ZNP	4,500	4,500	4,500	13,500
R81 ZUY	–	–	5,250	5,250
TOTAL	9,000	9,000	9,750	27,750

Vehicles Account

Dr		£			Cr £
1996			1996		
24 Jan	Bank	15,000	31 Dec	Balance c/d	30,000
24 Jan	Bank	15,000			
		30,000			30,000
1997			1997		
1 Jan	Balance b/d	30,000	31 Dec	Balance c/d	30,000
1998			1998		
1 Jan	Balance b/d	30,000	13 Oct	Disposals	15,000
17 Feb	Bank	17,500	31 Dec	Balance c/d	32,500
		47,500			47,500
1999			1999		
1 Jan	Balance b/d	32,500			

Depreciation Account – Vehicles

Dr		£			Cr £
1996			1996		
31 Dec	Provision for dep'n	9,000	31 Dec	Profit and loss account	9,000
1997			1997		
31 Dec	Provision for dep'n	9,000	31 Dec	Profit and loss account	9,000
1998			1998		
31 Dec	Provision for dep'n	9,750	31 Dec	Profit and loss account	9,750

Provision for Depreciation Account – Vehicles

Dr		£			£ Cr
1996		£	1996		£
31 Dec	Balance c/d	9,000	31 Dec	Dep'n account: vehicles	9,000
1997			1997		
31 Dec	Balance c/d	18,000	1 Jan	Balance b/d	9,000
			31 Dec	Dep'n account: vehicles	9,000
		18,000			18,000
1998			1998		
13 Oct	Disposals	9,000	1 Jan	Balance b/d	18,000
31 Dec	Balance c/d	18,750	31 Dec	Dep'n account: vehicles	9,750
		27,750			27,750
1999			1999		
			1 Jan	Balance b/d	18,750

Disposals Account – Vehicles

Dr					Cr
1998		£	1998		£
13 Oct	Vehicles	15,000	13 Oct	Provision for dep'n	9,000
13 Oct	Profit and loss (profit on sale)	500	13 Oct	Bank	6,500
		15,500			15,500

16.7 (a) See text, page 255

(b) **Alternative 1**

- Write off all research and development revenue expenditure costs to profit and loss account:

	£000s
– pure research	45
– applied research	172
– development	49
	266

- The effect of this will be to reduce the profit for 1998 by £266,000
- Profits for future years will not be affected by this year's revenue expenditure

Alternative 2

- Write off pure and applied research revenue expenditure costs to profit and loss account:

	£000s
– pure research	45
– applied research	172
	217

- The effect of this will be to reduce the profit for 1998 by £217,000
- The development expenditure may be capitalised and treated as an intangible fixed asset if it relates to an ultimately profitable project (see page 256 for criteria)
- If this is done, there will be no effect on the 1998 profit; in future years, however, the intangible fixed asset of development expenditure will be amortised in proportion to sales of the product as they materialise – thus profits in the future will be reduced by the amount of the amortisation

appendix

SOLE TRADER PROFIT AND LOSS ACCOUNT - EXAMPLE LAYOUT

This example layout for final accounts is for sole trader businesses; for partnerships, the layout will need to be adjusted to take note of the partners' capital and current accounts (see Chapter 14).

PROFIT AND LOSS ACCOUNT OF .... (name)
FOR THE YEAR/PERIOD ENDED ....(date)

	£	£	£	
Sales			x	
Less Sales returns			x	
Net sales			x	(a)
Opening stock		x		
Purchases*	x			
Carriage in	x			
Less Purchases returns	x			
Net purchases		x		
		x		
Less Closing stock		x		
Cost of sales			x	(b)
Gross profit (a) – (b)			x	(c)
Add other income, eg				
Discount received			x	(d)
Provision for bad debts (reduction)			x	(d)
Profit on sale of fixed assets			x	(d)
Other income			x	(d)
(c) + (d)			x	(e)
Less overheads, eg				
Vehicle running expenses		x		
Rent		x		
Rates		x		
Heating and lighting		x		
Telephone		x		
Salaries and wages		x		
Discount allowed		x		
Carriage out		x		
Depreciation		x		
Loss on sale of fixed assets		x		
Bad debts written off		x		
Provision for bad debts (increase)		x		
			x	(f)
Net profit (e) – (f)			x	(g)

* for a manufacturing business, production cost of goods completed is shown instead of (or as well as) purchases – see Chapter 15

SOLE TRADER PROFIT AND LOSS ACCOUNT - EXPLANATION

The amounts for **sales** and **purchases** include only items in which the business trades – eg a clothes shop buying clothes from the manufacturer records the amount incurred in its purchases figure; when the clothes are sold the amount is recorded as sales. The amounts of sales returns and purchases returns are deducted from the amounts of sales and purchases. Note that the cost of having purchases delivered (eg post and packing) – called 'carriage in' – is added to the cost of purchases (but the expense of carriage out is included amongst the overheads – see below).

Cost of sales represents the cost to the business of the goods which have been sold in this financial year. Cost of sales is:

	opening stock
plus	*purchases, minus purchases returns
minus	closing stock
equals	cost of sales

* including the cost of 'carriage in' (see above), if appropriate

Gross profit is calculated as:

sales (less sales returns) – cost of sales = gross profit

If cost of sales is greater than sales, the business has made a gross loss.

Overheads are the expenses of running the business – *revenue expenditure*. The categories of expenses used vary according to the needs of each business. If there are any small amounts of income, such as rent received or discount received, they are usually added below gross profit. Amongst the overheads will be included the expenses of carriage out and discount allowed, together with depreciation of fixed assets, loss on sale of fixed assets, bad debts written off and increase in provision for bad debts.

Net profit is calculated as:

gross profit – overheads = net profit

If overheads are greater than gross profit, the business has made a net loss.

The net profit is the amount the business earned for the owner during the year, and is subject to taxation. The owner can draw some or all of the net profit for personal use in the form of *drawings*. Part of the profit might well be left in the business in order to help build up the business for the future. Profit does not necessarily equal cash in the bank available for spending; it may already have been invested back in the business.

SOLE TRADER BALANCE SHEET - EXAMPLE LAYOUT

BALANCE SHEET OF .... (name) AS AT .... (date)

		£	£	£	
Fixed assets		Cost (a)	Prov for dep'n (b)	Net	(a) – (b)
Intangible:	Goodwill	x	x	x	
Tangible:	Premises	x	x	x	
	Equipment	x	x	x	
	Vehicles	x	x	x	
	etc	x	x	x	
		x	x	x	(c)
Current assets					
Stock (closing)			x		
Debtors		x			
Less provision for bad debts		x			
			x		
Prepayments			x		
Bank			x		
Cash			x		
			x		(d)
Less Current liabilities					
Creditors		x			
Accruals		x			
Bank overdraft		x			
			x		(e)
Working capital (d) – (e)				x	(f)
(c) + (f)				x	(g)
Less Long-term liabilities					
Loans				x	(h)
NET ASSETS (g) – (h)				x	(i)
FINANCED BY					
Capital					
Opening capital				x	
Add net profit (from profit and loss account)				x	
				x	
Less drawings				x	
				x	(i)

Note: balance sheet balances at points (i)

Practical point: When preparing handwritten final accounts it is usual practice to underline all the headings and sub-headings shown in bold print in the example layout.

SOLE TRADER BALANCE SHEET - EXPLANATION

Fixed assets comprise the long-term items owned by a business which are not bought with the intention of early resale in the near future, eg premises, machinery, motor vehicles, office equipment, shop fittings, etc.

Tangible assets are assets which have physical form, eg buildings, vehicles, computers.

Intangible assets are assets which have value but no physical form, eg goodwill (reputation).

Current assets comprise short-term assets which change regularly, eg stocks of goods for resale, debtors, bank balances and cash. These items will alter as the business trades, eg stocks will be sold, or more will be bought; debtors will make payment to the business, or sales on credit will be made; the cash and bank balances will alter with the flow of money paid into the bank account, or as withdrawals are made.

By accounting tradition, fixed and current assets are listed starting with the most permanent, ie premises, and working through to the most liquid, ie nearest to cash: either cash itself, or the balance at the bank.

Current liabilities are due for repayment within twelve months of the date of the balance sheet, eg creditors, Value Added Tax due to Customs and Excise, and bank overdraft (which is technically repayable on demand, unlike a bank loan which is negotiated for a particular time period).

Working capital is the excess of current assets over current liabilities, ie current assets minus current liabilities = working capital. Without adequate working capital, a business will find it difficult to continue to operate. Working capital is also often referred to as net current assets.

Long-term liabilities are where repayment is due in more than one year from the date of the balance sheet; they are often described as 'bank loan', 'long-term loan', or 'mortgage'.

Net assets is the total of fixed and current assets, less current and long-term liabilities. The net assets are financed by the owner(s) of the business, in the form of capital. Net assets therefore equals the total of the 'financed by' section – the balance sheet 'balances'.

Capital is the owner's investment, and is a liability of a business, ie it is what the business owes the owner.

Note how net profit for the year is added to the owner's capital, while drawings – the amount withdrawn by the owner during the year – are deducted. This calculation leaves a closing capital at the balance sheet date which balances with the net assets figure – the balance sheet *balances.*

Note that drawings must not be included amongst the overheads in the profit and loss account because they are a payment to the owner rather than being made to 'third parties'.

In partnership balance sheets (see Chapter 15) the same details, ie capital, net profit, and drawings, are shown for each partner, together with other items which relate specifically to the way in which the partners have agreed to share profits and losses.

PRO-FORMA EXTENDED TRIAL BALANCE

EXTENDED TRIAL BALANCE name.. date..

Description	Ledger balances		Adjustments		Profit and loss		Balance sheet	
	Dr £	*Cr* £	*Dr* £	*Cr* £	*Dr* £	*Cr* £	*Dr* £	*Cr* £
Closing stock: Profit and loss								
Closing stock: Balance sheet								
Accruals								
Prepayments								
Depreciation								
Bad debts								
Provision for bad debts:adjustment								
Net profit/loss								